The
Reference Shelf®

Representative American Speeches 2010–2011

Edited by

Brian Boucher

The Reference Shelf
Volume 83 • Number 6
H. W. Wilson
A Division of EBSCO Publishing, Inc.
Ipswich, Massachusetts
2011

The Reference Shelf

The books in this series contain reprints of articles, excerpts from books, addresses on current issues, and studies of social trends in the United States and other countries. There are six separately bound numbers in each volume, all of which are usually published in the same calendar year. Numbers one through five are each devoted to a single subject, providing background information and discussion from various points of view and concluding with a subject index and comprehensive bibliography that lists books, pamphlets, and abstracts of additional articles on the subject. The final number of each volume is a collection of recent speeches, and it contains a cumulative speaker index. Books in the series may be purchased individually or on subscription.

Library of Congress has cataloged this serial title as follows:

Representative American speeches. 1937 / 38–
New York, H. W. Wilson Co.™
v. 21 cm.—The Reference Shelf
Annual
Indexes:
Author index: 1937/38–1959/60, with 1959/60; 1960/61–1969/70, with 1969/70;
1970/71–1979/80, with 1979/80; 1980/81–1989/90, 1990.
Editors: 1937/38–1958/59, A. C. Baird.—1959/60–1969/70, L. Thonssen.—1970/ 71–1979/80, W. W. Braden.—1980/81–1994/95, O. Peterson.—1995/96–1998/99, C. M. Logue and J. DeHart.—1999/2000–2002/2003, C. M. Logue and L. M. Messina.—2003/2004–2005/2006, C. M. Logue, L. M. Messina, and J. DeHart.—2006/2007– , J. Currie, P. McCaffrey, L. M. Messina.—2007/ 2008–2010/2011, B. Boucher.
ISSN 0197-6923 Representative American speeches.
1. Speeches, addresses, etc., American. 2. Speeches, addresses, etc.
I. Baird, Albert Craig, 1883–1979 ed. II. Thonssen, Lester, 1904–III. Braden, Waldo Warder, 1911–1991 ed. IV. Peterson, Owen, 1924– ed. V. Logue, Calvin McLeod, 1935– , Messina, Lynn M., and DeHart, Jean, eds. VI. Series.
PS668.B3   815.5082   38-27962
                                                                                      MARC-S

Library of Congress [8503r85] rev4

Cover: Gloria Steinem delivers her keynote address at the 2010 Seattle Inspire Luncheon at the YWCA in Seattle, Washington. Courtesy of the Seattle YWCA.

Visit H. W. Wilson's Web site: www.hwwilson.com

Printed in the United States of America

Contents

Preface

The two years gone by reminded Thomas Blanton, one of the speakers in this year's volume, of a Chinese curse: "May you live in interesting times." This period saw continuing worldwide economic turmoil, the overthrow of several long-standing autocrats in the Middle East, the killing of al Qaeda leader Osama bin Laden, newsmaking revelations by the international organization WikiLeaks, the continued growth of the Tea Party movement, and the birth of the Occupy Wall Street (OWS) demonstrations, among other historic developments. Many of these are addressed in *Representative American Speeches 2010–2011*.

Probably no one could have guessed, when Tunisian produce vendor Mohamed Bouazizi set himself on fire in protest on December 17, 2010, that his actions would ignite a chain of popular uprisings across the Middle East. This ongoing period of upheaval came to be called the Arab Spring, and it forms the subject of our first chapter. In January 2010, Tunisian president Zine el Abidine Ben Ali stepped down, followed in February by Egyptian president Hosni Mubarak. Libyan dictator Muammar al-Gaddafi was killed in October 2011 after months of civil war. Syria, Yemen, and several other nations in the region have also seen widespread unrest. Whether these conflagrations will topple the old regimes, as in Tunisia, Egypt, and Libya, remains an open question as of this writing. Also unanswered is whether the Arab Spring will usher in a new democratic era in the Middle East, a region often described as immune to democracy. Lively debates have concerned the role of the U.S. invasion of Iraq and that of social media in these uprisings. In this chapter, Council on Foreign Relations (CFR) president Richard N. Haass questions the Obama administration's participation in a NATO operation to assist the uprising in Libya. Analyst and writer Paul A. Goble describes the impact of the Arab Spring on autocratic regimes in Central Asia. President Barack Obama discusses American policies relating to the changes in the Middle East, and in the chapter's final speech, Georgetown professor Daniel Byman describes the implications of the death of bin Laden and of the Arab Spring for U.S. counterterrorism.

Meanwhile, China has continued a period of dramatic economic growth and increasing international influence. Consequently, our second chapter is devoted to the rise of the People's Republic. In 2010 Goldman Sachs projected that by 2030, China's gross domestic product (GDP) would exceed that of the United States. Especially when viewed against the great economic instability in the United States and Europe, this has led to a certain amount of hand-wringing: The historian Niall Ferguson, as quoted by Princeton professor John Ikenberry in *Foreign Affairs* (January/February 2008), has written that the bloody 20th century witnessed "the descent of the West" and "a reorientation of the world" toward the East. In the first speech in this chapter, historian Joseph S. Nye, Jr. questions this view, arguing that relative decline is not necessarily absolute decline. Erica S. Downs offers a perspective on how China's business interests are helping to drive its foreign and domestic policies. Speaking at the Heritage Foundation, Franklin Lavin offers an optimistic view of the future of U.S.-China relations, noting that the two countries have long focused on internal issues. Echoing Nye's optimism, Harvard economist Martin Feldstein frames China's rise not as a threat to America, but as a challenge.

Many observers of American politics point out that bitter partisan divides create gridlock and foster an atmosphere of distrust. When a mentally disturbed young man, Jared Lee Loughner, killed six people and severely wounded Arizona Democratic representative Gabrielle Giffords in Tucson, Arizona, it revived a debate over partisanship, with both sides leveling charges of overheated rhetoric, media bias, and excessive divisiveness. Our third chapter is devoted to commentary on these concerns. Several days after Loughner's shooting spree, President Obama traveled to Tucson to deliver yet another address heralded as the speech of his career. Speaking the next month at the American Enterprise Institute (AEI), New Jersey's Republican governor Chris Christie, often cited as a leading light of the party and a potential presidential candidate, asserts that there is a place for vigorous debate over budgetary matters. Indiana governor Mitch Daniels, speaking at the Conservative Political Action Conference (CPAC), presents what he describes as the Republican Party's core beliefs and delivers a pointed rebuke to the left.

Advocates of government transparency have seen the post-9/11 age as a dark time for freedom of information in the United States, alleging that increased government secrecy has made it easier to cover up official malfeasance. As a response, WikiLeaks, according to its own Web site, "publishes and comments on leaked documents alleging government and corporate misconduct." Speeches in the fourth chapter turn to questions about government secrecy and transparency in the age of WikiLeaks. Perhaps the organization's most dramatic disclosure thus far has been the 2010 release of thousands of diplomatic cables supplied to it by a 22-year-old U.S. Army intelligence analyst, PFC Bradley Manning. Responses to this release have included calls for the arrest and even the assassination of the WikiLeaks founder, Australian activist Julian Assange. In the first talk in this chapter, Congressman Ron Paul poses a number of rhetorical "questions to consider" about the ethical and legal dimensions of the WikiLeaks disclosures and gives his response. Taking a very different tack at a hearing before Congress, author and former Harvard professor Gabriel Schoenfeld gives cautionary testimony about past disclosures that have caused harm to American interests and cost American lives. At the same forum, Blanton, director of George Washington University's National Security Archive, testifies amid an atmosphere of what he terms "Wikimania," and warns against many "WikiMyths" being spread by alarmists.

In a dramatically titled article published in *The Atlantic* magazine in July/August 2010, writer Hanna Rosin posited "The End of Men." In it, she writes, "Man has been the dominant sex since, well, the dawn of mankind. But for the first time in human history, that is changing—and with shocking speed." She wonders whether conditions in post-industrial society are more favorable to women globally, pointing out, for example, that men have suffered three-quarters of the job losses in the recent recession. In a more humorous vein, Dan Abrams of ABC News published a book this year titled *Man Down: Proof Beyond a Reasonable Doubt That Women Are Better Cops, Drivers, Gamblers, Spies, World Leaders, Beer Tasters, Hedge Fund Managers, and Just About Everything Else*. In a September 2011 debate on this issue, arguing along with Rosin, Abrams pointed out that "Between 1995 and 2008, 82 percent of lightning strikes were on men." Against this backdrop, our next chapter addresses feminism in the 21st century. Feminist icon Gloria Steinem imagines a world run by the YWCA and reflecting its values, while writer Courtney Martin gives voice to a new generation of feminists, who may just as likely start a blog as organize a protest march. Speaking at a TEDWomen conference in 2010, Rosin offers data to support her thesis for "The End of Men," as well as some theories about what has led to this global societal shift. Activist Phyllis Schlafly, by contrast, asserts that feminism is not truly aimed at creating opportunities for women; it is, in her view, first and foremost a tool to shift political power to the left.

According to the Centers for Disease Control and Prevention (CDC), about one-third of U.S. adults are obese, as are approximately 17 percent of children and adolescents—12.5 million people aged 2–19. *The New York Times*, meanwhile, reports that the American diet consists of 31 percent more packaged foods than fresh foods. Growing numbers of Americans, though, are shopping for organic produce, just as books like Michael Pollan's *The Omnivore's Dilemma* have Americans thinking more carefully about what they eat. In our final chapter, several speakers address our vexed relationship with food, and what food represents in terms of how we treat each other. In his TEDTalk, chef Dan Barber speaks about a delectable fish he ate that comes from a truly innovative farm that strives for sustainability and to work in harmony with natural processes. The Rev. David Beckmann, addressing the National Press Club, says that Americans of faith have to urge their governments to provide food assistance for the poor. Professor Aaron Bobrow-Strain uses the historical introduction of processed bread into the American diet as a way to talk about our emotional relationship to food and issues of race and class. Finally, Secretary of Agriculture Tom Vilsack describes scientific initiatives that will help to feed a growing global population.

Brian Boucher
December 2011

1

The Arab Spring:
The United States and the Middle East

"Foreign Policy Must Be About Priorities"*

Richard N. Haass

President, Council on Foreign Relations (CFR), 2003– ; born Brooklyn, NY, July 28, 1951; B.A., Oberlin College, 1973; master's degree, 1975, and D.Phil., 1982, Oxford University; Director, Office of Regional Security Affairs, U.S. Department of State, 1981–82; Deputy Director for European Affairs, Special Cyprus Coordinator, U.S. Department of State, 1982–85; lecturer, Kennedy School of Government, Harvard University, 1985–88; special assistant to President George H. W. Bush and Senior Director for Near East and South Asian Affairs, National Security Council (NSC), 1989–1993; senior associate, Carnegie Endowment for International Peace, 1993–94; senior fellow and director of national security programs, Council on Foreign Relations (CFR), 1994–96; vice president and director of policy studies, Brookings Institution, 1996–2000; Director of Policy Planning, U.S. Department of State, 2000–03; au-thor or editor of eleven books on American foreign policy, including The Bureaucratic Entrepreneur: How to Be Effective in Any Unruly Organization *(1999);* War of Necessity, War of Choice: A Memoir of Two Iraq Wars *(2009).*

Editor's introduction: Speaking before a U.S. Senate Committee on Foreign Relations hearing on the crisis in Libya, Richard N. Haass takes a skeptical view toward the U.S. intervention in the North African nation, suggesting that deploying military forces to counteract the imminent slaughter of civilians assumes too much certainty about future developments. He further contends that due to its Muammar al-Qaddafi-induced isolation, Libya is of little strategic importance to the future of the Middle East. In response to praise for the multilateral intervention, he states that "multilateralism is not a reason for doing something," rather it is only "a mechanism for distributing burdens." Haass points out what he perceives as a discrepancy between the declared objectives of the United States in Libya and the means it is prepared to deploy to achieve them. In view of this discrepancy, he recommends the adoption of more modest goals.

Richard N. Haass's speech: Mr. Chairman:

---

* Delivered on April 6, 2011, at Washington, D.C.

Thank you for asking me to appear before this committee to discuss recent U.S. policy toward Libya. Let me make two points at the outset. First, my statement and testimony reflect my personal views and not those of the Council on Foreign Relations, which as a matter of policy takes no institutional positions. Second, I will address today's topic from two perspectives: first, the lessons to be learned from recent U.S. policy toward Libya, and second, my recommendations for U.S. policy going forward.

Analysis must be rigorous. In two critical areas, however, I would suggest that what has been asserted as fact was in reality closer to assumption. First, it is not clear that a humanitarian catastrophe was imminent in the eastern Libyan city of Benghazi. There had been no reports of large-scale massacres in Libya up to that point, and Libyan society (unlike Rwanda, to cite the obvious influential precedent) is not divided along a single or defining fault line. Gaddafi saw the rebels as enemies for political reasons, not for their ethnic or tribal associations. To be sure, civilians would have been killed in an assault on the city—civil wars are by their nature violent and destructive—but there is no evidence of which I am aware that civilians per se would have been targeted on a large scale. Muammar Gaddafi's threat to show no mercy to the rebels might well have been just that: a threat within the context of a civil war to those who opposed him with arms or were considering doing so.

Armed intervention on humanitarian grounds can sometimes be justified. But before using military force to save lives, we need to be sure of the threat; the potential victims should request our help; the intervention should be supported by significant elements of the international community; the intervention should have high likelihood of success at a limited cost, including the cost to our other interests; and other policies should be judged to be inadequate. Not all of these conditions were satisfied in the Libyan case. Such an assessment is essential if we are asking our troops to put their lives at risk, if we are placing other important interests at risk, and if we are using economic and military resources that puts our future more at risk.

Second, it was (and is) not obvious that what happened or happens in Libya would or will have significant repercussions for what happens elsewhere in the region. Libya is not a particularly influential country; indeed, Gaddafi's isolation in no small part explains why it was possible to get Arab League and UN support for a resolution supporting armed intervention. The dynamics in Syria or Bahrain or Egypt, not to mention Iran, Iraq, and Saudi Arabia, will be determined mostly by local factors and forces and not by what happens in Libya.

American policymakers erred in calling explicitly early on in the crisis for Gaddafi's removal. Doing so made it far more difficult to employ diplomacy to help achieve U.S. humanitarian goals without resorting to military force. It removed the incentive Gaddafi might have had to stop attacking his opponents. The call for Gaddafi's ouster also put the United States at odds with much of the international community, which had only signed on to a humanitarian and not a political mission when voting for UN Security Council resolution 1973. It increased the odds the intervention would be seen as a failure so long as Gaddafi remained in power. And, as I shall discuss, requiring Gaddafi's removal actually makes it more difficult to effect the implemention of UN Security Council Resolution 1973 and stop the fighting.

Multilateralism is not a reason for doing something. Multilateralism is a mechanism, no more and no less, for distributing burdens. It can add to the legitimacy of an action; it can also complicate policy implementation. Such pros and cons need to be assessed. But multilateral support does not make a policy that is questionable on its merits any less so. To think otherwise is to confuse ends and means.

Inconsistency is unavoidable in foreign policy, and in and of itself is not a reason for rejecting doing something that makes sense or for undertaking something that does not. Some humanitarian interventions may be warranted. But inconsistency is not cost free, as it can confuse the American public and disappoint people in other countries, in the process opening us up to charges of hypocrisy and double standards.

It is acceptable in principle to intervene militarily on behalf of interests deemed less than vital, but in such cases—what I would deem "wars of choice"—it must be shown that the likely costs are commensurate with the interests involved and that other policies would not have done equally well or better in the way of costs and outcomes. Otherwise, a war of choice cannot be justified.

As I expect you have gathered from what I have said here today and both said and written previously, I did not support the decision to intervene with military force in Libya. But we are where we are. So what would I suggest the United States do in Libya going forward?

We must recognize that we face a familiar foreign policy conundrum, namely, that there is a large gap between our professed goals and the means we are prepared to devote to realizing them. The goals are ambitious: protecting the Libyan people and bringing about a successor regime judged to be preferable to what now exists. But the means are limited, as the president is clearly looking to our partners in NATO to assume the major military role and has ruled out the introduction of American ground forces.

Whenever there is such a gap between ends and means, a government has two choices: it can either reduce the ends or elevate the means. The Obama administration has up till now mostly emphasized the latter course. The no-fly zone was quickly augmented by additional air operations designed to degrade Libyan government forces. This proved insufficient to tilt the battlefield decisively in favor of regime opponents.

Now there is apparent interest in arming opposition forces. I would advise against taking this path. We cannot be confident of the agenda of the opposition towards either the Libyan people or various U.S. interests, including counter-terrorism. Nor can we be certain as to which opposition elements with which set of goals might in the end prove dominant. Arms once transferred can be used for any purpose. Bad situations can always get worse.

The only way to ensure the replacement of the current Libyan regime with something demonstrably better would be through the introduction of ground forces that were prepared to remain in place to maintain order and build capacities in the aftermath of ousting the government. As we have seen in Afghanistan and Iraq, the only thing certain about such a policy trajectory is its human, economic, and military cost. U.S. interests in Libya simply do not warrant such an investment on our part. And it is obviously far from certain whether any other outside party has both the will and the capacity to introduce ground forces on a scale likely to make a decisive military difference.

There is little reason to conclude that the Libyan opposition will any time soon be able to defeat the Libyan government. It appears to lack the requisite cohesiveness and skill. The combination of a no-fly zone, bombing, and arming might, however, have the effect of leveling the playing field and prolonging the civil war, leading to more civilian casualties in the process. This would be an ironic result of an intervention designed to promote humanitarian ends. The Libyan government may implode, but we cannot base our policy on this hope.

This all argues for reducing the immediate aims of American foreign policy and giving priority to humanitarian as opposed to political goals. This would entail undertaking or supporting a diplomatic initiative to bring about the implementation of UN Security Council resolution 1973 and, most importantly, a cease-fire. A narrow cease-fire is probably unrealistic, though. What would also be required to gain the support of the opposition would be a set of political conditions, possibly including specified political reforms and a degree of autonomy for certain areas. Sanctions could be added or removed to affect acceptance and compliance. Gaddafi might remain in office, at least for the time being. The country might effectively be divided for some time. An international force could well be required on the ground to keep the peace.

Such an outcome would be derided by some. But it would stop the civil war and keep many people alive who would otherwise perish. It would create a window for political reform and possibly over time lead to a new government without Muammar Gaddafi. The United States could use this time to work with Libyans in the opposition and beyond to help build national institutions without the added weight of ongoing fighting.

A compromise, negotiated outcome would also be good for this country, as it would allow the United States to focus its resources—economic, diplomatic, military, and political—elsewhere. Far more important than Libya for U.S. interests in the region are Egypt, Syria, Bahrain, Saudi Arabia, Iraq, Jordan, and Iran. The United States also needs to reserve resources for other parts of the world (the Korean Peninsula comes to mind), for possible wars of necessity, for military modernization central to our position in the Pacific, and for deficit reduction.

Foreign policy must be about priorities. The United States cannot do everything everywhere. This consideration would have argued for avoiding military intervention in Libya; now it argues for limiting this intervention in what it seeks to accomplish and what it requires of the United States.

Thank you for this opportunity to appear before this committee. I look forward to your questions.

A Renewed Sense of the Possibility of Change[*]

The Peoples of Central Asia Respond to the Arab Spring

Paul A. Goble

Editorial and research coordinator, Azerbaijan Diplomatic Academy, 2007– ; born Hamilton, OH, January 13, 1949; B.A., Miami University of Ohio, 1970; M.A., University of Chicago, 1973; Soviet affairs analyst, Central Intelligence Agency (CIA), 1979–1980; Soviet media analyst, Foreign Broadcast Information Service (FBIS), 1980–82; analyst, then special assistant for Soviet nationalities, Bureau of Intelligence and Research (INR), U.S. Department of State, 1982–89; acting director of research, Radio Liberty, 1989–1990; Special Advisor on Soviet Nationality Problems and Baltic Affairs and Desk Officer for Estonia, Latvia and Lithuania, U.S. Department of State, 1990–91; senior associate, Carnegie Endowment for International Peace, 1992–95; director of research, Jamestown Foundation, 1995; director of communications and technology, Radio Free Europe/Radio Liberty, 1996–2001; senior sdvisor to the director of the International Broadcasting Bureau (IBB) and Voice of America, 2001–04; senior fellow, EuroCollege, University of Tartu, Estonia, 2004–06; associate dean, Audentes University, Tallinn, Estonia, 2005–06; editor or co-editor of five books on ethnic and religious affairs in the post-Soviet states; author of more than 150 articles for journals and chapters in books, and of more than 250 op-ed articles in American and European newspapers and magazines.

Editor's introduction: Speaking at a hearing of the U.S. Commission on Security and Cooperation in Europe on "Central Asia and the Arab Spring: Growing Pressure for Human Rights?" analyst and writer Paul A. Goble asserts that the post-Soviet states of Central Europe have taken heart from the events of the Arab Spring. These peaceful, non-Islamist revolutions have given the lie to autocrats' claims, he argues. He predicts that a Central Asian Spring will follow. Goble goes on to outline, nation by nation, the particular risks of regime change in the countries of that

---

[*] Delivered on May 11, 2011, at Washington, D.C.

region and offers advice for the United States and the international community to help ensure progress toward genuine freedom for Central Asian countries.

Paul A. Goble's speech: Nowhere in the world has the Arab Spring given greater promise of real political change toward democracy and freedom than in the authoritarian states of post-Soviet Central Asia. The reasons for that are clear but not always clearly understood. It is not because these countries are also Muslim majority states, and it is not because they too are ruled by brittle authoritarian regimes. There are Muslim majority states where the Arab Spring has not had an impact, and there are authoritarian regimes which, either by brutality or accident, have blocked the spread of the idea people in the Middle East are seeking to promote.

Rather it is because the events in the Arab world have dispelled the myth promoted by these governments that fundamental change is impossible or dangerous and that the populations must put up with the status quo because these regimes enjoy international support as bulwarks against Islamist fundamentalism and supporters of the international effort against terrorism in Afghanistan and elsewhere.

Those arguments did not save the authoritarian regimes in Egypt, Tunisia, Libya, and elsewhere in the Middle East, and they will not save the authoritarian regimes in post-Soviet Central Asia. The peoples of those countries have been transfixed and transformed by the Arab Spring. They see that the arguments of their rulers no longer are convincing, and they see that the West and above all the United States, which often has pursued a policy of convenience with regard to these regimes, has changed as well. As a result, an increasing number of the people of these countries are ready to try to gain what is their natural right, freedom and democracy.

But just as the Arab Spring has affected the people, so too it has impressed the rulers in Central Asia. It has convinced them that they must take even more draconian measures in order to retain their hold on power. And the changes the Arab Spring have wrought in the consciousness of the peoples of Central Asia thus pose a serious challenge to Western governments including our own. Some of the regimes in that region may believe that they can get away with suppressing the opposition with extreme violence and that as long as they blame Islamists or outside agitators, as Uzbekistan president Islam Karimov did this week, all will be well. Consequently, the United States must find a way of encouraging these governments to give way to democracy rather than taking actions to defend their own power that will ultimately lead to a conflagration.

That is no easy task, but the Obama administration deserves a great deal of credit for the way in which it managed the situation in Egypt. And that approach, one that led to the exit of an increasingly weak authoritarian president and opened the way to the possibility of genuine democratic change, in which the next elections will not be the last ones, provides a serious model for how the United States should behave when, as I hope and believe, the Arab Spring will be succeeded by a Central Asian Spring, allowing the peoples of that region at last to gain what they were denied in 1991—genuine freedom, real democracy, and the human rights that all peoples should enjoy.

In my brief remarks today, I would like to focus on three things: first, the way in which the Arab Spring has affected thinking in Central Asia both among the populations and among the powers that be, underscoring the differences among the peoples of those states; second, the particular risks of regime change in the countries of that region, again country by country; and third, the way in which the U.S. and the international community can best proceed to ensure the next step toward genuine freedom for the peoples of this region.

SPRING IS NOT AN IMPOSSIBLE DREAM

The peoples of the post-Soviet countries of Central Asia have been told by their rulers that they must accept the status quo both because it is the only one that can prevent still worse things, including the imposition of Islamism, and because it enjoys widespread international support from Western democracies who for one reason or another believe that such authoritarian regimes are either useful or even more necessary for peoples like themselves. But the events in the Arab Spring have made such arguments less compelling than they were. After all, the governments that have been toppled in the Arab world made exactly the same arguments with perhaps even greater effect—until it became obvious that the peoples of that region no longer accepted them and that the West had begun to recognize that these claims were unjustified and wrong.

The reason that authoritarian leaders use such arguments and come down so hard on any display of collective demands for freedom is that such demands are contagious. When people in [any] country dare to be free, to live not by lies, and to not be afraid, others elsewhere are inspired to do the same. That is why there have been waves of democratization across large parts of the world at various points in the last generation, and it is why there is a new wave which has started in the Middle East but which will not end there.

In defense of their positions, authoritarian regimes rely not only on propaganda and police methods. They also rely on direct control of what people can find out about what is going on elsewhere. But the ability of these regimes to do that is small and declining. The Internet and other forms of social media mean that it is almost impossible to cut key groups off from learning what others are doing in other countries. That does not mean that regimes won't try—almost all of the regimes in Central Asia are doing so—but rather it means that they will not succeed. And the splash effect of such knowledge is larger than many understand.

Statistics on Internet penetration are less important than the fact of such penetration. If a few people can learn the truth, they can tell others. And that process means that even if the number of Web surfers in Central Asia is still small, the number of those who benefit from such knowledge is far larger. Indeed, one can argue that in many of these countries, it has reached critical mass. And to the extent that the Internet is supplemented by international broadcasting, both radio—and for obvious reasons, it has to be shortwave—and direct-to-home television broadcasting, the expansion in the spread of information will lead over time to the expansion of human freedom.

On this as on all other measures, there are enormous differences among the countries of this region, just as there are enormous differences among the countries of the Arab world. Consequently, just as the outcomes at any one point in the Arab world have ranged from quiescence to peaceful demonstrations to mass violence, so too the range of patterns in the Central Asian countries is likely to be large. At the same time, however, because within the Arab world and within the Central Asian world, people in one country often take their cue from what is happening in another in their region, so too a breakthrough in one Central Asian country, such as Kyrgystan, in response to developments in the Arab world, is likely to play out across the other Central Asian states more or less quickly.

ELECTIONS RATHER THAN BULLETS DEFEAT ISLAMISM

As an increasing number of American commentators are now pointing out, the execution of Osama bin Laden is likely to have a smaller [effect] on the future of terrorism than are the actions of Egyptians, Tunisians, and Libyans who are pressing for democratic rights. Indeed, the least reflection will lead to the conclusion that the actions on the streets of Cairo are a more definitive defeat of Al Qaeda than even the liquidation of bin Laden. This message is increasingly being absorbed among U.S. government leaders, who are ever more inclined to recognize that the purchase of short-term stability through reliance on authoritarian rulers gives a false sense of security.

That eliminates one of the key arguments that authoritarian rulers in Central Asia have advanced, many Central Asian populations have accepted, and that many Western governments including our own have made the basis of policy. Supporting a dictator who claims he can hold off Islamist extremism is a fool's errand: Such regimes are more likely to produce Islamist responses than are democratic ones. That does not mean that managing the transition from dictatorship to democracy is easy: It is obvious that those who support democracy must ensure that no free election will be the last one in any country.

But as Washington's approach in Egypt has shown, that is not an impossible task. There are ways to develop safeguards against backsliding, and there are ways to marginalize the extremists. That is one of the things that democracy truly understood does best. Another thing democracy does extremely well is allow for succession, an issue that arose in the first instance in Egypt and that will arise soon in many Central Asian countries whose presidents are aging Soviet-era officials. If such individuals can be led to see that they will be remembered as fathers of their countries if they allow the emergence of a genuine opposition via elections, they will be more likely to take that step than if they are encouraged to "keep the lid on" Islamic assertiveness.

EVERYONE NEEDS FRIENDS

As the events of the Arab Spring show, people who aspire to democracy need friends abroad, but they need friends who understand that support from abroad must be carefully calibrated lest it allow authoritarian regimes to claim that the democratic movement is a cat's paw for foreigners or it provoke the regimes into even more violent action in "defense of the nation." The United States showed that kind of understanding in the case of Egypt, carefully calibrating its statements and actions to the situation on the ground. But it has been less successful elsewhere in the Arab world not only because the leaders are less willing to see reason and yield to the people but also because the United States has either immediate interests it wants to protect or has less knowledge of the situation.

Unfortunately for the peoples of Central Asia, both of those factors are even more on view there. The US relies on several of the Central Asian countries for the passage of logistical support to the US-led effort in Afghanistan and not surprisingly does not want to see anything happen that might disrupt the flow of needed military supplies. And the US knows far less about Central Asia than it does about the Arab world. Few American representatives there speak the national languages, instead continuing to rely on the former imperial one; few US officials appear to view the Central Asian countries as independent actors in their own right, instead viewing them as part of Moscow's droit de regard. (The infamous case in which an American president thanked the Russian president in public for allowing a US base in Uzbekistan but did not thank the president of Uzbekistan is a symbol of this.)

There is little appreciation of the nature of Central Asian societies and the opportunities they have for development in a positive way. Instead, the focus in Washington is almost exclusively on the problems they represent: drug flows, human trafficking, corruption, violence, and unemployment among the urban young. All of these things are true, but they are neither the whole story nor can they be adequately addressed by authoritarian measures. Indeed, addressed in the ways that the regimes of this region have, these problems collectively can be the breeding ground for further violence and the replacement of the current authoritarian regimes by perhaps even more authoritarian Islamist ones.

That is something that the US does not yet appear to grasp, but if we are to be a friend to these peoples, we must understand that the only approach which gives hope of a truly better future for them is a commitment by us to the careful and continuing promotion of human rights and demography. Our doing that will add to the courage of those who are already inspired by the Arab Spring and will thus promote a change of seasons in Central Asia as well.

The authoritarian governments of Central Asia have maintained themselves not only by pointing to the threat that any change would bring Islamist regimes to power—something they make more likely the longer they are in office—but also by arguing that they have provided security and increasing prosperity for their peoples. In fact, they have provided neither. The peoples of Central Asia are less secure and less well off than they were. But even if it were true that they had done so, that is not enough for the peoples of the region, and it should not be enough for us.

In thinking about the situation in the post-Arab Spring Central Asia, one cannot fail to recall a Soviet anecdote from 1968. The story has it that two dogs meet at the border of Poland and Czechoslovakia. The Polish dog is sleek and fat, while the Czechoslovak dog is skin and bones. The Czechoslovak dog who is heading toward Poland asks the Polish dog why he is heading toward Czechoslovakia. The Polish dog replies he is doing so because he would like, for once in his life, to bark.

That message reverberated through Eastern Europe and then through the USSR with increasing power. It convinced many that, in Mikhail Gorbachev's words, "we cannot continue to live like that"—and more important still it led them to conclude that they didn't have to any more. That is what the peoples of Central Asia are learning from the Arab Spring. They want what all people want and deserve, and with the help of the people and government who pioneered human rights, they have a chance to gain sometime soon what they were promised but did not get twenty years ago.

Remarks on the Middle East and North Africa*

Barack Obama

President of the United States, 2009– ; born Honolulu, HI, August 4, 1961; early education in Jakarta, Indonesia, and Honolulu; B.A., Columbia University, 1983; J.D., Harvard Law School, 1992; first African-American president of the Harvard Law Review; *community organizer and civil rights lawyer in Chicago; senior lecturer, University of Chicago Law School, specializing in constitutional law; state senator, representing the South Side of Chicago, Illinois State Senate, 1997–2004; U.S. senator (D), Illinois, 2005–2008; author,* Dreams from My Father: A Story of Race and Inheritance *(1995, reprinted 2004);* The Audacity of Hope: Thoughts on Reclaiming the American Dream *(2006).*

Editor's introduction: In the face of revolutionary change in the Middle East and North Africa, President Obama describes the forces driving these shifts and how America must respond in this speech, delivered at the U.S. State Department. Obama assesses the condition of al Qaeda in the Middle East after the killing of Osama bin Laden and describes how, beginning with a street vendor in Tunisia who set himself alight in response to government abuse, demonstrations spread to Egypt, Yemen, Libya, and Syria, as people stood up to oppressive regimes. Obama outlines several principles that must guide the American response to these developments, including opposing repression and supporting universal human rights. He defends the U.S. military action against the Libyan government on humanitarian grounds. In reference to Syrian President Bashar Assad, whose people demand a transition to democracy, Obama says, "He can lead that transition, or get out of the way." He similarly addresses the leaders of Yemen and Bahrain. Finally, he outlines policies to support trade in the region and to promote peace in the Middle East.

Barack Obama's speech: Thank you. Thank you. (Applause.) Thank you very much. Thank you. Please, have a seat. Thank you very much. I want to begin by thanking Hillary Clinton, who has traveled so much these last six months that she

---

* Delivered on May 19, 2011, at Washington, D.C.

is approaching a new landmark—one million frequent flyer miles. (Laughter.) I count on Hillary every single day, and I believe that she will go down as one of the finest Secretaries of State in our nation's history.

The State Department is a fitting venue to mark a new chapter in American diplomacy. For six months, we have witnessed an extraordinary change taking place in the Middle East and North Africa. Square by square, town by town, country by country, the people have risen up to demand their basic human rights. Two leaders have stepped aside. More may follow. And though these countries may be a great distance from our shores, we know that our own future is bound to this region by the forces of economics and security, by history and by faith.

Today, I want to talk about this change—the forces that are driving it and how we can respond in a way that advances our values and strengthens our security.

Now, already, we've done much to shift our foreign policy following a decade defined by two costly conflicts. After years of war in Iraq, we've removed 100,000 American troops and ended our combat mission there. In Afghanistan, we've broken the Taliban's momentum, and this July we will begin to bring our troops home and continue a transition to Afghan lead. And after years of war against al Qaeda and its affiliates, we have dealt al Qaeda a huge blow by killing its leader, Osama bin Laden.

Bin Laden was no martyr. He was a mass murderer who offered a message of hate—an insistence that Muslims had to take up arms against the West, and that violence against men, women, and children was the only path to change. He rejected democracy and individual rights for Muslims in favor of violent extremism; his agenda focused on what he could destroy—not what he could build.

Bin Laden and his murderous vision won some adherents. But even before his death, al Qaeda was losing its struggle for relevance, as the overwhelming majority of people saw that the slaughter of innocents did not answer their cries for a better life. By the time we found bin Laden, al Qaeda's agenda had come to be seen by the vast majority of the region as a dead end, and the people of the Middle East and North Africa had taken their future into their own hands.

That story of self-determination began six months ago in Tunisia. On December 17th, a young vendor named Mohammed Bouazizi was devastated when a police officer confiscated his cart. This was not unique. It's the same kind of humiliation that takes place every day in many parts of the world—the relentless tyranny of governments that deny their citizens dignity. Only this time, something different happened. After local officials refused to hear his complaints, this young man, who had never been particularly active in politics, went to the headquarters of the provincial government, doused himself in fuel, and lit himself on fire.

There are times in the course of history when the actions of ordinary citizens spark movements for change because they speak to a longing for freedom that has been building up for years. In America, think of the defiance of those patriots in Boston who refused to pay taxes to a King, or the dignity of Rosa Parks as she sat courageously in her seat. So it was in Tunisia, as that vendor's act of desperation tapped into the frustration felt throughout the country. Hundreds of protesters took to the streets, then thousands. And in the face of batons and sometimes bullets, they refused to go home—day after day, week after week—until a dictator of more than two decades finally left power.

The story of this revolution, and the ones that followed, should not have come as a surprise. The nations of the Middle East and North Africa won their independence long ago, but in too many places their people did not. In too many countries, power has been concentrated in the hands of a few. In too many countries, a citizen like that young vendor had nowhere to turn—no honest judiciary to hear his case; no independent media to give him voice; no credible political party to represent his views; no free and fair election where he could choose his leader.

And this lack of self-determination—the chance to make your life what you will—has applied to the region's economy as well. Yes, some nations are blessed with wealth in oil and gas, and that has led to pockets of prosperity. But in a global economy based on knowledge, based on innovation, no development strategy can be based solely upon what comes out of the ground. Nor can people reach their potential when you cannot start a business without paying a bribe.

In the face of these challenges, too many leaders in the region tried to direct their people's grievances elsewhere. The West was blamed as the source of all ills, a half-century after the end of colonialism. Antagonism toward Israel became the only acceptable outlet for political expression. Divisions of tribe, ethnicity, and religious sect were manipulated as a means of holding on to power, or taking it away from somebody else.

But the events of the past six months show us that strategies of repression and strategies of diversion will not work anymore. Satellite television and the Internet provide a window into the wider world—a world of astonishing progress in places like India and Indonesia and Brazil. Cell phones and social networks allow young people to connect and organize like never before. And so a new generation has emerged. And their voices tell us that change cannot be denied.

In Cairo, we heard the voice of the young mother who said, "It's like I can finally breathe fresh air for the first time."

In Sanaa, we heard the students who chanted, "The night must come to an end."

In Benghazi, we heard the engineer who said, "Our words are free now. It's a feeling you can't explain."

In Damascus, we heard the young man who said, "After the first yelling, the first shout, you feel dignity."

Those shouts of human dignity are being heard across the region. And through the moral force of nonviolence, the people of the region have achieved more change in six months than terrorists have accomplished in decades.

Of course, change of this magnitude does not come easily. In our day and age—a time of 24-hour news cycles and constant communication—people expect the transformation of the region to be resolved in a matter of weeks. But it will be years before this story reaches its end. Along the way, there will be good days and there will bad days. In some places, change will be swift; in others, gradual. And as we've already seen, calls for change may give way, in some cases, to fierce contests for power.

The question before us is what role America will play as this story unfolds. For decades, the United States has pursued a set of core interests in the region: countering terrorism and stopping the spread of nuclear weapons; securing the free flow of commerce and safeguarding the security of the region; standing up for Israel's security and pursuing Arab-Israeli peace.

We will continue to do these things, with the firm belief that America's interests are not hostile to people's hopes; they're essential to them. We believe that no one benefits from a nuclear arms race in the region, or al Qaeda's brutal attacks. We believe people everywhere would see their economies crippled by a cut-off in energy supplies. As we did in the Gulf War, we will not tolerate aggression across borders, and we will keep our commitments to friends and partners.

Yet we must acknowledge that a strategy based solely upon the narrow pursuit of these interests will not fill an empty stomach or allow someone to speak their mind. Moreover, failure to speak to the broader aspirations of ordinary people will only feed the suspicion that has festered for years that the United States pursues our interests at their expense. Given that this mistrust runs both ways—as Americans have been seared by hostage-taking and violent rhetoric and terrorist attacks that have killed thousands of our citizens—a failure to change our approach threatens a deepening spiral of division between the United States and the Arab world.

And that's why, two years ago in Cairo, I began to broaden our engagement based upon mutual interests and mutual respect. I believed then—and I believe now—that we have a stake not just in the stability of nations, but in the self-determination of individuals. The status quo is not sustainable. Societies held together by fear and repression may offer the illusion of stability for a time, but they are built upon fault lines that will eventually tear asunder.

So we face a historic opportunity. We have the chance to show that America values the dignity of the street vendor in Tunisia more than the raw power of the dictator. There must be no doubt that the United States of America welcomes change that advances self-determination and opportunity. Yes, there will be perils that accompany this moment of promise. But after decades of accepting the world as it is in the region, we have a chance to pursue the world as it should be.

Of course, as we do, we must proceed with a sense of humility. It's not America that put people into the streets of Tunis or Cairo—it was the people themselves who launched these movements, and it's the people themselves that must ultimately determine their outcome.

Not every country will follow our particular form of representative democracy, and there will be times when our short-term interests don't align perfectly with our long-term vision for the region. But we can, and we will, speak out for a set of core principles—principles that have guided our response to the events over the past six months:

The United States opposes the use of violence and repression against the people of the region. (Applause.)

The United States supports a set of universal rights. And these rights include free speech, the freedom of peaceful assembly, the freedom of religion, equality for men and women under the rule of law, and the right to choose your own leaders—whether you live in Baghdad or Damascus, Sanaa or Tehran.

And we support political and economic reform in the Middle East and North Africa that can meet the legitimate aspirations of ordinary people throughout the region.

Our support for these principles is not a secondary interest. Today I want to make it clear that it is a top priority that must be translated into concrete actions, and supported by all of the diplomatic, economic, and strategic tools at our disposal.

Let me be specific. First, it will be the policy of the United States to promote reform across the region, and to support transitions to democracy. That effort begins in Egypt and Tunisia, where the stakes are high—as Tunisia was at the vanguard of this democratic wave, and Egypt is both a longstanding partner and the Arab world's largest nation. Both nations can set a strong example through free and fair elections, a vibrant civil society, accountable and effective democratic institutions, and responsible regional leadership. But our support must also extend to nations where transitions have yet to take place.

Unfortunately, in too many countries, calls for change have thus far been answered by violence. The most extreme example is Libya, where Muammar Qaddafi launched a war against his own people, promising to hunt them down like rats. As I said when the United States joined an international coalition to intervene, we cannot prevent every injustice perpetrated by a regime against its people, and we have learned from our experience in Iraq just how costly and difficult it is to try to impose regime change by force—no matter how well-intentioned it may be.

But in Libya, we saw the prospect of imminent massacre, we had a mandate for action, and heard the Libyan people's call for help. Had we not acted along with our NATO allies and regional coalition partners, thousands would have been killed. The message would have been clear: Keep power by killing as many people as it takes. Now, time is working against Qaddafi. He does not have control over his country. The opposition has organized a legitimate and credible Interim Council. And when Qaddafi inevitably leaves or is forced from power, decades of provocation will come to an end, and the transition to a democratic Libya can proceed.

While Libya has faced violence on the greatest scale, it's not the only place where leaders have turned to repression to remain in power. Most recently, the Syrian regime has chosen the path of murder and the mass arrests of its citizens. The United States has condemned these actions, and working with the international community we have stepped up our sanctions on the Syrian regime—including sanctions announced yesterday on President Assad and those around him.

The Syrian people have shown their courage in demanding a transition to democracy. President Assad now has a choice: He can lead that transition, or get out of the way. The Syrian government must stop shooting demonstrators and allow peaceful protests. It must release political prisoners and stop unjust arrests. It must allow human rights monitors to have access to cities like Dara'a; and start a serious dialogue to advance a democratic transition. Otherwise, President Assad and his regime will continue to be challenged from within and will continue to be isolated abroad.

So far, Syria has followed its Iranian ally, seeking assistance from Tehran in the tactics of suppression. And this speaks to the hypocrisy of the Iranian regime, which says it stand for the rights of protesters abroad, yet represses its own people at home. Let's remember that the first peaceful protests in the region were in the streets of Tehran, where the government brutalized women and men, and threw innocent people into jail. We still hear the chants echo from the rooftops of Tehran. The image of a young woman dying in the streets is still seared in our memory. And we will continue to insist that the Iranian people deserve their universal rights, and a government that does not smother their aspirations.

Now, our opposition to Iran's intolerance and Iran's repressive measures, as well as its illicit nuclear program and its support of terror, is well known. But if America is to be credible, we must acknowledge that at times our friends in the region have not all reacted to the demands for consistent change—with change that's consistent with the principles that I've outlined today. That's true in Yemen, where President Saleh needs to follow through on his commitment to transfer power. And that's true today in Bahrain.

Bahrain is a longstanding partner, and we are committed to its security. We recognize that Iran has tried to take advantage of the turmoil there, and that the Bahraini government has a legitimate interest in the rule of law.

Nevertheless, we have insisted both publicly and privately that mass arrests and brute force are at odds with the universal rights of Bahrain's citizens, and we will—and such steps will not make legitimate calls for reform go away. The only way forward is for the government and opposition to engage in a dialogue, and you can't have a real dialogue when parts of the peaceful opposition are in jail. (Applause.) The government must create the conditions for dialogue, and the opposition must participate to forge a just future for all Bahrainis.

Indeed, one of the broader lessons to be drawn from this period is that sectarian divides need not lead to conflict. In Iraq, we see the promise of a multiethnic, multi-sectarian democracy. The Iraqi people have rejected the perils of political violence in favor of a democratic process, even as they've taken full responsibility for their own security. Of course, like all new democracies, they will face setbacks. But Iraq is poised to play a key role in the region if it continues its peaceful progress. And as they do, we will be proud to stand with them as a steadfast partner.

So in the months ahead, America must use all our influence to encourage reform in the region. Even as we acknowledge that each country is different, we need to speak honestly about the principles that we believe in, with friend and foe alike. Our message is simple: If you take the risks that reform entails, you will have the full support of the United States.

We must also build on our efforts to broaden our engagement beyond elites, so that we reach the people who will shape the future—particularly young people.

We will continue to make good on the commitments that I made in Cairo—to build networks of entrepreneurs and expand exchanges in education, to foster cooperation in science and technology, and combat disease. Across the region, we intend to provide assistance to civil society, including those that may not be officially sanctioned, and who speak uncomfortable truths. And we will use the technology to connect with—and listen to—the voices of the people.

For the fact is, real reform does not come at the ballot box alone. Through our efforts we must support those basic rights to speak your mind and access information. We will support open access to the Internet, and the right of journalists to be heard—whether it's a big news organization or a lone blogger. In the 21st century, information is power, the truth cannot be hidden, and the legitimacy of governments will ultimately depend on active and informed citizens.

Such open discourse is important even if what is said does not square with our worldview. Let me be clear, America respects the right of all peaceful and law-abiding voices to be heard, even if we disagree with them. And sometimes we profoundly disagree with them.

We look forward to working with all who embrace genuine and inclusive democracy. What we will oppose is an attempt by any group to restrict the rights of others, and to hold power through coercion and not consent. Because democracy depends not only on elections, but also strong and accountable institutions, and the respect for the rights of minorities.

Such tolerance is particularly important when it comes to religion. In Tahrir Square, we heard Egyptians from all walks of life chant, "Muslims, Christians, we are one." America will work to see that this spirit prevails—that all faiths are respected, and that bridges are built among them. In a region that was the birthplace of three world religions, intolerance can lead only to suffering and stagnation. And for this season of change to succeed, Coptic Christians must have the right to worship freely in Cairo, just as Shia must never have their mosques destroyed in Bahrain.

What is true for religious minorities is also true when it comes to the rights of women. History shows that countries are more prosperous and more peaceful when women are empowered. And that's why we will continue to insist that universal rights apply to women as well as men—by focusing assistance on child and maternal health; by helping women to teach, or start a business; by standing up for the right of women to have their voices heard, and to run for office. The region will never reach its full potential when more than half of its population is prevented from achieving their full potential. (Applause.)

Now, even as we promote political reform, even as we promote human rights in the region, our efforts can't stop there. So the second way that we must support positive change in the region is through our efforts to advance economic development for nations that are transitioning to democracy.

After all, politics alone has not put protesters into the streets. The tipping point for so many people is the more constant concern of putting food on the table and providing for a family. Too many people in the region wake up with few expectations other than making it through the day, perhaps hoping that their luck will change. Throughout the region, many young people have a solid education, but closed economies leave them unable to find a job. Entrepreneurs are brimming with ideas, but corruption leaves them unable to profit from those ideas.

The greatest untapped resource in the Middle East and North Africa is the talent of its people. In the recent protests, we see that talent on display, as people harness technology to move the world. It's no coincidence that one of the leaders of Tahrir Square was an executive for Google. That energy now needs to be channeled, in country after country, so that economic growth can solidify the accomplishments of the street. For just as democratic revolutions can be triggered by a lack of individual opportunity, successful democratic transitions depend upon an expansion of growth and broad-based prosperity.

So, drawing from what we've learned around the world, we think it's important to focus on trade, not just aid; on investment, not just assistance. The goal must be a model in which protectionism gives way to openness, the reins of commerce pass from the few to the many, and the economy generates jobs for the young. America's support for democracy will therefore be based on ensuring financial stability, promoting reform, and integrating competitive markets with each other and the global economy. And we're going to start with Tunisia and Egypt.

First, we've asked the World Bank and the International Monetary Fund to present a plan at next week's G8 summit for what needs to be done to stabilize and modernize the economies of Tunisia and Egypt. Together, we must help them recover from the disruptions of their democratic upheaval, and support the governments that will be elected later this year. And we are urging other countries to help Egypt and Tunisia meet its near-term financial needs.

Second, we do not want a democratic Egypt to be saddled by the debts of its past. So we will relieve a democratic Egypt of up to $1 billion in debt, and work with our Egyptian partners to invest these resources to foster growth and entrepreneurship. We will help Egypt regain access to markets by guaranteeing $1 billion in borrowing that is needed to finance infrastructure and job creation. And we will help newly democratic governments recover assets that were stolen.

Third, we're working with Congress to create Enterprise Funds to invest in Tunisia and Egypt. And these will be modeled on funds that supported the transitions in Eastern Europe after the fall of the Berlin Wall. OPIC will soon launch a $2 billion facility to support private investment across the region. And we will work with the allies to refocus the European Bank for Reconstruction and Development so that it provides the same support for democratic transitions and economic modernization in the Middle East and North Africa as it has in Europe.

Fourth, the United States will launch a comprehensive Trade and Investment Partnership Initiative in the Middle East and North Africa. If you take out oil exports, this entire region of over 400 million people exports roughly the same amount as Switzerland. So we will work with the EU to facilitate more trade within the region, build on existing agreements to promote integration with U.S. and European markets, and open the door for those countries who adopt high standards of reform and trade liberalization to construct a regional trade arrangement. And just as EU membership served as an incentive for reform in Europe, so should the vision of a modern and prosperous economy create a powerful force for reform in the Middle East and North Africa.

Prosperity also requires tearing down walls that stand in the way of progress— the corruption of elites who steal from their people; the red tape that stops an idea from becoming a business; the patronage that distributes wealth based on tribe or sect. We will help governments meet international obligations, and invest efforts at anti-corruption—by working with parliamentarians who are developing reforms, and activists who use technology to increase transparency and hold government accountable.

Let me conclude by talking about another cornerstone of our approach to the region, and that relates to the pursuit of peace.

For decades, the conflict between Israelis and Arabs has cast a shadow over the region. For Israelis, it has meant living with the fear that their children could be blown up on a bus or by rockets fired at their homes, as well as the pain of knowing that other children in the region are taught to hate them. For Palestinians, it has meant suffering the humiliation of occupation, and never living in a nation of their own. Moreover, this conflict has come with a larger cost to the Middle East, as it impedes partnerships that could bring greater security and prosperity and empowerment to ordinary people.

For over two years, my administration has worked with the parties and the international community to end this conflict, building on decades of work by previous administrations. Yet expectations have gone unmet. Israeli settlement activity continues. Palestinians have walked away from talks. The world looks at a conflict that has grinded on and on and on, and sees nothing but stalemate. Indeed, there are those who argue that with all the change and uncertainty in the region, it is simply not possible to move forward now.

I disagree. At a time when the people of the Middle East and North Africa are casting off the burdens of the past, the drive for a lasting peace that ends the conflict and resolves all claims is more urgent than ever. That's certainly true for the two parties involved.

For the Palestinians, efforts to delegitimize Israel will end in failure. Symbolic actions to isolate Israel at the United Nations in September won't create an independent state. Palestinian leaders will not achieve peace or prosperity if Hamas insists on a path of terror and rejection. And Palestinians will never realize their independence by denying the right of Israel to exist.

As for Israel, our friendship is rooted deeply in a shared history and shared values. Our commitment to Israel's security is unshakeable. And we will stand against attempts to single it out for criticism in international forums. But precisely because of our friendship, it's important that we tell the truth: The status quo is unsustainable, and Israel too must act boldly to advance a lasting peace.

The fact is, a growing number of Palestinians live west of the Jordan River. Technology will make it harder for Israel to defend itself. A region undergoing profound change will lead to populism in which millions of people—not just one or two leaders—must believe peace is possible. The international community is tired of an endless process that never produces an outcome. The dream of a Jewish and democratic state cannot be fulfilled with permanent occupation.

Now, ultimately, it is up to the Israelis and Palestinians to take action. No peace can be imposed upon them—not by the United States; not by anybody else. But endless delay won't make the problem go away. What America and the international community can do is to state frankly what everyone knows—a lasting peace will involve two states for two peoples: Israel as a Jewish state and the homeland for the Jewish people, and the state of Palestine as the homeland for the Palestinian people, each state enjoying self-determination, mutual recognition, and peace.

So while the core issues of the conflict must be negotiated, the basis of those negotiations is clear: a viable Palestine, a secure Israel. The United States believes that negotiations should result in two states, with permanent Palestinian borders with Israel, Jordan, and Egypt, and permanent Israeli borders with Palestine. We believe the borders of Israel and Palestine should be based on the 1967 lines with mutually agreed swaps, so that secure and recognized borders are established for both states. The Palestinian people must have the right to govern themselves, and reach their full potential, in a sovereign and contiguous state.

As for security, every state has the right to self-defense, and Israel must be able to defend itself—by itself—against any threat. Provisions must also be robust enough to prevent a resurgence of terrorism, to stop the infiltration of weapons, and to provide effective border security. The full and phased withdrawal of Israeli military forces should be coordinated with the assumption of Palestinian security responsibility in a sovereign, non-militarized state. And the duration of this transition period must be agreed, and the effectiveness of security arrangements must be demonstrated.

These principles provide a foundation for negotiations. Palestinians should know the territorial outlines of their state; Israelis should know that their basic security concerns will be met. I'm aware that these steps alone will not resolve the conflict, because two wrenching and emotional issues will remain: the future of Jerusalem, and the fate of Palestinian refugees. But moving forward now on the basis of territory and security provides a foundation to resolve those two issues in a way that is just and fair, and that respects the rights and aspirations of both Israelis and Palestinians.

Now, let me say this: Recognizing that negotiations need to begin with the issues of territory and security does not mean that it will be easy to come back to the table. In particular, the recent announcement of an agreement between Fatah and Hamas raises profound and legitimate questions for Israel: How can one negotiate with a party that has shown itself unwilling to recognize your right to exist? And in the weeks and months to come, Palestinian leaders will have to provide a credible answer to that question. Meanwhile, the United States, our Quartet partners, and the Arab states will need to continue every effort to get beyond the current impasse.

I recognize how hard this will be. Suspicion and hostility has been passed on for generations, and at times it has hardened. But I'm convinced that the majority of Israelis and Palestinians would rather look to the future than be trapped in the past. We see that spirit in the Israeli father whose son was killed by Hamas, who helped start an organization that brought together Israelis and Palestinians who had lost loved ones. That father said, "I gradually realized that the only hope for progress was to recognize the face of the conflict." We see it in the actions of a Palestinian who lost three daughters to Israeli shells in Gaza. "I have the right to feel angry," he said. "So many people were expecting me to hate. My answer to them is I shall not hate. Let us hope," he said, "for tomorrow."

That is the choice that must be made—not simply in the Israeli-Palestinian conflict, but across the entire region—a choice between hate and hope; between the shackles of the past and the promise of the future. It's a choice that must be made by leaders and by the people, and it's a choice that will define the future of a region that served as the cradle of civilization and a crucible of strife.

For all the challenges that lie ahead, we see many reasons to be hopeful. In Egypt, we see it in the efforts of young people who led protests. In Syria, we see it in the courage of those who brave bullets while chanting, "peaceful, peaceful." In Benghazi, a city threatened with destruction, we see it in the courthouse square where people gather to celebrate the freedoms that they had never known. Across the region, those rights that we take for granted are being claimed with joy by those who are prying loose the grip of an iron fist.

For the American people, the scenes of upheaval in the region may be unsettling, but the forces driving it are not unfamiliar. Our own nation was founded through a rebellion against an empire. Our people fought a painful Civil War that extended freedom and dignity to those who were enslaved. And I would not be standing here today unless past generations turned to the moral force of nonviolence as a way to perfect our union—organizing, marching, protesting peacefully together to make real those words that declared our nation: "We hold these truths to be self-evident, that all men are created equal."

Those words must guide our response to the change that is transforming the Middle East and North Africa—words which tell us that repression will fail, and that tyrants will fall, and that every man and woman is endowed with certain inalienable rights.

It will not be easy. There's no straight line to progress, and hardship always accompanies a season of hope. But the United States of America was founded on the belief that people should govern themselves. And now we cannot hesitate to stand squarely on the side of those who are reaching for their rights, knowing that their success will bring about a world that is more peaceful, more stable, and more just.

Thank you very much, everybody. (Applause.) Thank you.

Denying Terrorist Safe Havens[*]

Homeland Security Efforts to Counter Threats from Pakistan, Yemen and Somalia

Daniel L. Byman

Professor, 2009– , School of Foreign Service, Georgetown University; research director, 2011– , senior fellow, 2003– , Saban Center for Middle East Policy, Brookings Institution; born Chicago, IL, July 12, 1967; B.A., Amherst College, 1989; Ph.D., Massachusetts Institute of Technology (MIT), 1997; political analyst, Central Intelligence Agency (CIA), 1990–93; policy analyst and director for research, Center for Middle East Public Policy, The RAND Corporation, 1997–2002; professional staff member, Joint 9/11 Inquiry, U.S. House and Senate Intelligence Committees, 2001–02; professional staff member, National Commission on Terrorist Attacks on the United States (the "9/11 Commission"), 2003–04; assistant professor, 2003–05, associate professor, 2005–09, School of Foreign Service, Georgetown University; director, Center for Peace and Security Studies and the Security Studies Program, Georgetown University, 2005–10.

Editor's introduction: Testifying before the House Committee on Homeland Security, Daniel L. Byman discusses the implications of the death of Osama bin Laden and the Arab Spring on American counterterrorism policy and on U.S. security. Describing a still-aggressive al Qaeda core, he offers a measured assessment of the impact of bin Laden's death and urges a campaign of drone attacks. Byman discusses affiliated groups such as al Qaeda in the Arabian Peninsula and their relationship with the al Qaeda core. Byman goes on to assess the level of safety in the United States relative to the time before 9/11. Byman describes the possible effects on al Qaeda of the Arab Spring, which could deprive the terrorist organization of a rallying cry against despotism and may also encourage democracy, which the Islamist group considers blasphemous. Nevertheless, he observes, the unrest in the Middle East may allow al Qaeda more operational freedom.

---

[*] Delivered on June 3, 2011, at Washington, D.C.

Daniel L. Byman's speech: I would urge this subcommittee to consider several recommendations as it strives to improve U.S. homeland security. Fighting the al Qaeda core in Pakistan should remain at the center of U.S. counterterrorism policy, even after bin Laden's death. With the death of bin Laden there is an additional opportunity to weaken al Qaeda's relationship with affiliate groups, one of the core's most important sources of strength. The aggressive U.S. drone campaign in Pakistan has played an important role in weakening al Qaeda and should be continued. The drone campaign will not end the al Qaeda presence in Pakistan, but it does keep the organization on the run and reduces its operational effectiveness.

The "Arab spring" also requires fundamental changes in U.S. counterterrorism policy. The change sweeping the Arab world undermines al Qaeda's message but, at the same time, offers terrorists more operational freedom. The United States must exploit the threat to al Qaeda's message and encourage a smooth transition to democracy while continuing counterterrorism partnerships and building new ones.

In addition to aggressive efforts abroad, U.S. officials must consider how American foreign policy can lead to domestic radicalization and ensure that U.S. policy does not unnecessarily alienate key domestic constituencies. At home the FBI and state officials should redouble efforts to know local Muslim communities and gain their trust.

In the end, however, it is difficult to separate "over there" from "here." U.S. intelligence and homeland defense should focus on "seam" areas—where the United States is attackable outside of U.S. soil, such as on airplanes transiting from airports overseas to airports in the United States.

My testimony will address several issues: 1. The danger from the al Qaeda core in Pakistan after the death of bin Laden; 2. The importance of the drone campaign; 3. The role of al Qaeda-linked affiliate groups; 4. The nature of the threat to the U.S. homeland; 5. The impact of the "Arab spring" on counterterrorism; and 6. Policy recommendations for increasing the security of the U.S. homeland.

I. THE STATE OF THE AL QAEDA CORE

Despite claims that the al Qaeda core became largely irrelevant after 9/11, in reality it remained active in proselytizing, plotting anti-Western terrorist attacks, and supporting insurgencies in the Muslim world.[1] The al Qaeda core revived after the collapse of the Taliban in 2001 and its loss of a haven in Afghanistan. Over time, the group became more entrenched in parts of Pakistan. While Islamabad had made fitful efforts to uproot it, some of the jihadist groups that the regime nurtured and tolerated to fight India and advance Pakistani interests in Afghanistan have turned against the regime. Al Qaeda now has close ties to Laskkar-e Janghvi, Jaish-e Mohammed, and other groups that have tens of thousands of supporters in Pakistan, and its reach is considerable in non-tribal parts of the country.

In this sanctuary al Qaeda has planned, recruited, issued propaganda, and trained the next round of attackers. Al Qaeda played a major role in the 2005 attacks on the transportation system in London.[2] Writing in 2008, terrorism expert Peter Bergen describes the bombings as "a classic al Qaeda plot."[3] Al Qaeda appears to have organized, coordinated, or otherwise played a major role in foiled 2004 attacks in the United Kingdom on a nightclub or a shopping mall; plans to bomb economic targets in several American cities; and the 2006 plan to simultaneously blow up perhaps ten airplanes as they went from the United Kingdom to the United States.[4] Press reporting indicates that operatives with links to Pakistan played a role in the spring 2009 Manchester plot that British security services disrupted—all those alleged to be involved were of Pakistani origin.[5] Terrorism expert Bruce Hoffman found that al Qaeda was actively involved in virtually all major terrorist plots in the United Kingdom since 2003.[6]

Outside of the United Kingdom, German government officials claimed that they disrupted a plot to attack U.S. and German targets in Germany in 2007 involving three men, none of whom were of Pakistani origin, who trained at camps in Pakistan.[7] The Danish government also reported a disrupted plot linked to Pakistan in 2007. France and Italy have also reported al Qaeda-linked plots.

Al Qaeda has carried out numerous terrorist attacks in Pakistan today, working both on its own and with various Pakistani groups. It tried to kill former President Pervez Musharraf several times and probably was responsible for the assassination of Benazir Bhutto in 2007.[8]

Al Qaeda's own thinkers stress the importance of maintaining a haven and seem to have little faith in decentralized, bottom-up efforts. Al Qaeda itself was consciously constituted as a vanguard. Bin Laden's deputy and heir-apparent, Ayman al-Zawahiri, contended even as his movement was being expelled from Afghanistan that "the mujahid [fighter for the faith] Islamic movement will not triumph against the world coalition unless it possesses an Islamist base in the heart of the Islamic world."[9]

The al Qaeda core issues propaganda to radicalize Muslims and helps recruit potential terrorists, trains them, and offers guidance for specific attacks. As a result, local individuals become far more dangerous when they are able to interact with al Qaeda core members.

IMPACT OF THE DEATH OF BIN LADEN

Bin Laden's death is a significant blow to al Qaeda. Bin Laden, Hoffman notes, "played an active role at every level of al Qaeda operations: from planning to targeting and from networking to propaganda."[10] Beyond his operational role, his survival was a form of successful defiance. The world's biggest military and most powerful country made him public enemy number one for almost 10 years and failed to find him. To bin Laden's supporters, only God's protection explained this mystery.

Because of the successful U.S. attack, the aura of divine protection has diminished not only for bin Laden, but by association his cause. A new leader like Zawahiri is an effective operator but has far less starpower than bin Laden and is unlikely to inspire Muslims as effectively. More prosaically, but no less importantly, al Qaeda will find it hard to recruit and fundraise without bin Laden to lead their cause.

Within the jihadist movement, bin Laden often pushed back against the tendency toward slaughter that manifested in Iraq and Algeria. In such countries, so-called "taqfiris" (who saw other Muslims who did not adhere to their extreme views as apostates) made war on their own societies, killing other Muslims and often making civil strife a priority over striking U.S. or regime targets. Bin Laden counseled against this tendency and tried to put his resources behind leaders who embraced his agenda rather than killed their co-religionists on a mass scale.

In short, bin Laden was both a symbol of the movement and an effective strategic and operational leader. It would be glib to assume his death means the movement is finished. At the same time, however, the organization has suffered a tremendous blow.

II. THE IMPORTANCE OF THE DRONE CAMPAIGN

The U.S. drone campaign against al Qaeda, begun under Bush and put on steroids under Obama, has taken out dozens of al Qaeda figures, primarily in Pakistan. In 2010, the United States launched over 100 drone attacks in Pakistan, according to the New America Foundation.[11] Those killed were far less prominent than bin Laden, but in many cases their skills were in short supply and difficult to replace. Al Qaeda struggles to find seasoned and skilled new leaders, and even when it can it takes time to integrate them into the organization. Even more important, but even harder to see, al Qaeda lieutenants must limit communications to stop U.S. eavesdropping that could lead to airstrikes, reduce their circle of associates to avoid spies, and avoid public exposure, all of which make them far less effective as leaders. This makes it harder, though not impossible, for them to pull off sophisticated attacks that require long-term planning.

Although innocent civilians do die in these attacks, the number of non-combatant deaths is often exaggerated and has been declining. According to Peter Bergen and Katherine Tiedemann, "According to our estimates, the nonmilitant fatality rate since 2004 is approximately 25 percent, and in 2010, the figure has been more like 6 percent—an improvement that is likely the result of increased numbers of U.S. spies in Pakistan's tribal areas, better targeting, more intelligence cooperation with the Pakistani military, and smaller missiles."[12] Such innocent deaths are still considerable, and errant strikes have the potential to worsen U.S.-Pakistan relations, but drone strikes are often far less bloody than alternatives such as Pakistani military attacks or U.S. attacks by manned fixed-wing aircraft. In addition, drone strikes involve no risk of U.S. personnel.

Killing terrorist group lieutenants on a large scale can devastate a group. There may still be thousands of people who hate the United States and want to take up arms, but without bomb-makers, passport-forgers, and leaders to direct their actions they are often reduced to menacing bumblers, easier to disrupt and often more a danger to themselves than to their enemies.

III. AL QAEDA AFFILIATES

Because of the blows the al Qaeda core has suffered, attention is increasingly focused on al Qaeda affiliates. The most notable of these affiliates include al Qaeda in the Arabian Peninsula (AQAP), al Qaeda of Iraq (AQI), al Qaeda of the Islamic Maghreb (AQIM), and al-Shabaab in Somalia. Al Qaeda also has ties to a range of other salafi-jihadist groups, at times working with them against U.S. or allied interests and in other cases simply supporting the local groups' struggles against various regimes.[13]

The Yemen-based AQAP began to receive far more attention from U.S. homeland security officials after the 2009 Christmas Day bombing plot, in which a Nigerian recruit almost blew up a passenger airplane landing in Detroit. Al Qaeda has long had operatives and associates in Yemen, but for most of the last decade they focused on targets in Yemen or in the region. The Yemeni regime effectively crushed the threat after 9/11, but a 2006 jailbreak and a lapse in U.S. and Yemeni attention reinvigorated the jihadists.[14] At the same time the Saudi government successfully suppressed what had briefly seemed to be a serious jihadist threat to the regime, and many Saudi fighters fled to Yemen. In 2009 the Saudi and Yemeni branches claimed to merge under the AQAP banner and took a more global focus, attacking not just Yemeni and Western targets in the region but also conducting international terrorism such as the Christmas bombing plot and the October 2010 plan to blow up two cargo planes as they neared U.S. cities.[15] Some U.S. officials claim that AQAP is more dangerous than al Qaeda.

It is difficult to come to firm conclusions about how to view al Qaeda affiliates.[16] There is no single way to join al Qaeda, nor is it always clear when a group should be viewed as under the al Qaeda core's control. Al Qaeda does not demand sole allegiance: it supports local struggles even as it pursues its own war against the United States and its allies. So group members can be part of al Qaeda's ranks and loyal fighters in their local organizations.

Groups often straddle their old and new identities, trying to keep up their local activities while also attacking more global targets. Often this is a time of infighting within a group, with key leaders pulling in different directions. Somalia's al-Shabaab, for instance, appears to be in such a phase today.[17] Some parts of the organization cooperate with al Qaeda, with foreign jihadis playing leading roles in tactics and operations. But others within the movement—probably the majority, in fact—oppose the control of the foreigners, with some even publicly condemning terrorism and even working with international humanitarian relief efforts. Al-Shabaab could become "al Qaeda of the Horn of Africa," but this is not yet a done deal. And if it happens, it could split the group.[18]

THE BENEFITS AND RISKS OF AFFILIATION

Al Qaeda seeks not only to change the Islamic world, but also to shift the orientation of jihad from the local to the global—and here affiliates play a crucial role. Historically, most jihadist resistance movements have focused on their own territory or on throwing out foreign troops, but bin Laden successfully convinced groups that striking the United States and its allies is more important to this victory than fighting more proximate enemies.

For the al Qaeda core, affiliates provide hundreds or even thousands of fighters, donors, smuggling networks, and sympathetic preachers who offer religious legitimacy. For example, when al Qaeda needed to get its fighters out of Afghanistan after the fall of the Taliban, they relied on the logistical assistance of Sunni radicals in Pakistan; the Libyan Islamic Fighting Group helped them obtain false travel documents.

Al Qaeda affiliates also offer access to immigrant and diaspora communities—a group like Somalia's al-Shabaab, with its connections to the Somali-American population, would be a prize asset. In 2010 a Somali-American from Portland was arrested for planning to bomb a Christmas tree lighting ceremony in Portland.[19] (There is no indication I have seen, however, that the individual was linked to the al Qaeda core.)

Al Qaeda franchises, in turn, often get money from the al Qaeda core or others in its fundraising network. Al Qaeda also has web and media specialists, recruiters, trainers, and other experts in its global rolodex, all available to help a local franchise.

In the past, an al Qaeda label is also a potential recruiting boon—it may help a group attract new members who hate the West and the United States but were not motivated by the group's past, more local, rhetoric. Less tangibly, the al Qaeda brand also can give credibility to groups struggling at home. Groups like al-Shabaab often have an inchoate ideology; al Qaeda offers them a coherent alternative. The death of bin Laden, for now at least, diminishes the attractiveness of the al Qaeda brand.

Gaining affiliates may raise al Qaeda's profile and extend its reach, but it also poses risks for the core. The biggest is the lack of control. Nowhere was this more apparent than Iraq. Beginning at least in 2005, al Qaeda core leaders tried to push Iraqi fighters waging guerrilla war under the banner of al Qaeda in Iraq not to slaughter Shi'a Muslims, and especially not Sunni civilians, but to no avail. As the bloodshed rose, al Qaeda funders and supporters pointed their fingers not only at AQI leaders, but also at the al Qaeda core.

The risk is even greater for affiliates. When they take on the al Qaeda label, they also take on al Qaeda enemies. The United States not only conducts direct attacks on al Qaeda–related individuals and targets their recruiting and financial infrastructure, but Washington also can offer its allies intelligence, financial support, paramilitary capabilities, and other vital forms of assistance, creating new headaches for groups that are already beleaguered. They also move farther away from their original goal of fighting the local regime. Because of these risks, the decision to join al Qaeda's ranks often angers more sensible group members who retain local ambitions.

IV. THE NATURE OF THE THREAT TO THE U.S. HOMELAND

The U.S. homeland is safer than it was in the months before 9/11, and the death of bin Laden is a further blow to al Qaeda. Yet the danger of terrorism remains real. As I and others have noted, there is a real chance that in revenge an al Qaeda sympathizer or member will attack a U.S. target, ideally (from the terrorists' point of view) in the U.S. homeland but also, primarily for operational reasons, on U.S. persons and facilities overseas. Al Qaeda itself also has a strong incentive to conduct an attack in order to prove its relevance at a time when many question whether it can continue after bin Laden's death.

There have been few attacks on the U.S. homeland since 9/11, and only one serious terrorist success—Major Nidal Malik Hasan's shooting of 13 Americans at Fort Hood in Texas. Hasan does not appear to have any direct linkages to the al Qaeda core, but he was in email contact with AQAP member, and U.S. citizen, Anwar al-Awlaki, the ideologue and operator who was also linked to AQAP's attempted attacks on U.S. aviation targets in 2009 and 2010.

Despite Hasan's action, in general the U.S. homeland has enjoyed far more freedom from terrorism than I and many experts predicted in the months after 9/11. I believe this good fortune stems from several factors. The destruction of al Qaeda's haven in Afghanistan and the global intelligence and law enforcement hunt for group members and supporters dealt major blows to the core's operational capability and global reach. At home, the FBI and other organizations focused intensely on al Qaeda, making it harder for the terrorists to pass unnoticed. Although there are individual exceptions, the U.S. Muslim community is not radicalized. Indeed, in several important terrorism cases community members have worked with U.S. law enforcement, providing invaluable tips.

Ironically, the terrorism charges levied against various Americans in the years immediately after 9/11 seemed to confirm how much safer our country was. The FBI would often announce arrests of suspects with great drama, but those charged were often common criminals or unskilled dreamers, talking big but with little ability to carry out their schemes. Those arrested had little or no training, and— just as importantly—they did not seem to know how to get in touch with the al Qaeda core. In the end, the government would often charge them with minor, non-terrorism related crimes such as fraud or violating their immigration status.

Yet there is reason to believe that all these factors are changing for the worse in recent years. As discussed above, al Qaeda has revived somewhat in Pakistan, enabling it to plan and train more effectively than it could in the years after losing its base in Afghanistan. This revival is why the September 19, 2009, arrest of

Najibullah Zazi is so disturbing to homeland defense officials. Zazi, a legal Afghan resident of the United States for many years, pled guilty in 2010 to planning to bomb several targets in New York. Unlike the unskilled attackers who were arrested in the past, Zazi admitted he was trained in Pakistan where he was instructed to carry out a suicide bombing.[20]

Nor is Pakistan the only problem. On October 28, 2008, Shirwa Ahmed became the first American suicide bomber, killing himself in Somalia's civil war on behalf of the Islamist group al-Shabaab.[21] Ahmed was part of two groups of perhaps 20 Somali-Americans who grew up in Minneapolis and became radicalized after the Ethiopian invasion of Somalia in 2006. The Somali-American community from which he came has more in common with the Algerians in the banlieues in Paris than the affluent Arab Muslim community of the U.S. By one estimate 60 percent of the Somalis in the U.S., a community estimated as high as 200,000 people, live in poverty, and many young men drop out of school and turn to crime.

While the conflict in Somalia may seem distant to most Americans, the U.S. role there is considerable—and Somali-Americans know it well. In the minds of many Somalis, the 2008 U.S. airstrike that killed Aden Hashi Ayro, a Shabaab leader, fused Somalia's historic enemy Ethiopia and the United States. The result, in Somalia expert Ken Menkhaus' words, was that "fierce levels of anti-Americanism took root among many Somalis at home and abroad."[22] In September 2009, the United States struck again, killing another al Qaeda figure there, Saleh Ali Saleh Nabhan. So far, none of the Somali-Americans who went overseas have planned to return home and attack, but the Shabaab's move toward al Qaeda and the anger at U.S. policy are a disturbing combination.

One of the biggest dangers involves "seam" areas that involve borders, airspace, and other security spots that are the responsibility of multiple countries—areas where homeland security meets foreign policy. Al Qaeda and affiliate groups have far more sympathizers in foreign countries and better logistics networks there as well, making it easier for them to launch attacks from there rather than in the United States. Several of the most deadly terrorist plots in the last decade—the 2003 "shoebomber" attempt to blow up American Airlines flight 63 in 2001, the 2009 and 2010 AQAP attempts on civil and commercial aviation, a United Kingdom cell's 2006 plan to bomb as many as ten transatlantic flights—would have had devastating effects on the U.S. homeland but were not based in the United States. Instead, these involved the al Qaeda core in Pakistan working with members and sympathizers, usually in Europe, to attack the U.S. homeland.[23]

Radicalization from abroad is another homeland security problem. Anwar al-Awlaki left the United States in 2002 and went to Yemen in 2004. From there, his fluent English and comprehensive understanding of U.S. culture enabled him to radicalize individuals like Major Hasan and perhaps others—activities that would have led to his arrest had he remained in the United States.

V. COUNTERTERRORISM AND THE ARAB SPRING

Al Qaeda is dangerous not just because it has hundreds of skilled fighters under arms, but also because tens of thousands of Muslims have found its calls for violent change compelling. When dictators reigned supreme in Arab lands, al Qaeda could score points by emphasizing its struggle against despotism. When dictators like Mubarak fall, however, al Qaeda loses one of its best recruiting pitches: the repression Arab governments inflict on their citizens and the stagnant societies that result. The possible emergence of less repressive and more dynamic leaders would remove a popular issue from al Qaeda propagandists.

Although the word democracy itself often means different things to different audiences, polls suggest that the generic concept is quite popular in the Arab world, as befits a region that knows first-hand how brutal autocracy can be.[24] In contrast, al Qaeda believes that democracy is blasphemous because it places man's word above God's.

Even more ominous for al Qaeda is the way in which Mubarak and Ben Ali fell. Al Qaeda's narrative is that violence carried out in the name of God is the only way to force change. Further damaging al Qaeda's message, change occurred without blows being struck first at the United States. Al Qaeda has long insisted that you must first destroy the region's supposed puppetmaster in Washington (or Jerusalem) before change will come to Cairo or Tripoli. Events have shown idealistic young people dreaming of a new order—in, say, Jordan or Morocco—that you do not need to strike at Westerners and that peaceful change is possible.

Finally, bin Laden must also have lamented that the youth of various Arab countries are leading the revolution. Young people, especially young men, are al Qaeda's key demographic, the ones al Qaeda propagandists expect to take up arms. For over a decade, al Qaeda portrayed its fighters as audacious and honorable defenders of Muslim lands. In some circles they are cool. Now youth in the Arab world are afire with ideas of freedom and non-violent action.

Though the revolutions make al Qaeda's message less compelling, it may still gain traction in the Arab world through greater freedom of operation. Arab tyranny often served U.S. purposes. U.S. counterterrorism officials have long praised countries like Egypt for their aggressive efforts against terrorism and their cooperation with the United States. Even Qaddafi—long derided as the "Mad Dog of the Middle East"—since 9/11 has been valued as a partner against al Qaeda.

New governments in the Arab world will not necessarily be anti-American, but if they take popular opinion into account, cooperation will not be as close as it had been with governments like Mubarak's. The security services that have fought al Qaeda and its affiliates have also imprisoned peaceful bloggers, beat up Islamist organizers to intimidate them, and censored pro-democracy newspapers. Indeed, one measure of how much progress the Arab regimes are making toward democracy will be how much these services are purged. New security officials will be inexperienced, and conspiracy theories about U.S. intelligence have run amok in the Arab world. U.S. intelligence officers would probably be seen as coup plotters rather than partners. Islamists are likely to be particularly suspicious of intelligence cooperation.

In addition, during the unrest some jails in Libya and Egypt have emptied, and the ranks of newly freed jihadists multiplied. In both countries, many of the jailed jihadists turned away from violence in the last decade, producing bitter polemics against al Qaeda (and an even more vitriolic al Qaeda response) in recent years. Nevertheless, among those released are some true believers in jihad who are willing to wreak havoc upon their perceived enemies.

Even in countries where the autocrats cling to power, security services are likely to be less effective against jihadists. At the very least, the security services of Morocco, Algeria, and other countries that have seen protests will make the democratic dissenters their top priority, not suspected terrorists.

For now, there is reason to hope that revolutions in the Arab world will end up a net plus for counterterrorism. But hope should be balanced with the recognition that in the short-term al Qaeda will gain operational freedom and that the United States and its allies need to act now if they are to prevent al Qaeda from reaping long-term benefits from the upheavals.

VI. POLICY RECOMMENDATIONS

I would urge this subcommittee to consider several recommendations as it strives to improve U.S. homeland security. First, fighting the al Qaeda core in Pakistan should remain at the center of U.S. counterterrorism policy, even after bin Laden's death. Having a secure haven is often a make or break issue for terrorist groups, and al Qaeda's strength there is a deadly danger. Because of the danger this haven presents, and because Pakistan is at best a fitful counterterrorism partner, the United States must continue an aggressive drone campaign. Drone strikes, however, are not a substitute for forcing Pakistan to crack down on terrorist groups and secure its own territory. Zazi, for example, managed to receive training after the drone strikes began in earnest, and other terrorist recruits can do so too.

Second, we need to consider how American foreign policy can lead to domestic radicalization. Killing an al Qaeda leader in Somalia can be a blow to the organization there, but the decision on whether to pull the trigger or not should also factor in the risk of radicalizing an immigrant group here at home, not just the operational benefit of removing one leader from the organization.

Third, bin Laden's death also offers a further opportunity to reduce links between the al Qaeda core and al Qaeda affiliates. Zawahiri does not have bin Laden's charisma, and in the past his leadership has been more polemical and divisive. Affiliates may be more reluctant to follow him, particularly if al Qaeda core fundraising efforts suffer after bin Laden's death and the drone campaign makes it difficult for Zawahiri to communicate regularly with affiliate leaders. Conversely, atrocities by one branch of al Qaeda discredit the core, as has happened with AQI.

Fourth, the United States needs to prepare for low-end threats as well as high-level dangers. For homeland defense purposes, the al Qaeda core represents an unusual set of leaders and operatives: most are highly skilled and dedicated, well-trained, and meticulous about operational security. Affiliate members, however, are often less careful—their organizations grew up amidst a civil war, and accordingly focused more on maintaining an insurgency as opposed to a limited number of high profile terrorist attacks.

A vexing dilemma for U.S. policy concerns groups that may be moving toward al Qaeda but have not yet made the leap. Many al Qaeda affiliates always hated the United States and its allies and, even before they took on the al Qaeda label, had members who trained or worked with al Qaeda in a limited way. Their focus, however, was primarily on local issues. Because their groups had some ties to al Qaeda, the Bush and Obama administrations began to target them and encourage others to do so. As a result, the groups became more anti-American, creating a vicious circle. Administrations are damned either way: ignoring the group allows potential threats to grow worse and risks an attack from out of the blue. But taking them on may mean driving some deeper into al Qaeda's fold.

Fourth, U.S. intelligence and homeland defense should focus on "seam" areas—where the U.S. homeland is attackable from outside the country, such as on airplanes transiting from airports overseas to U.S. soil. U.S. officials should continue to try to improve integration between domestic and foreign-focused agencies and, at the same time, ensure that domestic-focused agencies are in touch with the relevant non-U.S. agencies in key countries.

Fifth, at home the FBI and state officials should redouble efforts to know local Muslim communities and gain their trust. Counterterrorism involves not only drone attacks, but also social services for immigrant communities and courtesy calls to local religious leaders to hear their concerns and assure them that the United States continues to welcome them. Whether it be concerns over radicalization of Somali-Americans or other recent immigrant groups, outreach and successful immigration is vital for counterterrorism.

Finally, U.S. counterterrorism policy must incorporate the "Arab spring" into its strategic planning, and U.S. regional policy toward the new regimes (and surviving old ones) must continue to emphasize counterterrorism. U.S. public diplomacy efforts should relentlessly highlight al Qaeda's criticisms of democracy and emphasize the now-credible argument that reform can come through peaceful change. The message should be spread by television and radio, as always, but specific attention should be given to the Internet given the importance of reaching young men in particular.

Washington also needs a new policy towards Islamists. Ignoring the Muslim Brotherhood and other Islamist movements seemed prudent to both Republican and Democratic administrations when they had little chance of gaining power. In particular, the United States should make it clear that it does not want these movements frozen out of government, but rather wants them to participate. The price for this participation is more moderate policies at home and abroad. Inevitably, this will lead to tension, as these Islamist groups seek policies that do not jibe with U.S. preferences, but their alienation could be a disaster for U.S. counterterrorism.

More quietly, the United States should renew efforts to train the intelligence and security forces of new regimes, particularly if there are widespread purges. The first step is simply to gain their trust, as the new leaders are likely to see their U.S. counterparts as bulwarks of the old order and a possible source of counterrevolution. Many of the security services' leaders will be new to counterterrorism. Even more important, they will be unaccustomed to the difficult task of balancing civil liberties and aggressive efforts against terrorism. Here the FBI and Western domestic intelligence services have much to offer.

Recognizing these dilemmas and implementing (or continuing to implement) these policy recommendations will not end the threat from terrorism. However, they can make the United States more secure as the terrorism threat continues to evolve.

FOOTNOTES

1 For a leading proponent of the view that al Qaeda was weak and decentralized, see Marc Sageman, *Leaderless Jihad: Terror Networks in the 21st Century* (Philadelphia: University of Pennsylvania Press, 2008). However, several official U.S. and U.K. government statements and documents support the assessment that the al Qaeda core remains active. National Intelligence Council, "National Intelligence Estimate: The Terrorist Threat to the U.S. Homeland," unclassified key judgments (July 2007), p. 1; Dennis C. Blair, "Annual Threat Assessment of the Intelligence Community for the Senate Select Committee on Intelligence," February 12, 2009, pp. 5-6; "Speech by the Director General of the Security Service," Queen Mary's College, London, November 9, 2006; and Jonathan Evans, "Intelligence, Counter Terrorism and Trust," November 5, 2007. Available at:www.mi5.gov.uk.

2 See "Were They Directed from Abroad?" Honourable House of Commons, Report of the Official Account of the Bombings in London on the July 2005 (London: The Stationary Office, May 2006), pp. 20-21; Robert Winnett and David Leppard, "Leaked No 10 Dossier Reveals Al-Qaeda's British Recruits," *Sunday Times*, July 10, 2005 available at: http://www.timesonline.co.uk/tol/news/uk/article542420.ece; Bruce Riedel, *The Search for Al Qaeda* (Brookings, 2008); Bruce Hoffman, "Challenges for the U.S. Special Operations Command Posed by the Global Terrorist Threat: Al Qaeda on the Run or on the March?" written testimony submitted to the U.S. House of Representatives Committee on Armed Services Subcommittee on Terrorism, Unconventional Threats, and Capabilities, February 14, 2007," pp. 11-13; Bruce Hoffman, "Radicalization and Subversion: Al Qaeda and the 7 July 2005 Bombings and the 2006 Airline Bombing Plot," *Studies in Conflict and Terrorism*, 32 (2009), p. 1102; and Bruce Hoffman, "The 7 July 2005 Bombings," unpublished paper.

3 Peter Bergen, "Al Qaeda, the Organization: A Five Year Forecast," *Annals of the American Association of Political Science* (July 2008), p. 15.

4 Hoffman, "Challenges for the U.S. Special Operations Command," pp. 11, 13-14; Richard Greenberg, Paul Cruickshank, and Chris Hansen, "Inside the Terror Plot that 'Rivaled 9/11,'" MSNBC.com, September 16, 2008.

5 Sarah Laville, Richard Norton-Taylor, and Vikram Dodd, "Student visa link to terror raids as Gordon Brown points finger at Pakistan," Guardian, available at: http://www.guardian.co.uk/uk/2009/apr/10/student-visa-terror-arrests-link; House of Commons, "Examination of Witnesses," statement of James Fergusson, available at: http://www.publications.parliament.uk/pa/cm200809/cmselect/cmfaff/302/9042103.htm

6 Hoffman, "Challenges for the U.S. Special Operations Command," p. 11.

7 Craig Whitlock, "Germany Says It Foiled Bomb Plot," *Washington Post*, September 6, 2007.

8 Riedel, *The Search for Al-Qaeda*, p. 125.

9 Zawahiri, Knights under the Prophet's Banner. Serialized in *Al-Sharq al Awsat* (London) 2-10 December 2001, trans. Foreign Broadcast Information Service, document FBIS-NES-2001-1202, maintained on-line by the Federation of American Scientists, http://fas.org/irp/world/para/aymanh_bk.html

10 Bruce Hoffman, "The Leaderless Jihad's Leader," *Foreign Affairs*, May 13, 2011, http://www.foreignaffairs.com/articles/67851/bruce-hoffman/the-leaderless-jihads-leader

11 See data compiled by Peter Bergen and Katherine Tiedemann, "The Year of the Drone" at http://counterterrorism.newamerica. net/drones.

12 Peter Bergen and Katherine Tiedemann, "There Were More Drone Strikes — And Far Fewer Civilians Killed," *Foreign Policy*, December 22, 2010, available at: http://newamerica.net/node/41927

13 AQIM remains focused on the greater Maghreb area, but it is more anti-Western in its operations than in the past. On the road to becoming AQIM the GPSC expanded its primary focus to include France as well as the Algerian regime. The group also began to strike U.N. and Israeli targets and go after Algeria's energy infrastructure, none of which were a priority in the past. Suicide bombings, hitherto one of the few horrors the GSPC did not inflict, grew more frequent, along with Iraq-style car bombs. In addition, with the NATO intervention in Libya AQIM should be a concern to Western officials. In Pakistan, where al Qaeda's influence has spread since 9/11, there were two suicide attacks in 2002; by 2010 there were over 50, which killed over 1,000 people. Al Qaeda allies in Pakistan attack both the Pakistani state and support anti-U.S. forces in Afghanistan. And AQI, of course, attacks U.S. forces in Iraq. See Lianne Kennedy Boudali, "The GSCP: Newest Franchise in Al-Qa'ida's Global Jihad," April 2, 2007, available at: http://www.ctc.usma.edu/posts/the-gspc-newest-franchise-in-al-qaidas-global-jihad; "2010 bloodiest year in Pakistan since 2001," The Economic Times Online, December 24, 2010, available at http://articles.economictimes.indiatimes. com/2010-12-24/news/27599872_1_suicide-khyber-pakhtunkhwa-province-personnel

14 See in particular "Testimony of Gregory D. Johnsen," before the Senate Foreign Relations Committee, January 20, 2010.

15 For an overview of this danger, see Christopher Boucek, "Terrorist Threat to the U.S. Homeland – Al-Qaeda in the Arabaian Peninsula (AQAP)," Testimony before the House Committee on Homeland Security Subcommittee on Counterterrorism and Intelligence, March 2, 2011.

16 For an excellent recent review of how al Qaeda views affiliation, see Barak Mendelsohn, "Al-Qaeda's Franchising Strategy," *Survival* (Summer 2011), http://www.iiss.org/publications/survival/survival-2011/year-2011-issue-3/al-qaedas-franchising-strategy/

17 International Crisis Group, "Somalia's Divided Islamists," May 18, 2010.

18 See Bronwyn Burton, "In the Quicksands of Somalia," *Foreign Affairs* (November/December 2009), available at http://www. foreignaffairs.com/articles/65462/bronwyn-bruton/in-the-quicksands-of-somalia

19 See "Somali-American accused of plotting to bomb Oregon tree-lighting event," November 27, 2010. http://articles.cnn. com/2010-11-27/justice/oregon.bomb.plot_1_tree-lighting-justice-department-portland-resident?_s=PM:CRIME

20 United States Department of Justice, "Najibullah Zazi Pleads Guilty to Conspiracy to Use Explosives Against Persons or Property in U.S., Conspiracy to Murder Abroad, and Providing Material Support to Al-Qaeda," February 22, 2010.

21 In 2009, al Qaeda's No. 2 Zawahiri called Shabaab advances in Somalia "a step on the path of victory of Islam," while Shabaab would pledge allegiance to Bin Laden. The group even used Alabama native Omar Hammani, who spoke under the name Abu Mansoor al-Amriki ("the American"), to do a video critique of President Barack Obama's speech in Cairo earlier in the year.

22 Testimony of Ken Menkhaus, "Violent Islamic Extremism: Al-Shabaab Recruitment in America," before the Committee on Homeland Security and Governmental Affairs, United States Senate, March 11, 2009.

23 BBC News, "'Airliners Plot': The Allegations," April 3, 2008, available at: http://news.bbc.co.uk/2/hi/uk_news/7329221.stm; Riedel, The Search for Al-Qaeda, p. 131.

24 See for example http://pewresearch.org/pubs/1874/egypt-protests-democracy-islam-influence-politics-islamic-extremism

2

The Rise of China

The Future of Power[*]

Joseph S. Nye, Jr.

University Distinguished Service Professor, Harvard University, 2005– ; born South Orange, NJ, January 19, 1937; A.B., Princeton University, 1958; B.A., Oxford University, 1960; Ph.D., Harvard University, 1964; instructor, assistant, associate, and full professor of government, Harvard University, 1964–1995; Deputy Undersecretary of State for Security Assistance, Science and Technology, U.S. State Department, 1977– 79; director, Center for Science and International Affairs (CSIA), Kennedy School of Government, Harvard University, 1978–1984; director, CSIA, Kennedy School of Government, Harvard University, 1985–1990; Associate Dean for International Affairs, Harvard University, 1989–1992; director of the CSIA and Clarence Dillon Professor of International Affairs, Harvard University, 1989–1993; chairman, National Intelligence Council, 1993–94; U.S. Assistant Secretary of Defense for International Security Affairs, U.S. State Department, 1994–95; dean and Don K. Price Professor of Public Policy, Kennedy School of Government, Harvard University, 1995–2004; au-thor of books, including Pan Africanism and East African Integration *(1965);* Peace in Parts: Integration and Conflict in Regional Organization *(1971);* Power and Interdependence: World Politics in Transition, *co-authored with Robert O. Keohane (1977; 3rd edition with additional material, 2000);* Living with Nuclear Weapons. A Report by the Harvard Nuclear Study Group *(1983);* Hawks, Doves and Owls: An Agenda for Avoiding Nuclear War, *co-authored with Graham Allison and Albert Carnesale (1985);* Bound to Lead: The Changing Nature of American Power *(1990);* Nuclear Ethics *(1986);* The Paradox of American Power: Why the World's Only Superpower Can't Go it Alone *(2002);* Power in the Global Information Age: From Realism to Globalization *(2004);* Soft Power: The Means to Success in World Politics *(2004);* The Power Game: A Washington Novel *(2004);* The Powers to Lead *(2008); editor of numerous books; author of numerous articles and book chapters.*

---

[*] Delivered on February 16, 2011, at Cambridge, Massachusetts. Reprinted by permission.

Editor's introduction: In a talk given at the American Academy of Arts and Sciences and featured in his 2011 book *The Future of Power*, Joseph S. Nye, Jr. discusses two large shifts in how power is deployed in international relations. The first of these is the migration of power from state to nonstate actors. The second is the rise of Asia, though Nye characterizes this shift of power eastward as a restoration of historically normal conditions. He discusses the growth of the Internet and its role in the diffusion of influence and offers some definitions of power, touching on the notion of soft power. Nye maintains that perceptions of American decline in relation to China's recent ascent are faulty, and counsels against an organic model based on the rise and fall of nations. He further suggests that China's increasing influence will be hampered by state censorship, which Nye believes will inhibit its development of soft power.

Joseph S. Nye, Jr.'s speech: What is power, and why does it matter? I define power as the ability to affect others to get the things you want. You can do that in three ways: you can use coercion, sticks; you can use payments, carrots; or you can use attraction and persuasion, soft power. In the 21st century the ability to combine these as smart power will be one of the main challenges not just for the United States but for any actor in international politics. Today we are seeing two big shifts in how power is used in international politics and world affairs. These shifts, which are the result of the information revolution and globalization, are power transition among states and power diffusion from states to nonstate actors.

The power transition occurring in this century is sometimes called the rise of Asia, but it is more accurately called the recovery of Asia. In 1800, more than half of the world's population was in Asia and more than half of the world's product was in Asia. One hundred years later, more than half of the population was still in Asia, but only about 20 percent of world product was. Now, in the 21st century, we are getting back to proportions that are historically more normal. The shift began in the 20th century with Japan after World War II, moved on to Korea, and then to the so-called smaller East Asian states. Now it is in China, and it is about to be in India. In the days of Teddy Roosevelt, the American view was that power would migrate around the globe from east to west; that is, from Europe to the United States. That view was realized, only the migrating didn't end here. Power continues to migrate westward. In the 21st century, we are going to see more of the world's economic activity centered in Asia.

The other great power shift, power diffusion, is the movement of power from governments, whether East or West, to nongovernmental actors or nonstate actors. Nongovernmental actors have always played important roles, but their development and the growth of their influence has become much more rapid and much more widespread as a result of the information revolution. Information revolution is just a fancy term for the extraordinary decrease in the costs of computing and communications. From 1970 to 2000, the cost of computing decreased a thousand-fold. If the price of an automobile had decreased as rapidly as the price of computing power, you could buy a car today for five dollars. One consequence of the information revolution has thus been a significant lowering of the barriers to entry to the stage of world politics. Consider the ability to communicate simultaneously to all points of the globe. In 1970, if you wanted to be in Cambridge and communicate with Johannesburg, Beijing, Moscow, and London all at the same time, you could do so; it was technically possible but very, very expensive. Today, anybody can do so for the price of entry to an Internet café or, if you use Skype at home, for free. Consider also something that was a deep secret and cost billions of dollars when I was serving in the State Department in the 1970s: the ability to take a picture of any place on Earth with one meter resolution. At the time only the United States and the Soviets had this capability. Today, anybody can view such images by using Google Earth, a free program. This is an extraordinary lowering of the barriers to entry. And with such changes you get a different kind of politics. Sometimes people say these changes portend the decline or even the end of the nation-state, but that is not the right way to think about what is happening. The state and governments remain the most powerful actors in international politics, but they are no longer alone on the stage, and sharing the stage with many new actors makes for a different type of politics. As we try to think our way through this, we have to realize that we haven't quite caught up with this diffusion of power, and while we know a lot about power transition through history, we don't know anything about such rapid power diffusion.

The recent events in Egypt, Tunisia, and the rest of the Middle East are illuminating in that sense. The conventional wisdom among those who looked at the Middle East used to be that you had a choice either of supporting the autocrat or being stuck with the religious extremists. The extraordinary diffusion of information created in Egypt and other Middle Eastern countries reveals a strong middle that we weren't fully aware of. What is more, new technologies allow this new middle to coordinate in ways unseen before Twitter, Facebook, and so forth, and this could lead to a very different politics of the Middle East. This introduces a new complexity to our government's dealings with the region. With Egypt we watched the Obama administration try to deal with the hard power elements, with issues such as military assistance to the government, peace with Israel, the balancing of Iranian power, and so forth—issues that can't just be ignored and that thus force us to deal with governments. But at the same time, the Obama administration had to deal with civil society, with what was going on in Tahrir Square, with a new generation. If we think of stability as dealing only with existing institutions and the government and don't think about the future, we are missing dynamic stability. We will fall behind the curve. To deal with a government and with a civil society requires an extraordinary ability to use both hard and soft power—on the one hand, to use the threat of reduced or eliminated military assistance to encourage the Egyptian army not to shoot people; on the other hand, to craft a narrative that will attract young people of the new generation. The Obama administration had to walk a policy tightrope and, although it wobbled a bit along the way, by and large it crossed the chasm—likely the first of many that will characterize this new and different type of politics—successfully.

We forget how new cyber is. Yes, the Internet may be 40 or so years old, but the Web is only about 20 years old, and the millions of people who were on the Web in the 1990s has today grown to 1.7 billion people. This is an extraordinary pace of change, and it means the entry into the game of a lot of actors who previously were not able to play. Recall that wonderful *New Yorker* cartoon with the caption, "On the Internet, nobody knows you're a dog." Well, if you are attacked and something happens to your systems, you don't know who the attacker is—probably it isn't a dog, but you don't know whether it is a hacker, a criminal group, a terrorist group, or another government, and if a government, a large or small government. People can now send electrons across borders to do things that you previously had to do by sending bombers or spies who could be caught or defended against. Stuxnet, the worm that essentially disabled Iran's uranium centrifuges—an attack probably mounted by a government or governments, though we don't know for certain—illustrates the type of attack that could also be mounted against us.

The United States may be ahead of other countries in its offensive capabilities in cyber, but because it depends so much on cyber, it is also more vulnerable. What, then, should our policy be? When it comes to thinking about cyber, we are at about the same place people were in 1950 when thinking about the nuclear revolution. We know it is something new and big and that it is transformative, but we haven't thought out what offense means, what defense means. What is deterrence in such a world? What is strategy? How do we fit the pieces together? Can we establish rules of the road? Can we find an analogue in arms control, or is that an unlikely model for something that is apparently unverifiable? The first efforts at arms control didn't bear fruit until 20 years after the first nuclear explosion and came about largely to deal with third parties (the Nuclear Nonproliferation Treaty) or because of concerns with environmental fallout (the Limited Test Ban Treaty). Not until the 1970s, some 30 years after the technology emerged, were the first bilateral arms control agreements signed, and not until the 1980s did leaders of the two superpower nations proclaim that nuclear war cannot be won and must never be fought. Forty years were needed to develop a powerful basic normative agreement. In cyber, we are still around 1950. What this means is that we can no longer treat cyber and the other aspects of power diffusion as something to be left to the technocrats or the intelligence specialists.

We have to develop a broader awareness in the public and in the policy community to be able to think clearly about how we trade off different values and develop sensible strategies for cyber.

In learning to deal with the problems, many of them unprecedented, raised by power diffusion, we will need a much better account of what power is. We still tend to think of power in old-fashioned ways, as hard power, discounting soft power. We often use definitions like the one Robert Dahl, the distinguished Yale political scientist, proposed in the late 1950s: "Power is the ability to get others to do what they otherwise wouldn't do." That is a good definition for one part of power, but it doesn't encompass all of power; it misses the ability to set the agendas, which determine how others see issues. And it misses the ability to establish the preferences of others, to affect minds, so that you might not have to twist arms when push comes to shove.

Our way of thinking about the great powers is also old-fashioned. The British historian A. J. P. Taylor wrote in his wonderful book *The Struggle for Mastery in Europe* that "The mark of a great power is the ability to prevail in war." Well, the ability to prevail in war remains important in the 21st century, but in an information age it is not just whose army wins; it is whose story wins, and if you don't understand the importance of that narrative in shaping preferences and setting agendas, then you are going to have a foreign policy that relies on only one part of the spectrum of power, that uses only some of the tools in the toolbox. Sometimes this seems to be understood better in countries other than the United States. In 2007, Hu Jintao told the 17th Party Congress of the Communist Party of China that China had to invest more in its soft power. That is a smart strategy. If your economic and military hard power is increasing, you are going to scare others, and they will form coalitions against you. But if you can accompany your hard power with soft power so you look attractive and friendly, you are less likely to create these countervailing coalitions. After Hu Jintao urged China to invest more in soft power, the nation followed up with billions of dollars of expenditures—not only things like the Beijing Olympics and the Shanghai Expo but Confucius Institutes around the world.

In the United States, however, where we are sometimes good at soft power—all the way back to John Winthrop and the "City upon a Hill"—we don't discuss it in our public discourse. I once talked to a congresswoman, a friend of mine, who said, "You know, you're absolutely right about the importance of soft power, but I can't get up on a political platform and say the word soft, because I will not be elected." In practical terms this leads to situations like the one in which Hillary Clinton, the secretary of state, and Bob Gates, the secretary of defense (who does talk about soft power) agreed to transfer an aid program from the Defense Department to the State Department so that these tools of soft and hard power could be more effectively integrated. But after the program was transferred from Defense to State, Congress cut the budget in half—but not because anything had changed in the program. Rather, the cut is a reflection of a political culture and discourse in the United States that makes developing a balanced strategy difficult. Clinton talked about smart power during her confirmation hearings for secretary of state, about the need to balance hard and soft power and, as she put it, to "use all the tools in the toolbox." But how little that discussion enters our broader political discourse is remarkable. To stand on a stump and get money for defense is still a lot easier than to get money for exchange programs or aid programs in the State Department. But if we are going to succeed in this world of diffusion of power, we are going to have to think much more subtly about what is involved in power, and we will need a public that is educated to understand and engage in this broader discussion of our policies.

Unfortunately, one of the narratives currently being used to help us try to understand the power transition that I called the recovery of Asia is the narrative of

American decline. We are told that countries have lifecycles, America is past its peak, we are now in decline, and that is the narrative of the 21st century. I think using such narratives is a big mistake because countries don't have natural life-cycles, so the organic metaphor of natural decline is misleading when applied to countries. Yes, the 2008 financial crisis was a disaster, much of it made in America, but I suspect the idea that this shows the beginning of American decline—as President Medvedev of Russia has suggested—will be proven wrong as the economy recovers. In the 18th century, after Britain had lost its American colonies, Horace Walpole lamented, "We shall be reduced to a miserable little island; and from a mighty empire sink into as insignificant a country as Denmark or Sardinia." Of course, he missed the point that Britain was on the verge of its second century of ascendancy because of the Industrial Revolution. Rome went on for some 300 years after the apogee of its power, and when it finally did collapse, it collapsed not before another country but because of internal decay and the onslaught of barbarians. We don't know where America is in the trajectory of its history. Thus, the metaphor of organic decline misleads us into conflating relative and absolute decline when we ought to think of these two separately.

Absolute decline is not what we are seeing in America. The severe problems we face—including the budget deficit and the issues of secondary education—do not prove absolute decline. These are problems that, in principle, have solutions. That doesn't mean we will necessarily achieve a solution, but we shouldn't pretend that no solutions are possible. The Bowles and Simpson commission shows that solutions to, for example, the deficit problem are possible. That possibility doesn't mean we will have the will to put solutions into effect; just that it is not a situation where you can't imagine solutions. Throughout American history people have expressed concern that the country is in decay, but if you compare American society today to that of the McCarthy period or the 1920s or the beginning of the century, we have a healthier society today. We have always complained about immigration, and yet immigration is what we are. We are a nation of immigrants, and fortunately we will be inefficient enough that we won't be able to stop the flow of newcomers.

Once when I was talking with former Singaporean prime minister Lee Kuan Yew about his projections of what would happen in the contest between the United States and China in the 21st century, he said, "You know, the Americans have a unique advantage. The Chinese can draw from the talents of 1.3 billion people; the Americans can draw upon the talents of 7 billion people. And what's more, when the Americans take these talented people, they recombine them with diversity to create a new and creative generation, which the Chinese can't do because of ethnic Han nationalism." To the extent the United States maintains that openness, worries about American society being in absolute decay are probably overstated. The World Economic Forum's latest Global Competitiveness Report places the United States fourth on its competitiveness index behind Switzerland, Sweden, and Singapore. China is ranked 27th. We are still the innovation leaders in areas like nanotechnology and biotechnology, and American universities and higher education lead the world. The United States has its share of problems at the moment, but the picture they paint is not of absolute decay. Yes, we are going through a miserable trough of extreme partisanship in our political debate, but we have seen worse periods. The 1930s were one. Even among the founding fathers we can find examples of extreme partisanship—look at the relations between Adams and Jefferson and Hamilton. This type of political debate comes from deep in our roots as a people and does not lead me to believe we are in absolute decline.

Our present mood is one of declinism, and it is a mood we have felt before. After Sputnik we thought the Russians were ten feet tall. In the 1980s it was the Japanese. Now, after the 2008 financial crisis, the Chinese are ten feet tall. You can find polls showing that a majority of people think the Chinese economy is now larger than the American economy. We will outgrow this. These cycles of declinism tell us more about the American psyche than about reality.

China will decrease the gap between its power and that of the United States, but I don't think it is likely to surpass the United States in the next few decades. On one measure, size of economy, the Chinese probably will pass the United States sometime in the 2020s, and that stands to reason. With 1.3 billion people and a growth rate of 10 percent, China is bound to get bigger. But having similarly sized economies does not mean having economies equal in composition. Per capita income is a better measure of the sophistication or composition of an economy, and China is not likely to equal the United States in per capita income until close to the middle of the century, if then. The other mistake people make is to look only at one-dimensional projections of power. Most people, when they talk about China passing the United States, are looking only at growth in gross domestic product (GDP) and the size of the economy. They neglect military power and soft power. In military power, however, the Americans are well ahead of the Chinese, and the Chinese are unlikely to catch up in the ability to project military power globally for several decades. China is investing billions of dollars to increase its soft power, but they are limited by the characteristics of their domestic political society. An authoritarian system has a hard time generating soft power because much of soft power is generated by civil society, not by governments. American soft power comes from Hollywood and Harvard and the Bill and Melinda Gates Foundation and from many, many others. The Chinese have been unwilling to unleash their civil society. I was once asked by a Chinese student at Beijing University, "How can we increase our soft power?" I said, "By relaxing your censorship. Look at India. Bollywood makes more movies than Hollywood, but if you compared India's directors, actors, and actresses to those in China, you wouldn't say India's film professionals are more talented—but they do have fewer censors." I think that was the right advice to give my Chinese interlocutor, even if it was totally useless as advice!

You can see the difficulties China will have in generating soft power in the problems it has faced in the last year. After all its efforts to invest in soft power with the Olympics and the Shanghai Expo, they lock up Liu Xiaobo and prevent him from going to the Nobel Peace Prize ceremony, essentially shooting themselves in the foot. The Chinese are unlikely to equal the Americans in soft power until you see a transformation of the political system in China, and I don't think that is likely to come quickly. Recent polls taken by the Chicago Council on Global Affairs show that, even after the disastrous first part of this past decade for American soft power, the United States is still ahead of China and the other Asian countries when it came to measuring or judging soft power.

Finally, when considering whether China will pass the United States in overall power, you have to take into account the geopolitical circumstances in Asia. Asia is not monolithic. Bill Emmott, in his fine book *Rivals*, points out that Japan, India, Vietnam, and others have quite different views of the rise of Chinese power than China does, which makes them natural allies for the United States. The situation is analogous to Canada and Mexico inviting China to come in to North America to balance American power. Fortunately, because of our soft power, that is not a problem with our neighbors, but China does have that problem. The argument that China is bound because of its GDP growth to pass the United States seems to me a rather simplistic, unidimensional view of power.

Why does all of this matter? Certainly, power is not about being able to brag we are number one. We are not the Green Bay Packers of world politics. Instead it matters because power is not good or bad per se. Power is a lot like calories in a diet—too little and you expire; too much and you become obese. Understanding the different dimensions of power and the right strategy for using it is what we need to look at. Understanding our own power, its strengths and its limits, and having others understand it, is particularly important if we are to manage one of the great questions of power transition, the rise of China. Thucydides said that the Peloponnesian War, which tore apart the Greek city-state system, was caused by the rise of the power of Athens and the fear it created in Sparta. Many people have said World War I, which tore the European state system apart, was caused by the rise in the power of Germany and the fear this created in Britain. Some analysts today say this story will be repeated in the 21st century as the rise in the power of China creates fear in the United States. But that is bad history. By 1900, Germany had already surpassed Britain economically. If my analysis is correct and China will not surpass the United States for another decade, or even two or three decades, then we have time to deal with this change. We have time to manage the rise of China without succumbing to the second part of the Thucydidean trap: overreaction because of fear. But we face a concurrent problem, the danger of Chinese belief in American decline. Such belief could lead to Chinese hubris, which would make it even more difficult for us to then make compromises and accommodate China because every time we made a compromise it would be read in Beijing as proof of American decline. Managing well our relationship with China over the next decade or so is going to be extremely difficult, but we can succeed if we design our policies intelligently.

We need not repeat the mistakes that led to the great disaster of World War I. But avoiding a similar outcome will take a much more sophisticated understanding of the present power transition than the current commonplace narrative of American decline.

Power in world politics today resembles a three-dimensional chess game. On the top board of military power among states, the world is unipolar, and the United States is likely to remain the dominant power for another decade or two. On the middle board of economic relations among states, the world is multipolar and has been for two decades. In this domain, Europe can act as an entity, and when it does, its economy is larger than that of the United States. On the bottom board of transnational relations, things that cross borders outside the control of the government, whether terrorists or international cyber crime syndicates or whether impersonal forces like pandemics or global climate change, power is distributed chaotically; the traditional terminology of unipolarity and multipolarity makes no sense here. Dealing with the challenges that emerge from the bottom board of transnational relations requires cooperation, and that is where our soft power comes in. With many of these transnational issues, which pose serious challenges to us, power with others is as important as power over others. Therefore, we have to think of positive-sum and zero-sum games simultaneously. To deal with this world of power transition and power diffusion, we need to think more clearly about how we treat power. We have to understand that the rise of the rest is not necessarily a sign of American decline. We have to keep our wits about us if we are not to succumb to the fear that Thucydides warns against. When we deal with power diffusion issues, we have to think about how we can use the full set of tools in our toolbox, the soft-power instruments as well as the hard-power instruments. As Anne-Marie Slaughter of Princeton put it, the unique capacity of the United States to maintain alliances, to create networks, and to use institutions puts us in a good position to be the most powerful state. If we think in terms of the ability to coordinate collective action to deal with the diffusion of power rather than thinking in the old traditional terms of military hegemony, which I believe is an obsolete conception of power, then we might well get through these next decades of the 21st century in reasonable shape. But in dealing with power transition and power diffusion in the 21st century, we are going to have to learn as a people to think and talk about power in different ways and to become a truly smart power.

New Interest Groups in Chinese Foreign Policy[*]

Erica S. Downs

Fellow, John L. Thornton China Center, Brookings Institution; B.S., Georgetown University; M.A. and Ph.D., Princeton University; previously energy analyst, Central Intelligence Agency (CIA); analyst, RAND Corporation; lecturer, Foreign Affairs College, Beijing; author of numerous articles and book chapters.

Editor's introduction: Speaking before the U.S.-China Economic and Security Review Commission, Erica Downs testifies on the growing influence of Chinese business interests on Chinese foreign policy, which she says has resulted in the erosion of China's longstanding program of noninterference in other countries' internal affairs. The growing number of Chinese working abroad has spurred measures to protect those workers' safety, she points out. China's involvement in commerce with other countries likewise heightens China's interest in those countries' economic conditions, Downs asserts. The rising economic profile of the People's Republic has led to international pressure for it to assume a commensurate profile in global diplomatic efforts. Downs concludes, "the international expansion of Chinese companies is redefining China's national interests and the actions Beijing takes to protect them."

Erica S. Downs's speech: I first would like to thank the members of the Commission for the opportunity to testify. It is an honor to participate in this hearing.

My remarks today will focus on how Chinese companies are shaping China's diplomacy.

The international expansion of Chinese companies and their increasing influence on China's foreign policy is eroding a longstanding principle of Chinese diplomacy, noninterference in the internal affairs of other countries. The global business activities of Chinese firms are heightening domestic and international pressures on the Chinese government to protect Chinese assets and citizens abroad and to help resolve international crises. I will now discuss four ways in which the cross-border deals of Chinese firms, especially China's national oil companies and

---

[*] Delivered on April 13, 2011, at Washington, D.C.

China Development Bank, have prompted the Chinese government to move away from the principle of noninterference.

First, the global activities of Chinese companies are spurring the Chinese government to substantially increase its efforts to protect Chinese citizens abroad.

The expansion of Chinese companies around the world has increased the number of Chinese citizens working overseas, including in countries with elevated levels of political risk. The number of Chinese workers abroad is estimated to have increased from 3.5 million in 2005 to 5.5 million today.[1] This has prompted China's foreign policy establishment to step up its efforts to ensure the safety of Chinese citizens overseas.

The evacuation of nearly 36,000 Chinese citizens from Libya is the most prominent example of this phenomenon. It was the largest and most complicated overseas evacuation in the history of the People's Republic of China. The evacuation was also noteworthy because it involved military deployment beyond China's borders.

The Libya evacuation underscores the Chinese government's enhanced ability to protect its nationals abroad. The prominent coverage of the evacuation in the Chinese media was probably aimed in part at demonstrating to the Chinese public, which expects its government to take care of compatriots working overseas, that Beijing has improved its crisis management skills with respect to ensuring the safety [of] the Chinese people. Indeed, the swift and efficient rescue of Chinese citizens in Libya stands in contrast to the government's more tepid responses to previous situations in which Chinese nationals have found themselves in harm's way, such as when Chinese oil workers were kidnapped and killed in Ethiopia in 2007. That response triggered criticisms from Chinese Internet users, some of whom urged Beijing to dispatch the military to defend China's interests abroad.[2]

Second, the expanding global business portfolios of Chinese companies are prompting Beijing to seek to influence economic policies in other countries to protect investments made by Chinese firms and to ensure that loans extended by Chinese banks are repaid.

China Development Bank's loans to Venezuela are a case in point. In 2010, China Development Bank agreed to extend two lines of credit totaling $20.6 billion to the Venezuelan government. The bank's efforts to ensure repayment of its loans involve two noteworthy endeavors to shape Venezuela's economic policies and decisions.

First, in May 2010, a Chinese delegation comprised of more than 30 representatives of government bodies and state-owned enterprises spent 18 days in Venezuela, where they drafted plans to help Caracas improve its economy. The plans covered issues including the achievement of price stability, improving the investment climate, reforming the exchange rate, and developing selected industries. The healthier the Venezuelan economy, the more likely Venezuela will be able to repay its loans.

Second, China Development Bank is playing an active role in determining Venezuela's allocation decisions. Projects funded by the lines of credit require the bank's approval. China Development Bank probably wants to ensure that its loans are used to finance projects that will be perceived as benefitting the country of Venezuela as a whole and not just the administration of President Hugo Chavez. Chinese government officials and business leaders clearly calculate that the focus on such projects may also ensure that if China Development Bank is still owed money after Chavez leaves office, his successor will continue to repay the loans.[3]

Third, China Development Bank's cross-border deals provide Beijing with financial leverage over distressed borrowers to advance other Chinese interests.

This is especially true for Venezuela and Turkmenistan, where China Development Bank has leveraged its loans to advance other Chinese foreign policy objectives, including supporting the international use of Chinese currency and enhancing energy supply security.

In the case of Venezuela, China Development Bank has taken advantage of its status as Venezuela's largest foreign creditor to further the Chinese government's goal of promoting greater international use of the renminbi. More than half of the $20.6 loan from China Development Bank ($10.6 billion) is denominated in Chinese currency, which locks Venezuela into spending the money on Chinese suppliers of goods and services. China Development Bank was able to structure its loan in this way because Venezuela's high level of sovereign risk makes accessing international capital markets difficult and President Hugo Chavez has forsworn borrowing from the International Monetary Fund because the conditionalities imposed by the IMF would likely cause his government to fall.

In the case of Turkmenistan, China Development Bank has leveraged its role as a provider of emergency funds to enhance China's energy supply security. In 2009, the bank agreed to lend $4 billion after an explosion on Turkmenistan's natural gas export pipeline to Russia deprived Ashgabat of a major source of revenue for nine months. The loan is being used to finance the development of South Yolotan, one of the world's five largest natural gas fields. Not only did the loan help China Natural Petroleum Corporation secure a role in the development of South Yolotan, but some of the field's natural gas will eventually flow to China.

Fourth, the growing overseas activities of Chinese firms are contributing to increasing international pressure on Beijing to assume global responsibilities commensurate with China's global economic interests.

Two of the most high-profile examples involve Sudan and Iran. In the case of Sudan, Washington and other world capitals urged Beijing to use whatever influence it derived from China National Petroleum Corporation's substantial investments in Sudan to press Khartoum to stop the violence in Darfur. In the case of Iran, Washington and other world capitals have lobbied Beijing to prioritize curbing Tehran's nuclear ambitions over the expansion of China's national oil companies in Iran.

In both cases, international pressure appears to have modestly influenced China's diplomacy. With respect to Sudan, in 2006–2007, Beijing helped to persuade Khartoum to accept a hybrid African Union-United Nations peacekeeping force in Darfur. With respect to Iran, in 2010, China voted in support of United Nations

Security Council Resolution 1929. More recently, China's national oil companies appear to be following Washington's warning not to "backfill" oil and natural gas exploration and production projects abandoned by European and other firms.

In conclusion, the international expansion of Chinese companies is redefining China's national interests and the actions Beijing takes to protect them. Non-interference in the internal affairs of other countries is no longer an option for the Chinese government when events in other countries threaten the assets of Chinese companies and the lives of Chinese citizens. Indeed, the Libya evacuation is likely to elevate expectations within China that the Chinese government will similarly protect Chinese workers abroad in future crises. Moreover, as Chinese firms continue to expand overseas, Beijing is also likely to find itself under greater international pressure to influence the policies of countries in which Chinese firms are invested to help address global challenges involving these countries.

FOOTNOTES

1. "Libya a reminder that citizens must come first," *South China Morning Post*, March 4, 2011.

2. Edward Cody, "China Expansion Puts Workers in Harm's Way; Attack on Ethiopian Oil Fields Highlights Political Perils of Pursuing Resources Abroad," *Washington Post*, April 26, 2007; and Rowan Callick, "China's African venture is risky business," *The Australian*, April 30, 2007.

3. For more information on China Development Bank's loans to Venezuela, see Erica Downs, *Inside China, Inc: China Development Bank's Cross-Border Energy Deals*, John L. Thornton China Center Monograph Series, No. 3 (Brookings Institution, March 2011).

Consequential China[*]

U.S.-China Relations in a Time of Transition

Franklin Lavin

Chairman, Export Now, 2010– ; chairman, Public Affairs, Edelman Asia Pacific, 2009– ; born Canton, OH, October 26, 1957; B.Sc.F.S., 1980, M.A., 1985, Georgetown University; M.S. Johns Hopkins University, 1991; M.B.A., Wharton School, University of Pennsylvania, 1996; White House staff member, 1981; officer, U.S. State Department, 1982–83; assistant director, White House Office of Public Liaison, 1984–85; Deputy Executive Secretary, National Security Council (NSC), 1986–87; director, White House Office of Political Affairs, 1987–89; Deputy Assistant Secretary, U.S. Department of Commerce, 1991–93; vice president, Citibank, 1996–99; principal, Bank of America, 2000; U.S. Ambassador to Singapore, 2001–05; Undersecretary for International Trade, U.S. Department of Commerce, 2005–07; enlisted, U.S. Navy Reserves, 1987–2003.

Editor's introduction: In this speech, presented at the Heritage Foundation, China expert Franklin Lavin addresses the future of American-Chinese relations. Among the questions he asks: How will U.S. economic turmoil affect the Chinese economy? How will two countries with long histories of isolationism go forward into an increasingly interdependent future? How will China's leadership transition affect relations between the two countries? Though these are difficult questions, Lavin expresses an optimistic view about their potential outcomes.

Franklin Lavin's speech: Glad to spend some time today to talk about China. I have had the privilege of devoting most of my professional life to China, whether in academia, business or the public sector, and it is a double pleasure to have this discussion at The Heritage Foundation where we have a terrific combination of very serious policy experts and a lot of younger people who are starting to think seriously about policy. As we know, the magic that takes place at Heritage is not just the pure policy analysis, but also its application. I have had a chance to tell

---

[*] Delivered on April 20, 2011, at Washington, D.C. Reprinted by permission.

Heritage's president, Ed Feulner, and other people in Heritage leadership, that it is the extraordinary timeliness and succinctness of Heritage papers that have such an impact on people in government. Heritage papers were always an important reference point for me when I served in government—to be able to put your hands on something very timely and concise, and to go through it and have that as a foundation as you come to policy tradeoffs yourself. So it is a pleasure for me to pay respect to Heritage, to a group that has been a good partner in the policy business all these many years.

I mentioned that I have had the privilege of spending much of my professional life dealing with China and China-related matters, and maybe that is what makes me, in a broad sense, an optimist about China and U.S.-China relations. I think the more one watches China and works on U.S.-China relations, the more reason for optimism one sees, because China is going through quite significant changes, and I think they are overwhelmingly positive changes—not just for the people of China but also for U.S.-Chinese relations. But the size of China, as well as the size and complexity of the United States, means that this relationship might become the most complicated diplomatic relationship in the world.

There are any number of differences, challenges, and even friction points in the bilateral relations, but I want to underscore my optimism because the policy emphasis is such that it requires that most of our time be spent discussing the problems or challenges. However, before I get to that, I want to talk a bit about what is working. For example, it is interesting to me that both China and the U.S. have a national-interest-focused foreign policy. Neither country, I think, subscribes to a philosophy that threatens the other. Neither country, as they say in China, tries to put sand in the other's rice bowl. So I think there is a reasonably positive functional relationship between the two countries.

From a U.S. point of view, if we look over the modern era, since the Nixon-to-China moment, we have about four decades of relations, across eight presidents, both political parties, a range of philosophies, different challenges, and different times. But, there is a high degree of continuity in that relationship and I think there are two pillars that allow for that continuity. One is the pillar of engagement that, regardless of the issue or the challenge, we were not going to break off or try to diminish relations but always try to find a way to improve them. The second pillar is respect for China's one-China policy, that we would not seek to undermine that, although we certainly have interests vis à vis Taiwan. But we never tried to directly do something to diminish the one-China policy.

With that background in mind, let me turn to the U.S.-China relationship and some of the tests this relationship might encounter. That takes us really to the topic under discussion today and to my mind, "Consequential China" is a good way of framing the challenge. It is a challenge for both China and the U.S., and what I mean by this is simply that China is now, by virtue of economic success and other elements of state policy, more consequential that it has ever been. This new role, in which China is a leading economic and political power, does present a challenge to both China and the U.S. in terms of foreign policy management.

I would also say that I do not believe that either country has an extensive geopolitical tradition. The United States was generally an isolationist power until the Cold War, when it was forced to assume a global leadership position. I would say that holds true for much of China's history as well—that as a massive continental power, it focused on a range of domestic problems. When we look throughout China's history, much of Chinese foreign policy really comes down to simply dealing with border state issues. The Chinese wanted stability on their borders and did not necessarily have broad foreign policy issues beyond that. In recent times, China went through a century of decline and turmoil, which further limited its ability to look at foreign policy.

But now we have a new China. Over the last few decades, China has climbed out of the misery of the past century and is in the process of forging a modern nation—the fastest-growing economy in the world, a burgeoning middle class, more university graduates than ever, growing international political reach, more Internet users than any nation in the world, and the most powerful military China has ever seen. So there is a China that has extraordinary capabilities and a much greater sense of self-confidence.

And remember, all of this takes place against the backdrop of the financial turmoil the West has faced over the past two years. It is, then, not simply that China has been outperforming global economic norms; for the last two years the U.S. and other Western countries have been underperforming. To my mind, the set of developments in China is probably the most significant development in international relations since the end of the Cold War and the impact of that is something with which we are still grappling.

I would like to divide up the issues that come with that into two sets of issues, systemic and particular. Systemic issues are those that come about with the rise of a major power, and we could go through international relations history and come to any number of moments where the emergence of a new power had consequences for that country and for other countries as well. What I would like to focus on are the particular issues—issues that are particular to China's rise that might present a greater management challenge. I think these issues are all manageable, but that there are some challenges. Let me offer some illustrations.

THE PRIMACY OF DOMESTIC REQUIREMENTS

The core of foreign policy management for China is external equilibrium: How do you achieve your goals in a peaceful setting? But the policy decisions are driven by internal equilibrium, so we have an internal set of factors that limit, constrain, and define policy options, but those policy options are projected externally. It is not necessarily a contradiction, but it is a constraint. In other words, China seeks to advance its foreign policy goals through a set of policies and tools, but a primary determinant of these foreign policy decisions are domestic political and bureaucratic requirements. China is not alone in this respect; this is a phenomenon in the

United States as well, but sometimes the disconnect between internal requirements and external goals can be striking. To illustrate this point, let us look at some policy statements China made about South Korea late last year.

One of the key regional relationships for China is its relationship with South Korea, even though China has had a longer relationship with North Korea. In many respects, China has done a good job of cultivating South Korea, and there have been much closer economic and cultural ties with South Korea over the years than with North Korea. But late last year, a senior Chinese official gave a speech to a People's Liberation Army (PLA) audience at a Korean War anniversary event, where he stated that the war was "A great and just war for safeguarding peace and resisting aggression." He went on to praise the People's Republic of China's and North Korean actions as "a great victory in the pursuit of world peace and human progress." Well, let us just say that such remarks are unlikely to contribute to better relations with South Korea, and it raises the question of what would prompt these comments. Notably, the remarks did not contain even a courtesy reference to South Korea that we might expect, such as that even though this war was fought for the right reasons, it was over a long time ago and it does not define our relations today, or something of that nature, just some kind of gracious comment toward the other side. But those were not part of the remarks.

I think the answer is that, although these comments do not contribute to better relations with South Korea, they are a very powerful signal to the PLA, that the leadership understands and respects the PLA's role. So the internal requirement prevailed over the external goals.

Let me touch on how domestic political and bureaucratic requirements serve as a constraint on China policy formulation. I want to touch on five examples: internal cohesion, personalities, silos, amplification, and the Internet.

INTERNAL COHESION

Another example of the primacy of bureaucratic politics in China is that the number one criterion in the Chinese government is internal cohesion. One could argue that there is essentially one question during a job interview with the Chinese government, and it is a very simple one: Are you one of us? A capable Chinese government official essentially spends his entire life demonstrating that the answer to this question is "yes." Life is a job interview. Indeed, when you reflect on the raucous nature of the U.S. political process, it might strike the Chinese as very perplexing. Not only do U.S. political candidates avoid questions like, "Are you one of us," in some respects they are trying assiduously to demonstrate that they are contrarian or anti-establishment or representing a change, and the thrust of the campaign can very much be at odds with the established order and policies. However, in China, you must be able to demonstrate that you will be a responsible member of the team. The first question is not how capable you are or how creative you are or what your ideas are. The first question is: Are you one of us? You can call that the dead hand of Leninism because it forces on the system a high degree of homogeneity. This does not always get you the best outcome, and it militates against people who want to try a slightly different direction or throw in a different idea. Thus, China does not have much in the way of bottom-up experimentation, and you really have changes from the top down. And people have a need to demonstrate to a broader audience that they are part of the team. In fact, to go back to the Korean example, we might even have a circumstance in which a government official enhances his internal stature by consciously provoking criticism from South Korea or the U.S.

PERSONALITIES

A related phenomenon of which we should be aware is the end of the personality-led system and the emergence of a bureaucratic state in China. In some respects this could be reassuring because of the excesses of historic personality-led systems, but in some respects it can also augur a foreign policy drift, because it can require a strong personality at the top of the Chinese system to help shape outcomes that are in China's best interest. Think for a second what classic international relations theory teaches about ascendant powers: that if you are a country on the rise, it is in your best interest to defer challenges and problems for as long as possible. There is no strong argument for prematurely forcing an issue if your capabilities are on the upswing. The longer you put off an issue, the better off you are. Indeed, to most observers, this approach was captured pretty effectively by Deng Xiaoping during his tenure in leadership, what was typically in the U.S. referred [to] as the Charm Offensive, and what Deng himself called Tao Guan Yang Hui—to, basically, bide your time.

Yet when we look at the issues that have bubbled up over the last year or two, it looks as if there is almost a deliberate pattern of surfacing issues that did not need to be surfaced: harassment of U.S. ships in the South China Sea, the overly hostile reaction to U.S. arms sales to Taiwan, some of the unneighborly remarks by Chinese officials to foreign ministers from the Association of Southeast Asian Nations (ASEAN), the ramming of a Japanese coast guard vessel by a Chinese fishing boat. Any one of these actions from the Chinese side could have been stopped by a dominant personality, but, unfortunately, I think, for China, what transpired over the past few years was a series of arguably minor steps that cumulatively created a perception of a country that was taking an aggressive posture in the region.

There are different theories as to why China abandoned this seemingly successful Charm Offensive, which, to my mind, helped them a great deal in Southeast Asia. I believe there has been a combination of factors, some of which I have just articulated, along with the role of silos and the amplification effect.

SILOS

By silos, I am referring to the fact that the Chinese government is more com-partmentalized than other large governments, with ministries responsible for rela-tively narrow areas and without many interagency mechanisms for coordination. It is not always easy in the Chinese system to think through and argue costs and benefits of various government initiatives. There is a particular challenge if there are short-term or nominal benefits for one ministry and perhaps long-term costs borne by another ministry. For example, if a PLA navy vessel harasses a foreign ship in the South China Sea, that might help the naval command demonstrate that it is committed, that it is part of the team. However, this action could work very much to the long-term detriment of China's foreign policy. Still, the Foreign Ministry cannot countermand a PLA navy decision.

AMPLIFICATION

There is also an amplification effect, by which I mean that people tend not just to echo established policy but to amplify it in order to signal their allegiance to that policy. Thus, bad policy gets amplified through the system, not toned down as one would hope. It was interesting to me to try to understand what transpired in China after Liu Xiaobo was awarded the Nobel Peace Prize. From the Chinese point of view it was understandable that the award of the Nobel Prize was seen as a severe public insult, and their starting point was that they wanted to respond in kind, criticizing Liu Xiaobo and the Nobel Committee. But in what respects did that help them or hurt them? What other steps did they take and what were the eventual consequences of this for China's foreign policy? Not only did they not have to respond to the public criticism, but this did play to a domestic constitu-ency and did play to that cohesion point mentioned earlier. Then, after they went through the public criticism, they conjured up their own international prize, the Confucian Peace Prize, and awarded it to a Taiwanese dignitary who had not even been informed he had won. It was a somewhat embarrassing moment, I believe, for the people who orchestrated that event and even worse for Beijing—it just kept the issue alive. Instead of letting the issue fade, they responded because of the cohesion requirement, and matters were made worse because of the amplification effect. They ended up setting into play a set of activities which were not in their own self interest.

THE INTERNET

Let me make a final point on a policy constraint—the emergence of the Internet in China. In general, it has been a positive force and it certainly provides more lati-tude for discussion than we've ever seen. I am sure there are many people here who click around on Chinese blogs and chat rooms, and it is very interesting to follow some of the discussions. But I think we should also note that in some respects it might also serve as a constraint on policy because Internet chatter in China tends to be a bit unbalanced. On some sets of issues, open criticism of government policy is prohibited, so the audience only receives one point of view.

Beyond that, the Internet itself tends to be a medium, which, for whatever set of reasons, promotes comments that tend to be a bit emotional and maybe even a bit nationalistic. So, instead of thoughtful examination of an issue or the pros and cons, you can get this cheerleading effect. It was interesting to me when I looked at some of the discussions in the chat rooms about the incident when the Chinese fishing boat hit the Japan Coast Guard—that virtually none of the discussion had to do with cost and benefit. Was the incident helpful? What was the ultimate accomplishment? What is our goal, and did this take us to our goal? None of this discussion had to do with what we would say was a normal analytical approach. Almost all the comments were just cheerleading.

Some of this emotional response is to be expected because it is the Internet, not a graduate school seminar. But I do think that, cumulatively, this kind of emotionalism does not help China move to more productive outcomes in foreign policy management.

Let me close by saying that I think the Chinese system has many strengths. I think it provides a lot of consistency in foreign policy management. I think the Chinese government typically demonstrates a pretty strong understanding of national self-interest. I do think this understanding provides some strength to China and other countries who are trying to develop good relations with China. You always know where China stands on a set of issues.

My conclusion is that China and the U.S. face twin challenges when it comes to foreign policy management. As China emerges into this new major power role, I think it is going to enhance its own prospects for a successful foreign policy, showing subtlety and restraint that all great powers have to show, and I think this is difficult to do given China's domestic political environment. For its part, the United States needs to be able to display flexibility and goodwill in trying to work with China.

I think the biggest mistake China could make in foreign policy would be simply to assert its foreign policy goals without regard to other parties. An assertion of a point of view is not the same as the adoption of policies that would help you reach your objectives. Sometimes, I think those different concepts are blurred in China. We can understand that domestically they may be somewhat the same. You have a top-down system and if you assert a domestic policy goal, that is an important step on the way to achieving that policy goal. But, it does not work that way in foreign policy as there are other parties involved.

The United States has responsibilities as well. I think the biggest mistake the United States could make in dealing with China would be to view China through a deterministic lens, that China's economic rise inevitably means hostility. Sino–American relations are a mosaic of a thousand policies, initiatives, gestures, and meetings across a range of government and private sector activities. Relations are not pre-determined by GDP growth rates. Given the size and complexities of the two countries and the many differences between the two governments, it is no surprise there are different points of view and even occasional points of friction, but I also see significant progress in the relationship. If there is as much positive movement over the next 40 years as in the past 40 years, the leaders in both countries should be congratulated for their statesmanship.

Thank you very much for letting me talk with you.

America's Challenge[*]

Martin Feldstein

George F. Baker Professor of Economics, Harvard University, 1984– ; President Emeritus, National Bureau of Economic Research (NBER); born New York, NY, November 25, 1939; A.B., Harvard College, 1961; B. Litt., 1963, M.A., 1964, D. Phil., 1967, Oxford University; lecturer in public finance, Oxford University, 1965–67; research fellow, 1964–65, official fellow, 1965–67, Nuffield College, Oxford University; chairman, White House Council of Economic Advisers, 1982–84; assistant professor, 1967–68, associate professor, 1968–69, professor, 1969–1984, Harvard University; president and chief executive officer (CEO), NBER, 1977–1982, 1984–2008.

Editor's introduction: In this speech, delivered to the American Enterprise Institute (AEI), economist Martin Feldstein notes that China's economy, currently the second-largest in the world, is on pace to become larger than that of the United States. He outlines several challenges this presents to the United States, among them how to maintain overwhelming military supremacy in the face of China's rapidly developing armed forces. In the areas of trade and economic policy, he recommends free trade agreements with other Asian nations as a hedge against the growing influence of the massive Chinese consumer market. As for the challenge at home, he calls for a pro-growth economic policy that stresses productivity over competitiveness, and comments on the nation's educational system as well as its immigration and tax policy.

Martin Feldstein's speech: Thank you. I am very honored by this award and by the opportunity to deliver this year's Irving Kristol lecture.

I knew Irving Kristol for more than 30 years and admired him as a public intellectual who was devoted to the development of ideas that could shape public policy in favorable ways.

Irving also played an important part in my own life. I met him when I was a first-year assistant professor at Harvard. Someone had told him that I had some novel ideas about reforming health insurance and he encouraged me to write about

[*] Delivered on May 3, 2011, at Washington, D.C. Reprinted by permission.

them for the *Public Interest*. Over the years I found the *Public Interest* to be an excellent way to present ideas about a wide range of subjects to the relatively small but highly influential group of *Public Interest* readers who helped to shape conservative thinking and action about domestic policy. We should all be grateful to Irving for creating the *Public Interest* and for his devotion to maintaining its relevance and its impact.

I am also honored to be standing here tonight because of my admiration for the American Enterprise Institute. Many years ago, at a time when conservative ideas were scarce, particularly in the academic community, AEI brought rigorous debate to public policy issues. I saw many of those ideas come to fruition when I was in the Reagan White House. AEI continues to be a major contributor to public policy in a wide range of areas. We are all better off because of what AEI has done and what it continues to do.

CHINA'S RISE

Let me begin with an important—and to many people, disturbing—economic fact: sometime in the next 15 years China's economy will be bigger than that of the United States. That presents a major economic challenge, military challenge, political challenge, and psychological challenge. Those challenges are my subject this evening.

China is, of course, still a very poor country with a much lower average income than we enjoy in America. Real per-capita income in China is less than one-sixth of the U.S. level. But China's population of 1.3 billion people is more than four times ours and its per-capita income is growing rapidly. That makes it inevitable that the real value of China's GDP—the total value of goods and services produced in China (adjusted to U.S. prices)—will soon exceed America's GDP.

China's GDP recently exceeded Japan's, making China the second-largest economy in the world. Although we remember Japan's industrial expansion in the 1980s, its relatively small population means that Japan's economy could never become as large as ours.

According to official U.S. government estimates, China's real GDP is now about two-thirds of America's GDP. Over the past three decades, China's GDP has been growing at a 10 percent real rate while the U.S. GDP has been growing at about 3 percent. If those growth rates continue, China's GDP will exceed ours within just six years. But even if China's growth rate slows to 7 percent a year while ours accelerates to 4 percent, China's GDP will catch up to ours by 2025. So China's future place as the largest economy in the world is virtually inevitable.

I would not have believed that when I first visited China 30 years ago. China was then a desperately poor country in which the heavy hand of its communist government reduced productivity and prevented growth. It was then illegal for anyone to hire employees or to own production equipment. Agriculture was still collectivized. But all of that was about to change as the Chinese government began to recognize property rights and to welcome entrepreneurship.

Today's China is a strange mixture of entrepreneurial capitalism and state-owned enterprises. Anyone who now visits Beijing or Shanghai or dozens of other Chinese cities sees increasing prosperity and growth. China's real GDP is now about 20 times what it was when I visited there in 1982. The Chinese people have taken seriously the advice of Deng Xiaoping when he said, "To get rich is glorious." It's too bad that that sentiment is not advocated by some of our own senior political leaders.

But here is the important point: China's imminent overtaking of America's GDP does not diminish our ability to grow and to raise our standard of living. Even when China's total GDP catches up to ours, our per-capita income will be very much higher than China's. And the United States can continue to have the highest standard of living in the world if we pursue sound policies here at home.

But the rapid growth of China's total GDP does have important implications for America's military and foreign policy and for our policies toward trade and foreign investment. I'll begin my remarks by commenting on these military and trade challenges. I will then return to the challenge of achieving a strong rate of growth and a rising living standard here at home.

THE MILITARY CHALLENGE

The United States and China now have relatively good political relations and China is not a current military threat to the United States. There are tensions over Taiwan and Tibet and the South China Sea but these are being dealt with diplomatically. Today's leaders in China are focused on achieving economic growth, raising domestic living standards, and preserving internal stability. They want to engage with the United States in a positive way by promoting trade and investment in China. American administrations and businesses are responding in a similar positive way.

But China is building a military capability that will grow in scale and force as its total GDP grows. China's military spending has been growing at double-digit rates for decades. China is already a nuclear power, is developing a navy that can have global reach, is acquiring an aircraft carrier, has anti-ship missiles, has demonstrated a stealth fighter plane, and clearly has sophisticated skills in cyberspace.

The quality of China's military force is not currently up to U.S. standards. The United States now clearly has the world's strongest military. But no one doubts that China's defense budget will grow with its GDP. And while the U.S. political system has forced defense spending to shrink from nine percent of GDP in the Kennedy years to less than five percent of GDP now, China does not face the same political limits on the share of its GDP that it devotes to defense.

What are the implications of this for America's defense policy and defense spending? The key is to focus on the future and to recognize the virtual certainty of China's growing economic power. Our focus should be on the future generations of Chinese civilian and military leaders. The United States should maintain a military capability such that no future generation of Chinese leaders will consider a military challenge to the United States or consider using military force to intimidate the United States or our allies.

China's future military spending and its weapons development will depend on China's perception of what the United States is doing and what we will do in the future. If we show a determination to remain invincible, China will not waste resources on trying to challenge us in an arms race.

China is in many ways a resource-poor country that depends on imports of oil, iron, and other raw materials as well as on imports of food to feed its people. That is not likely to change. China is therefore now buying oil in the ground around the world and arable land in Africa to grow food for the Chinese people. Some countries in the past have used military force to gain secure access to such materials. China's future leaders should not be tempted to follow that path.

It is important that our allies and friends like Japan and Korea and Singapore and Australia see the commitment of the United States to remain strong and to remain present in Asia. Their relations with China and with us depend on what they can expect of America's future military strength.

The Navy has a particularly important role to play in this, including the Navy's presence in international waters to enforce freedom of the seas, naval visits to Asian ports, and joint exercises with the navies of other governments.

We cannot postpone implementing a policy of future military superiority until some future year. We have to work now to develop the weapon systems of the future. We have to maintain the industrial and technological capacity to produce those weapon systems. We have to make it clear by our budgets and by our actions that we are the global force now and will continue to be that in the future. While reducing fiscal deficits is very important, that task should not prevent the federal government from achieving its primary responsibility of defending this country and our global interests, both now and in the future.

And while my remarks have been focused on China, the United States now faces current global threats that cannot be ignored. We need a strong military force now and a budget that is adequate for current operations as well as for preparing for the future. The president's proposal to shrink defense spending to less than 4 percent of GDP in the current decade threatens our capabilities and sends the wrong message about our future strength.

And as we think about our military role in Asia and elsewhere, we have to ask ourselves whether we have a moral obligation to defend our allies. Or is our appropriate military policy just limited to protecting our trade, our foreign investments, and our access to oil? And as we think about our national interest, shouldn't we look ahead and consider how developments in any one country can eventually affect a broader geographic area?

There are those who say the United States should not be the global policeman. But if not us, who? As the only democratic superpower with the ability to defend and to punish, do we not have a moral obligation to be willing to use that power? Is anyone now proud of America's isolationism in the 1930s that prevented the United States from assisting European nations that were being overrun by Nazi Germany?

There are also those who say we cannot afford to be the global policeman. But should we really be deterred from that role when the cost of our entire military budget—including the actions in Iraq and Afghanistan—is now less than 5 percent of our GDP? There is no danger of bankrupting ourselves by so-called "imperial overreach" when we spend less than 5 percent of GDP on defense. And while there is no doubt waste in military budgets and military procurement, that is unfortunately inherent in the congressional appropriation process. Cutting the defense budget would reduce our military capabilities rather than just removing waste.

THE CHALLENGE TO TRADE AND INVESTMENT POLICY

Let me turn now from military issues to some brief comments on the challenge that China's economic growth poses for America's trade and investment policies. China, with more than $1.3 trillion of annual imports, has become the major customer for the exports of many companies and many countries. Many foreign firms also produce in China and sell to the Chinese market. It is a striking fact that General Motors now sells more vehicles in China than it does in the United States. The countries and companies that sell in China recognize that the size of China's market will continue to rise rapidly as China's GDP increases and its middle class grows. They want to continue to sell increasing amounts to those Chinese buyers.

Global companies also want to locate production facilities in China. They do that to be close to potential buyers but also to hire both low-skill and high-skill employees at more favorable wages than they can in the United States, Europe, or Japan. This will remain true even though rising wages and increasing property rents in China will erode some of the cost advantage of producing there.

The increasing size of the Chinese market creates a challenge for U.S. trade policy and for our related foreign policy. China will inevitably want to leverage its trade and investment relations with other countries in pursuit of its political, economic, and military aims. The best way to prevent a deterioration of Asia into a closed trading block and a China-centered political coalition is for the United States to expand free trade agreements and other trade arrangements with the countries of Asia.

The recent experience of U.S. manufacturers in China is an example of the risks that could lie ahead. Two years ago the Chinese government announced a policy that would allow only Chinese firms to sell products to the Chinese government and to all Chinese governmental entities. Moreover, the Chinese decree said that even U.S. firms that are producing in China would be classified as foreign and therefore not eligible to sell to government entities. Since so many Chinese firms— from state-owned enterprises to local hospitals—are technically government entities, this policy would exclude American firms from a large part of the Chinese market. Fortunately, in response to U.S. pressure, the Chinese government eventually revised the rules to treat American firms that are based in China as Chinese for the purpose of this restriction.

The Chinese government also declared a policy that would require foreign firms that want to manufacture in China to transfer their technology to a Chinese partner. American CEOs with whom I spoke about this were outraged but felt that they had no choice since they wanted to manufacture and sell in China. Pressure from the United States and other governments eventually caused a modification of this policy, but it is not clear how this will evolve in the future.

Although China is bound by WTO rules, policies of limiting market access for government purchases and requiring technology sharing are not technically prevented by WTO rules. As China flexes its economic muscles in the future, the United States and other countries will have to develop a strategy to protect the legitimate property rights of our firms when they invest in China.

THE CHALLENGE AT HOME: RAISING AMERICA'S STANDARD OF LIVING

Let me now turn to the challenge at home. At the beginning of my remarks I emphasized that China's growth and its eventual overtaking of U.S. total GDP does not diminish America's ability to grow and to remain the greatest economy in the world, the country to which people around the world want to come, and the country that is the global leader in science and culture and creative industry.

Our growth and our standard of living depend on what we do and not on what the Chinese do.

Although our economy has had its cyclical ups and downs, the 2.3 percent average annual growth rate of real per-capita GDP that America has experienced during my life has been enough to raise real per-capita income more than five fold during those years. In today's prices, per capita GDP rose from $9,070 in 1939 to more than $47,000 last year. The challenge is to maintain that rate of growth into the future or to raise it even higher.

Small differences in the growth rate can mean a great deal. If the average growth rate of GDP per capita had been 1 percent less during my lifetime, our income level today would be only half of what it actually is. And if we could have grown at 1 percent more per year, our incomes now would have twice today's buying power. So preserving or increasing our economic growth will have a powerful effect on our nation's future.

I fear that the policy path that our economy is now on will not permit strong future growth. If we want to achieve satisfactory growth, we need to shift to more pro-growth policies.

The key to our standard of living is productivity—that is, the quantity of goods and services produced per hour of employee work. The faster the growth of productivity, the faster will be the rise in real incomes and in our standard of living.

The growth of productivity depends on the quality of our workforce, the growth of our capital stock, the effectiveness of management, and the introduction of new technology and new products. Each of these can be influenced by government policies—by taxes, regulation, government programs, and fiscal deficits.

But while government policies cannot produce the creative drive that generates exciting new products—products that make American ingenuity the envy of the world—bad government policies can stifle that creativity and make it more difficult to convert new ideas into real products at prices that millions of people around the world can enjoy.

You may have noticed that I have not said anything about "competitiveness"—our national ability to export and to compete with imports from China and other countries. That wasn't an oversight. Our nation's ability to export and to replace imports with American-made goods and services does not raise our standard of living unless it is the result of higher productivity.

Productivity is fundamental, not competitiveness.

Indeed, raising America's competitiveness can actually depress our standard of living if it is the result of a weaker dollar rather than of greater American productivity. If the Chinese raise the value of the renminbi, as the current and previous administrations have urged, that would increase our ability to compete with China both at home and abroad. It would help American firms and workers that want to sell to China and that compete with Chinese products here in the United States. But the rise in the renminbi would increase the real cost of everything we buy from China. For Americans as a whole the increased competitiveness brought about by a stronger renminbi would mean a lower standard of living. So let's stop focusing on competitiveness and focus instead on raising our productivity—the amount that we produce per worker.

A fundamental source of American productivity is the quality of our workforce, and education is key to that quality. American higher education is very good. That reflects the tradition of independent private universities and the national market in higher education in which those institutions compete for students and faculty.

We could of course do better and I worry that our system of financing students in public postsecondary institutions is making it hard for the private institutions to survive and flourish.

Fewer than 30 percent of students are enrolled in private institutions. Wouldn't it be better if, instead of subsidizing their state public-sector universities and colleges directly, the state governments gave scholarship grants directly to students?

We are also failing to keep many of the talented foreign-born science and engineering graduates of our universities here in America because of our immigration policies. Nearly half of our nation's output of PhDs in science and engineering goes to foreign nationals, many of whom would like to stay in this country but are forced to leave. What's wrong with the idea of giving a green card to anyone who gets an American PhD in science or engineering?

But the real problem with our education system is in the primary and secondary schools. While there are some excellent schools, far too many of our schools are failing to educate the students that sit in their classrooms. The problem is not just in poor neighborhoods in central cities.

American students as a whole do poorly on standardized international tests of science and mathematics. The most recent OECD-sponsored test of science and math skills found American students below the average for all the OECD countries. Chinese students in Shanghai finished first. The scores of American students were well below those in such diverse countries as Korea, Canada, and Finland.

We know the primary reasons for this failure—the lack of choice that students and their parents have and the power of monopoly teachers unions. The result is that teaching does not attract talented college graduates and that schools do not weed out poor teachers. I can only hope that the accumulating evidence on the positive effects of school choice and the changes that computer technology will make possible in education will improve this situation in the future. The recent willingness of state governors to stand up to public unions over budget issues gives me some optimism that someday they will focus on the seniority rules and other features that handicap our educational system.

Our productivity growth also reflects the way that government policies, especially tax policies, influence what students do when they leave school and join the workforce. High tax rates affect the occupations they choose, the effort that they make on the job, their desire for promotion, their decisions to change jobs and to move in pursuit of better employment, and their willingness to take risks in pursuit of a good idea. The entrepreneurial drive is strong in America but it can be suppressed by high tax rates and complex regulations.

Let me spend a moment on the effect of tax policies on economic incentives, a subject that has been a focus of much of my research over the years.

Marginal tax rates on incremental earnings are too high. Consider a middle-income couple making $80,000 a year. They now face a marginal tax rate of 45 percent on every extra dollar that they earn because of the combined effect of the federal income tax, the payroll tax, and state taxes. But while 45 percent is a typical marginal tax rate on additional earnings, all of these personal taxes combined collect less than 15 percent of GDP.

The reason that we have such high marginal tax rates to collect 15 percent of GDP is that the tax code is full of special features that reduce revenue. Those features are really forms of government spending that have been built into the tax code.

Tax credits for buying hybrid cars or solar panels are just like government spending to subsidize their purchase. The exclusion from employees' taxable incomes of employer payments for health insurance is just like government spending on the same excessive first-dollar health insurance.

And the deductions for interest on home mortgages provide a government subsidy for excessive investment in homes and excessive mortgage leverage. Those overleveraged home mortgages were important contributors to the housing bubble and subsequent collapse.

These special features—known as tax expenditures—add more to the deficit each year than all the nondefense discretionary spending in the budget. Once enacted, the tax rules that create tax expenditures do not face any annual review as part of the appropriation process, a review that is in principle given to ordinary defense and nondefense outlays. Restricting the size of these tax expenditures would generate revenue that would permit reducing marginal tax rates while at the same time cutting the budget deficit.

Although limiting the use of tax expenditures produces additional tax revenue, it is very different from other revenue increases. It does not raise marginal tax rates, does not discourage work or entrepreneurship, and does not tax saving and risk taking. It is really a reduction in government spending.

It is possible to limit spending through the tax system without eliminating or reducing any specific tax expenditures. A better way is to allow individuals to have all of the current tax expenditures but just to limit the total tax saving of each individual to a maximum percentage of that individual's adjusted gross income. In other words, individuals can continue to have all of the current tax expenditures but cannot be too greedy about the total amount of tax they save in this way.

A 45 percent combined marginal tax rate may not discourage everyone but it is undoubtedly a drag on effort and entrepreneurship for the economy as a whole. The marginal tax rate on middle-income families has increased because of the rise in the payroll tax rate—from 6 percent in 1960 to more than 15 percent now. And the top federal income tax rate has risen from 28 percent after the Reagan tax cuts to more than 40 percent now.

While a fair distribution of tax burdens is important, we should reject the spiteful egalitarianism of those who would use high tax rates to reduce income inequality. We should insist that reducing poverty and maintaining income mobility, not limiting inequality, are the appropriate goals of government policy.

The productivity of the workforce depends also on the size of our capital stock—the equipment, software, and buildings. The size of the productive capital stock depends on how much we save as a nation and how we divide that saving between housing and productive business investment. We don't score well on either of these.

Many government policies depress our national saving rate, starting with our enormous fiscal deficit that offsets the positive saving of households and businesses. Our household saving rate of about 4 percent of GDP is low by both historic and international standards. A major reason why lower- and middle-income households save very little is that Social Security benefits replace about half of the preretirement income of an average earner, leaving much less incentive to save.

The household saving of higher-income individuals is depressed by high marginal taxes on interest, dividends, and capital gains. The capital gains tax not only discourages saving and risk taking but also locks investors into existing investments rather than freeing their capital to invest in new ventures. It is a very unfair tax: a double tax on incomes that have already been taxed at the corporate level, a tax on nominal gains that reflect inflation, and a tax on gains without allowing a full deduction for losses.

The estate tax also discourages saving and unfairly taxes funds that have previously been subject to the income tax. And by causing a large fraction of potential estates to go to charitable institutions, the estate tax destroys the future income tax revenue that would otherwise have been paid if those funds had remained in private hands. This loss of income tax revenue may actually exceed the revenue collected by the estate tax—making it a net revenue loser as well as an economically harmful and unfair tax.

The corporate tax—and America has the highest corporate tax rate in the world—reduces corporate saving, lowers the net return to individual savers, and drives capital into housing rather than more productive uses. And our corporate tax rules for foreign-source income induce American firms to leave profits abroad rather than bringing them back to invest in the United States.

It is clear that we need tax reform to lower marginal tax rates and improve incentives for saving and investment. Reforming all aspects of our tax system should be combined with bringing our budget deficits under control. The unprecedented deficits that are now projected for the current decade and beyond will absorb most of private saving, crowding out productive investment and keeping the United States dependent on unreliable capital inflows from abroad.

We cannot eliminate those deficits and the resulting explosion of the national debt by faster economic growth or by inflation. We have to slow the growth of spending, particularly of the so-called entitlement programs for the future aged. The right solution is to provide a basic level of tax-financed social security pensions and medical care for retirees and to encourage individuals to supplement those benefits by saving more in their preretirement years.

Reducing spending also means cutting the spending that is done through the tax code. Limiting those tax expenditures would allow raising revenue to reduce the budget deficit while lowering marginal tax rates at the same time. All of this is a tough political agenda. But it is doable.

It is worth remembering that after World War II we brought our national debt down from 109 percent of GDP to 46 percent of GDP in 1960. We did it by avoiding any growth of the government's debt during those years—that is, by balancing deficit years with surplus years.

And with the debt no longer growing, the combination of a 2.6 percent real growth rate and a 3.3 percent inflation rate was enough to bring the ratio of debt to GDP down to 46 percent over 15 years. We did that then and we can do it again.

A PICTURE OF SUCCESS

If we do the things that need to be done—improving education, reforming taxes, reducing government deficits, stabilizing the government debt, and eliminating damaging regulations—we will unleash the rising incomes that American creativity and a free enterprise system can produce.

We will have only ourselves to blame if the decades ahead do not experience the same rising standard of living that Americans have enjoyed during our lifetimes.

I have a new grandson, born just six months ago. So I think about what life could be like when young Otto is 30 years old. Just maintaining that same 2.3 percent a year growth of per-capita income would—in just those 30 years—double the level of individual real incomes in America.

And when Otto is as old as I am now, real incomes would be five times what they are today. The average income of about $45,000 today would be $90,000 in today's prices after 30 years and $225,000 in today's prices after 70 years.

Those income levels would make so many things possible that are not possible today. Otto and his generation would be able to take advantage of the remarkable improvements in health care that science will bring, spending a larger share of income on health care while still having very large amounts left to spend on everything else. They would be able to devote much more income to education, to cultural activities, to the environment, to maintaining America's security, and to virtually eliminating poverty.

But all of that will only happen if we act now to make it so. That is America's challenge.

Thank you.

3

Political Partisanship After Tucson

"This Is a Time to Make Peace in America"*

Raúl M. Grijalva

U.S. representative (D), Arizona, 2003– ; born Tucson, AZ, February 18, 1948; B.A., University of Arizona, 1986; member, 1974–1986, chairman, 1984–86, Tucson Unified School District Governing Board; director, El Pueblo Neighborhood Center, 1975–1986; supervisor, Pima County Board of Supervisors, 1989–2002.

Editor's introduction: On the morning of Saturday, January 8, 2011, in Tucson, Arizona, a mentally disturbed young man, Jared Lee Loughner, shot 20 people at a "Congress on Your Corner" event organized by U.S. Representative Gabrielle Giffords. Six were killed, including a young girl. Giffords was shot through the head at point-blank range, but survived. In the aftermath of the murders, many felt the tone of American political discourse, which had grown especially caustic during the tumultuous national health care debate the previous winter, had contributed to the tragedy, creating a poisonous environment where acts of violence were almost inevitable. In response, there were calls for a new national dialogue based on civility and restraint. Echoing this sentiment, in a speech delivered before the House of Representatives four days after the shootings in Tucson, Congressman Raúl M. Grijalva of Arizona issues a plea for national unity.

Raúl M. Grijalva's speech: Madam Speaker, I rise today to honor the memories of Gabe Zimmerman, Judge John Roll, Christina-Taylor Green, Dorothy Morris, Dorwan Stoddard, and Phyllis Schneck. I rise also to voice my sincere hope for the recovery of our friend and colleague, Representative Gabrielle Giffords, and the others who were injured in Saturday's terrible shooting. The loss to the Congressional community and to Tucson has already been great. We can only hope the loss will not become even greater.

Representative Giffords serves a politically divided community. As long as I have known her, she's worked honestly and tirelessly to bridge that divide. There are few greater goals in public life than bringing people together and creating unity. What-

---

* Delivered on January 12, 2011, at Washington, D.C.

ever your politics, Representative Giffords is a listener and a seeker of solutions. In politics and in life, that is a rare thing.

She spread that ethic to her staff, as Tucson knows very well. Gabe Zimmerman, her director of community outreach, had an incredible and contagious desire to help people and make their lives better. When we speak of public service, we sometimes forget the many unelected but no less dedicated men and women whose work enriches the city, district, state, or country they serve. Tucson, and I hope the country, will never forget public servants like Gabe. He will be missed by more people than he could ever know.

Judge Roll was a strong, honest and effective advocate for the American justice system, and his loss will be deeply felt. Christina Green, at only nine years old, had already made an impression on everyone around her and will be long remembered. Dorwan Stoddard, a committed and long-time church volunteer, reportedly died saving his wife's life by shielding her from gunfire. Dorothy Morris and her husband, George, were together on that tragic day as they had been for the past 55 years of their happy marriage, and her daughters and family will hold her memory very close. Phyllis Schneck was an outgoing mother and grandmother known for her generosity and devotion to her family, and our thoughts go out to her and her loved ones today.

Alongside the victims of this tragedy, I would like to take a moment to recognize the many heroes of that day—people who offered medical assistance, alerted law enforcement, prevented further violence or assisted in too many other ways to count. This resolution names Patricia Maisch, Army Col. Bill Badger, Roger Sulzgeber, Joseph Zimudio, and Daniel Hernandez, Jr. To that list we can add brave people like Steven Rayle, an MD who was at the event and offered emergency medical attention to the wounded, and many others whose names may emerge over time.

It is in the spirit of unity that we all go forward together. As difficult as this time has been for Tucson and the nation, this can be a moment when the best is truly in each of us. This can be a time when the truest values of humanity join us all—values that let us mourn appropriately, reflect together, take time for ourselves, and bring us closer. At this moment, there is no greater goal than to heal our wounds and grow stronger.

Out of great tragedy and sorrow, there will be a new America. Pain brings people together and reminds us of the time we all share on this Earth. It also reminds us of the value of being good to one another, and how easily we forget ourselves in a heated moment. Pain, as horrible as it is, is inevitable. Our lives cannot be free of it. What matters now—what always matters—is how we respond to it.

Our most important response will not be political—it will be simply human. It will be to build bridges and remember those who have died. Public life should be about bringing people together; so should private life. We are stronger and more human when we are together. That's true of a family, a community, and a country. In a very real sense, a country—our country—is a family. Families may fight, disagree, and say things they regret, but in the end, they come together. They rejoin their hands and make peace. This is a time to make peace in America.

There are few occasions to offer a call for national unity, and in our lifetimes there will be few others. I sincerely hope the next is not another tragedy. With that hope, today I add my voice to the many who call for a stronger national family. There is nothing more important.

"The Hopes of a Nation Are Here Tonight"*

Barack Obama

Editor's introduction: "We mourn with you," the president says in this speech, presented to a capacity crowd at the University of Arizona's McKale Memorial Center during a service honoring the victims of the January 8, 2011 massacre in Tucson. He describes the lives and accomplishments of the six who were killed, including a judge, a veteran, a grandmother, and a nine-year-old girl. Giffords's husband allowed Obama to inform the crowd that for the first time since the shooting, "Gabby opened her eyes." As Obama points out, the tragedy sparked a national conversation about gun laws andthe treatment of mental illness, as well as our "sharply polarized" discourse. It is important, he says, "that we are talking with each other in a way that heals, not in a way that wounds."

Barack Obama's speech: Thank you. (Applause.) Thank you very much. Please, please be seated. (Applause.)

To the families of those we've lost; to all who called them friends; to the students of this university, the public servants who are gathered here, the people of Tucson and the people of Arizona: I have come here tonight as an American who, like all Americans, kneels to pray with you today and will stand by you tomorrow. (Applause.)

There is nothing I can say that will fill the sudden hole torn in your hearts. But know this: The hopes of a nation are here tonight. We mourn with you for the fallen. We join you in your grief. And we add our faith to yours that Representative Gabrielle Giffords and the other living victims of this tragedy will pull through. (Applause.)

Scripture tells us:

> There is a river whose streams make glad the city of God,
> the holy place where the Most High dwells.
> God is within her, she will not fall;
> God will help her at break of day.

---

* Delivered on January 12, 2011, at Tucson, Arizona.

On Saturday morning, Gabby, her staff, and many of her constituents gathered outside a supermarket to exercise their right to peaceful assembly and free speech. (Applause.) They were fulfilling a central tenet of the democracy envisioned by our founders—representatives of the people answering questions to their constituents, so as to carry their concerns back to our nation's capital. Gabby called it "Congress on Your Corner"—just an updated version of government of and by and for the people. (Applause.)

And that quintessentially American scene, that was the scene that was shattered by a gunman's bullets. And the six people who lost their lives on Saturday—they, too, represented what is best in us, what is best in America. (Applause.)

Judge John Roll served our legal system for nearly 40 years. (Applause.) A graduate of this university and a graduate of this law school—(applause)—Judge Roll was recommended for the federal bench by John McCain 20 years ago—(applause)—appointed by President George H.W. Bush and rose to become Arizona's chief federal judge. (Applause.)

His colleagues described him as the hardest-working judge within the Ninth Circuit. He was on his way back from attending Mass, as he did every day, when he decided to stop by and say hi to his representative. John is survived by his loving wife, Maureen, his three sons, and his five beautiful grandchildren. (Applause.)

George and Dorothy Morris—"Dot" to her friends—were high school sweethearts who got married and had two daughters. They did everything together—traveling the open road in their RV, enjoying what their friends called a 50-year honeymoon. Saturday morning, they went by the Safeway to hear what their congresswoman had to say. When gunfire rang out, George, a former Marine, instinctively tried to shield his wife. (Applause.) Both were shot. Dot passed away.

A New Jersey native, Phyllis Schneck retired to Tucson to beat the snow. But in the summer, she would return East, where her world revolved around her three children, her seven grandchildren, and two-year-old great-granddaughter. A gifted quilter, she'd often work under a favorite tree, or sometimes she'd sew aprons with the logos of the Jets and the Giants—(laughter)—to give out at the church where she volunteered. A Republican, she took a liking to Gabby, and wanted to get to know her better. (Applause.)

Dorwan and Mavy Stoddard grew up in Tucson together—about 70 years ago. They moved apart and started their own respective families. But after both were widowed they found their way back here, to, as one of Mavy's daughters put it, "be boyfriend and girlfriend again." (Laughter.)

When they weren't out on the road in their motor home, you could find them just up the road, helping folks in need at the Mountain Avenue Church of Christ. A retired construction worker, Dorwan spent his spare time fixing up the church along with his dog, Tux. His final act of selflessness was to dive on top of his wife, sacrificing his life for hers. (Applause.)

Everything—everything—Gabe Zimmerman did, he did with passion. (Applause.) But his true passion was helping people. As Gabby's outreach director, he made the cares of thousands of her constituents his own, seeing to it that seniors got the Medicare benefits that they had earned, that veterans got the medals and the care that they deserved, that government was working for ordinary folks. He died doing what he loved—talking with people and seeing how he could help. And Gabe is survived by his parents, Ross and Emily, his brother, Ben, and his fiancée, Kelly, who he planned to marry next year. (Applause.)

And then there is nine-year-old Christina Taylor Green. Christina was an A student; she was a dancer; she was a gymnast; she was a swimmer. She decided that she wanted to be the first woman to play in the Major Leagues, and as the only girl on her Little League team, no one put it past her. (Applause.)

She showed an appreciation for life uncommon for a girl her age. She'd remind her mother, "We are so blessed. We have the best life." And she'd pay those blessings back by participating in a charity that helped children who were less fortunate.

Our hearts are broken by their sudden passing. Our hearts are broken—and yet, our hearts also have reason for fullness.

Our hearts are full of hope and thanks for the 13 Americans who survived the shooting, including the congresswoman many of them went to see on Saturday.

I have just come from the University Medical Center, just a mile from here, where our friend Gabby courageously fights to recover even as we speak. And I want to tell you—her husband Mark is here and he allows me to share this with you—right after we went to visit, a few minutes after we left her room and some of her colleagues in Congress were in the room, Gabby opened her eyes for the first time. (Applause.) Gabby opened her eyes for the first time. (Applause.)

Gabby opened her eyes. Gabby opened her eyes, so I can tell you she knows we are here. She knows we love her. And she knows that we are rooting for her through what is undoubtedly going to be a difficult journey. We are there for her. (Applause.)

Our hearts are full of thanks for that good news, and our hearts are full of gratitude for those who saved others. We are grateful to Daniel Hernandez— (applause)—a volunteer in Gabby's office. (Applause.)

And, Daniel, I'm sorry, you may deny it, but we've decided you are a hero because—(applause)—you ran through the chaos to minister to your boss, and tended to her wounds and helped keep her alive. (Applause.)

We are grateful to the men who tackled the gunman as he stopped to reload. (Applause.) Right over there. (Applause.) We are grateful for petite Patricia Maisch, who wrestled away the killer's ammunition, and undoubtedly saved some lives. (Applause.) And we are grateful for the doctors and nurses and first responders who worked wonders to heal those who'd been hurt. We are grateful to them. (Applause.)

These men and women remind us that heroism is found not only on the fields of battle. They remind us that heroism does not require special training or physical strength. Heroism is here, in the hearts of so many of our fellow citizens, all around us, just waiting to be summoned—as it was on Saturday morning. Their actions, their selflessness poses a challenge to each of us. It raises a question of what, beyond prayers and expressions of concern, is required of us going forward. How can we honor the fallen? How can we be true to their memory?

You see, when a tragedy like this strikes, it is part of our nature to demand explanations—to try and impose some order on the chaos and make sense out of that which seems senseless. Already we've seen a national conversation commence, not only about the motivations behind these killings, but about everything from the merits of gun safety laws to the adequacy of our mental health system. And much of this process, of debating what might be done to prevent such tragedies in the future, is an essential ingredient in our exercise of self-government.

But at a time when our discourse has become so sharply polarized—at a time when we are far too eager to lay the blame for all that ails the world at the feet of those who happen to think differently than we do—it's important for us to pause for a moment and make sure that we're talking with each other in a way that heals, not in a way that wounds. (Applause.)

Scripture tells us that there is evil in the world, and that terrible things happen for reasons that defy human understanding. In the words of Job, "When I looked for light, then came darkness." Bad things happen, and we have to guard against simple explanations in the aftermath.

For the truth is none of us can know exactly what triggered this vicious attack. None of us can know with any certainty what might have stopped these shots from being fired, or what thoughts lurked in the inner recesses of a violent man's mind. Yes, we have to examine all the facts behind this tragedy. We cannot and will not be passive in the face of such violence. We should be willing to challenge old assumptions in order to lessen the prospects of such violence in the future. (Applause.) But what we cannot do is use this tragedy as one more occasion to turn on each other. (Applause.) That we cannot do. (Applause.) That we cannot do.

As we discuss these issues, let each of us do so with a good dose of humility. Rather than pointing fingers or assigning blame, let's use this occasion to expand our moral imaginations, to listen to each other more carefully, to sharpen our instincts for empathy, and remind ourselves of all the ways that our hopes and dreams are bound together. (Applause.)

After all, that's what most of us do when we lose somebody in our family—especially if the loss is unexpected. We're shaken out of our routines. We're forced to look inward. We reflect on the past: Did we spend enough time with an aging parent, we wonder. Did we express our gratitude for all the sacrifices that they made for us? Did we tell a spouse just how desperately we loved them, not just once in a while but every single day?

So sudden loss causes us to look backward—but it also forces us to look forward; to reflect on the present and the future, on the manner in which we live our lives, and nurture our relationships with those who are still with us. (Applause.)

We may ask ourselves if we've shown enough kindness and generosity and compassion to the people in our lives. Perhaps we question whether we're doing right by our children, or our community, whether our priorities are in order.

We recognize our own mortality, and we are reminded that in the fleeting time we have on this Earth, what matters is not wealth, or status, or power, or fame—but rather, how well we have loved—(applause)—and what small part we have played in making the lives of other people better. (Applause.)

And that process—that process of reflection, of making sure we align our values with our actions—that, I believe, is what a tragedy like this requires.

For those who were harmed, those who were killed—they are part of our family, an American family 300 million strong. (Applause.) We may not have known them personally, but surely we see ourselves in them. In George and Dot, in Dorwan and Mavy, we sense the abiding love we have for our own husbands, our own wives, our own life partners. Phyllis—she's our mom or our grandma; Gabe our brother or son. (Applause.) In Judge Roll, we recognize not only a man who prized his family and doing his job well, but also a man who embodied America's fidelity to the law. (Applause.)

And in Gabby—in Gabby, we see a reflection of our public-spiritedness; that desire to participate in that sometimes frustrating, sometimes contentious, but always necessary and never-ending process to form a more perfect union. (Applause.)

And in Christina—in Christina we see all of our children. So curious, so trusting, so energetic, so full of magic. So deserving of our love. And so deserving of our good example.

If this tragedy prompts reflection and debate—as it should—let's make sure it's worthy of those we have lost. (Applause.) Let's make sure it's not on the usual plane of politics and point-scoring and pettiness that drifts away in the next news cycle.

The loss of these wonderful people should make every one of us strive to be better. To be better in our private lives, to be better friends and neighbors and co-workers and parents. And if, as has been discussed in recent days, their death helps usher in more civility in our public discourse, let us remember it is not because a simple lack of civility caused this tragedy—it did not—but rather because only a more civil and honest public discourse can help us face up to the challenges of our nation in a way that would make them proud. (Applause.)

We should be civil because we want to live up to the example of public servants like John Roll and Gabby Giffords, who knew first and foremost that we are all Americans, and that we can question each other's ideas without questioning each other's love of country and that our task, working together, is to constantly widen the circle of our concern so that we bequeath the American Dream to future generations. (Applause.)

They believed—they believed, and I believe that we can be better. Those who died here, those who saved life here—they help me believe. We may not be able to stop all evil in the world, but I know that how we treat one another, that's entirely up to us. (Applause.)

And I believe that for all our imperfections, we are full of decency and goodness, and that the forces that divide us are not as strong as those that unite us. (Applause.)

That's what I believe, in part because that's what a child like Christina Taylor Green believed. (Applause.)

Imagine—imagine for a moment, here was a young girl who was just becoming aware of our democracy; just beginning to understand the obligations of citizenship; just starting to glimpse the fact that some day she, too, might play a part in shaping her nation's future. She had been elected to her student council. She saw public service as something exciting and hopeful. She was off to meet her congresswoman, someone she was sure was good and important and might be a role model. She saw all this through the eyes of a child, undimmed by the cynicism or vitriol that we adults all too often just take for granted.

I want to live up to her expectations. (Applause.) I want our democracy to be as good as Christina imagined it. I want America to be as good as she imagined it. (Applause.) All of us—we should do everything we can to make sure this country lives up to our children's expectations. (Applause.)

As has already been mentioned, Christina was given to us on September 11th, 2001, one of 50 babies born that day to be pictured in a book called "Faces of Hope." On either side of her photo in that book were simple wishes for a child's life. "I hope you help those in need," read one. "I hope you know all the words to the National Anthem and sing it with your hand over your heart." (Applause.) "I hope you jump in rain puddles."

If there are rain puddles in Heaven, Christina is jumping in them today. (Applause.) And here on this Earth—here on this Earth, we place our hands over our hearts, and we commit ourselves as Americans to forging a country that is forever worthy of her gentle, happy spirit.

May God bless and keep those we've lost in restful and eternal peace. May He love and watch over the survivors. And may He bless the United States of America. (Applause.)

"It's Time to Do the Big Things"*

Chris Christie

Governor (R) of New Jersey, 2009– ; born Newark, NJ, September 6, 1962; B.A., University of Delaware, 1964; J.D., Seton Hall University School of Law, 1987; practicing attorney, 1987–1993, partner, 1993–2001, lobbyist, 1998–2001, law firm of Dughi, Hewit & Palatucci; freeholder, Morris County, New Jersey, Board of Chosen Freeholders, 1994–98; United States Attorney for the District of New Jersey, 2002–08.

Editor's introduction: In this speech, presented to the conservative American Enterprise Institute (AEI), New Jersey governor Chris Christie asserts that the main challenges facing his state are not partisan issues but fiscal problems. These are the same dilemmas confronting other states, whether their governors are Democratic or Republican. Christie draws a comparison between himself and Democratic governor Andrew Cuomo of New York. The essential problem, he observes, is that the country's greatest dilemmas—crises in funding for Social Security, Medicare, and Medicaid—will not be averted by following the politician's usual playbook. In debating solutions, he avers, there is a time for partisanship in the form of vigorous debate.

Chris Christie's speech: Thank you very much for the introduction and for the invitation to be here today. I came today because I really think it's extraordinarily important for those of us who believe that our country is off on the wrong track to begin the conversation and for New Jersey's sake to continue the conversation about how we fix the problems that ail our states and our country in a direct and blunt way. And I fear that after watching how things have been going over the last month or two, that we're missing a historic opportunity. And I will not be someone who will participate in silently missing that opportunity. A month ago, I gave my State of the State speech in New Jersey, and what I said during that speech was that I was not going to do the normal State of the State or State of the Union speech that you see. George Will put it better than I ever could, he said these speeches have become every politician's attempt to stroke the erogenous zones of every con-

---

* Delivered on February 16, 2011, at Washington, D.C.

stituency in their jurisdiction. They become these laundry list things that you do for your cabinet so that as they're sitting up in the balcony, and you mention the Department of Labor, that Commissioner can sit up straight and smile, because at the time his mother is going to see him on TV. I didn't think it was a good enough of a reason, as much as I love my Commissioner of Labor, to give a speech like that, especially during these times. During these times, as I said in that speech, it's time to do the big things, the really big things, and I don't think they're will be much disagreement in this room and I don't think there should be much disagreement across the country about what those things are—what they are for New Jersey and what they are for America. For us in New Jersey, it's three things: it's restoring and maintaining fiscal sanity; it's getting our pension and health benefits under control, reformed and have the cost lowered; and it's reforming an education system that costs too much and produces too little for our society today and for our children's future. Now if you look at those three issues, these are not in and of themselves Democratic or Republican issues. Each governor across America is confronting the same things that I'm confronting in New Jersey: a decade or more of out-of-control spending in many if not most states; state taxes that have been raised to new levels; debt loads that are out of control, both for state entitlements and for just general borrowing. Every governor, Republican or Democrat, is facing this problem. If you look at it, just look at our little area of the world. You have me in New Jersey, elected in 2009 as a conservative Republican in one of the bluest states in America, and across the river you have the son of a liberal icon who is saying the exact same things that I'm saying. I defy you to look at the first six weeks of the Cuomo administration in Albany and discern much of a difference between what Governor Andrew Cuomo is saying and what Governor Chris Christie is saying on these big issues. And it's not because all of a sudden Governor Cuomo and I have decided that we're members of the same party, we're not. But we are confronted with the same problems and these problems and issues are not partisan. They are obvious and long overdue to be solved and so that's why you see Andrew Cuomo, or for God's sake, even Jerry Brown in California talking about reducing salaries of state workers by 8–10 percent. Saying the same things that Scott Walker is fighting in Wisconsin, that John Kasich is fighting in Ohio, that Rick Snyder is fighting in Michigan, that Susana Martinez is fighting in New Mexico.

I said to the people of New Jersey when I ran for governor in 2009 that if they gave me the opportunity to be their governor, that not only would the state go on a path towards fiscal recovery, but we would also lead the nation because we would have a one-year head start on everybody because of our odd election year. We would have a one year head start on a huge new class of governors that would come in the election of 2010. Now you can imagine how that was received in New Jersey. Now this was a state that during my time as a United States Attorney was known predominantly for a few things: political corruption, "The Sopranos," "The Real Housewives of New Jersey," and now, most regrettably, "The Jersey Shore." Not a place that thought of itself as a national leader in something that would matter for our children's future. But I believe part of that leadership is understanding, articulating and believing in that which is special and unique about the people that you serve. And having been born in New Jersey and raised there and lived there all my life, I know that if presented with a challenge directly, without any sugarcoating, that the people of New Jersey would step up to the plate and answer the call. And after 13 months now as governor, I think we have plenty of evidence that we were right in 2009.

When I came into office we confronted a $2.2 billion budget deficit for fiscal year '10. The one that had five months left. The one that Governor Corzine told me was just fine, cruise path into the end of the fiscal year; Governor, don't worry about it, everything is fine. $2.2 billion. My chief of staff, in my first week as governor, brought me a sheet of paper that showed me that if I did not act immediately to stop the planned spending, that New Jersey would not meet its payroll for the second pay period in March. Imagine that. The state that has the second-highest per capita income in America had so over-spent, over-borrowed, and over-taxed that it would not meet payroll in March of 2010. So we acted immediately to use the executive authority of the governorship to impound $2.2 billion in projected spending. Without the permission of the legislature. Without compromise because it was not the time for compromise. And without raising taxes on the people of the state who had had their taxes raised and fees 115 times in the eight years preceding my governorship. One hundred fifteen tax and fee increases in eight years. So we impounded spending and we balanced the budget. And we turned immediately towards this fiscal year that we're in now. And were confronted with an $11 billion budget deficit on a $29 billion budget. The highest budget deficit by percentage of any state in America. And believe me: the partisan Democrats in my state believed they had me right where they wanted me—he would have to raise taxes. And they put it right down on the table and said they wanted to increase the tax that they love the most—the income tax and specifically they called it the millionaires' tax.

Now of course this leads me to have to give you an aside about New Jersey math. See, when Democrats in New Jersey call it a millionaires' tax, that's for anyone who makes $400,000 or over—that's called New Jersey math. So for businesses or individuals who have $400,000 in income or more, they wanted to raise their taxes, again, from a nine percent top marginal rate to nearly eleven percent. And they told me that if I did not agree they would close down the government. There would be no budget in 2011 without an income tax increase. Now you know, this had happened four years earlier in New Jersey under Governor Corzine. They were arguing how much to raise taxes. And the Democrat-controlled legislature closed down the government on the Democratic governor because they couldn't agree on how much to raise the sales tax. And Governor Corzine very famously invited the press into his office, now my office, and there was a cot in the office. I can tell you it's not normally there. And he said to them, "I'm going to be sleeping in this cot, right over here, until this crisis is averted." So I knew that these were the same fellows who had been in the legislature when he was there, now threatening to do the same thing. So I decided to call them down early on and advise them that the place was under new management. And what I said to them was listen, if you guys want to pass an income tax increase, you can. That's fine, I'm going to veto it. And if you want to close down the government because of that, that's fine. But I want to tell you something—I'm not moving any cot into this office to sleep in here. If you close down the government I'm getting into those black SUVs with the troopers and going to the governor's residence. I'm going to go upstairs, I'm going to open a beer, I'm going to order a pizza, I'm going to watch the Mets. And when you decide to reopen the government, give me a call and I'll come back. But don't think I'm sleeping on some cot. Take a look at me, you think I'm sleeping on a cot? Not happening.

So we stood up, we stood for our principles. We submitted a budget that cut real spending nine percent, year over year. Not projected growth—real spending, nine percent, every department of state government was cut. And we balanced the budget without any new or increased taxes on the people of the state of New Jersey for the first time in eight years. And the budget they called "dead on arrival without an income tax increase" was passed two days early with 99.8 percent of the line items exactly as they were when I submitted them back in March. With a Democratic legislature. Why? Because we stood up for what we believed in and we made it very clear that we would not compromise on our principles. We'd compromise on things that were not core principle items, but we were not going to compromise on raising taxes on the people of New Jersey. That leads us now to today. And that's why fiscal discipline is so important. Because just because we went through that once or one and a half if you count fiscal year '10—doesn't mean we should be self congratulatory, patting ourselves on the back, and take our eye off the ball. This is a problem that took a decade to develop and it's going to take longer than a year for us to fix it. Fiscal discipline is extraordinarily important not only for New Jersey but for America.

Now we have a whole new way of budgeting in New Jersey. We don't assume every program will be funded any longer. We don't assume a certain increase in every budget. The Democratic legislature will come out and say I have some $10 billion or so deficit for this year. That's because they're playing in the old playbook, which says that everything I did last year, of course, the next year I'd want to reverse and go right back. That is not going to happen. And it can't happen if states are going to progress and get out of this crisis. We now have to stick to a new type of approach to budgeting—budgeting from the bottom up. Requiring as I do now of everyone one of my cabinet officers, that they come to me and not tell me what each one of their programs cost and how much they're willing to cut it. But to say to me which one of your programs are absolutely necessary and how much do you need to fund them—this is how much money you're getting and whatever doesn't fit in your equation is out. We have to fund that which we really need, and to do that we have to cut that which is just what we'd like, rather than what we need.

And you'll hear this debate going on down here now. You'll have folks tell you that every bit of federal spending is absolutely necessary and laudatory. It's not. And in fact some of it's not even laudatory, let alone necessary. But we have to bring a new approach and new discipline to this. And when people say that you can't tackle these big problems, look at what we're doing on pensions and benefits. Pensions and benefits are the equivalent of federal entitlements at the state level. They are no different. They have no more vocal constituency at the federal level than they do at the state level. Take my word for it. I rolled out my pension and benefit reform in September on a Tuesday, and then that Friday I went to the firefighters' convention in Wildwood, New Jersey. Seven thousand five hundred firefighters at 2:00 on a Friday afternoon—I think you know what they had for lunch. And I rolled out a very specific pension and benefit reform proposal. On pensions: raise the retirement age, eliminate COLAs, increase the amount employees have to contribute to their pension every year. And roll back a nine percent increase that was given to them by a Republican governor and a Republican legislature and they had no way to pay for it. Those four reforms would take our current pension system, which is underfunded by $54 billion dollars, and in thirty years cut it in half to $28 billion dollars. Real reform getting us on the glide path to solvency. You can imagine how that was received by 7,500 firefighters. As I walked into the room and was introduced, I was booed lustily. I made my way up to the stage, they booed some more. I got to the microphone, they booed some more. So I said, come on, you can do better than that, and they did! They did. And then I said to them—I took away the prepared notes I had for the speech—I actually took them off of the podium, crumpled them up and threw them on the ground, so they could see that I would. And I said, here's the deal: I understand you're angry, and I understand you're frustrated, and I understand you feel deceived and betrayed. And the reason you feel all the things is because you have been deceived and you have been betrayed. And for twenty years, governors have come into this room and lied to you. Promised you benefits that they had no way of paying for, making promises they knew they couldn't keep, and just hoping that they wouldn't be the man or women left holding the bag. I understand why you feel angry and betrayed and deceived by those people. Here's what I don't understand. Why are you booing the first guy who came in here and told you the truth? See, there is no political advantage to me coming into that room and telling the truth. The way we used to think about politics and unfortunately the way I fear they're thinking about politics still in Washington, DC. See, the old playbook says lie, deceive, obfuscate and make it to the next election. You know, there's a study that says by 2020, New Jersey is one of eleven states whose pension could be bankrupt. And when I told a friend of mine about that study, he said to me, well, wait. By 2020, you won't be governor. What the hell do you care? That's the way politics has been practiced in our country for too long and practiced in New Jersey for too long. So I said to those firefighters, you may hate me now. But fifteen years from now, when you have a pension to collect because of what I did, you'll be looking for my address on the Internet so you can send me a thank you note.

Leadership, today in America, has to be about doing the big things and being courageous. That's what it has to be about. Same thing with health benefit reform, which is an analogy to Medicaid and Medicare here in Washington. And if you think that the public workers in New Jersey hold on any less strongly to the benefits that they get through the government—teachers in New Jersey who pay nothing for their health insurance, nothing, from the day they are hired until the day they die, for full family medical coverage that costs the state of New Jersey $24,000 per family. If you don't think they're holding on to that tight, you're not paying attention. The battles are similar. And here's the problem. You can't fix these problems if you don't talk about them. You cannot fix these problems without talking about them. And I look at what's happening in Washington, DC right now and I'm worried. I'm worried. And I think, you know, I heard the president's State of the Union speech, and it was two weeks after mine, and he said America was about doing the big things. Now I'm not saying he copied me. I've seen some writing about that, that's not what I'm saying. But I think it's important to note it because of what he says the big things are. He says the big things are high-speed rail. The big things are high speed internet access for almost eighty percent of America or something by some date. One million electric cars on the road by some date.

Ladies and gentlemen, that is the candy of American politics. Those are not the big things. Because let me guarantee you something, if we don't fix the real big things, there are going to be no electric cars on the road. There is going to be no high-speed Internet access, or if there is you're not going to be able to afford to get on it. We are not going to be able to care about the niceties of life, the investments that Washington wants to continue to make. That's not what we need to be talking about. No one is talking about it. And now what this has become, I read, is a political strategy. The president is not talking about it because he is waiting for the Republicans to talk about it. And our new bold Republicans that we just sent to the House of Representatives aren't talking about it because they are waiting for him to talk about it. Let me suggest to you, that my children's future and your children's future is more important than some political strategy. Let me suggest to you that what game is being played down here is irresponsible and it's dangerous. We need to say these things and we need to say them out loud. When we say we're cutting spending, when we say everything is on the table, when we say we mean entitlement programs, we should be specific. And let me tell you what is the truth. What's the truth that no one is talking about? Here is the truth that no one is talking about: you're going to have to raise the retirement age for Social Security. Oh, I just said it and I'm still standing here! I did not vaporize into the carpeting and I said it. We have to reform Medicare because it costs too much and it is going to bankrupt us. Once again lightning did not come through the windows and strike me dead. And we have to fix Medicaid because it's not only bankrupting the federal government, it's bankrupting every state government. There you go. If we're not honest about these things, on the state level about pensions and benefits and on the federal level about Social Security, Medicare, and Medicaid, we are on the path to ruin.

And you know now—I hear people saying—we're going too fast, we're going too fast. We need to slow down a little bit. I hear the same thing in New Jersey. In New Jersey, all the time the legislature says, the legislature is a deliberative body, we need to study the governor's proposals. You know, I never worked in Trenton before I became governor and they do speak a different language in state capitals and in this capital. They speak different languages. So you need to get—when you become governor, and no one tells you this—but you need to get your English-to-Trenton dictionary. Because the language in Trenton is just much different. See, when a legislature—and I don't care whether this is the Congress or whether this is the state legislature in New Jersey. When they say we need to study the executive's proposal, you think because you speak English, that means they're really going to take some time, consider it, and then act. No, no. What that means in Trenton, and what I suspect it means in Washington also, is this: it means we are going to drag our feet for as long as we can until we hope it dies a natural death because God knows we don't want our fingerprints on it for murdering it, but we also don't have the guts to do it. That's what "study" means in government parlance. So in New Jersey they call me impatient, they call me lots of other things too. But they call me impatient among other things. Ladies and gentlemen, I think it's time for some impatience. I think it's time for some impatience in America. Because if you think we're moving too slow, think about these statistics. The deficit stands at $1.6 trillion dollars, the Social Security system is going to be insolvent in 2037, and the Medicare system is expected to run out of money in 2017. So I'm impatient? Because I want them to act now. Because I want our healthcare system to be secure for the future. Because I want our retirement system to be secure for the future.

See, one of the things that the public sector unions don't understand about my approach in New Jersey is that they think I'm attacking them. I'm attacking the leadership of the union. Because they're greedy and they're selfish and self-interested. The members of that union are being ill-served by the leadership of that union. And so what I say, what I'm doing, is to save your pension, to save your healthcare for the rest of your life, and yeah, you're going to have to take a little less. That's the way it goes, we're in difficult times and there were promises made that couldn't be kept. But it's no longer time to wait. And leadership in my opinion is not about waiting. You know, I get four years as governor of New Jersey and I don't have time to wait. And anybody who leads a government, whether it's in another state or in America, has a defined period of time to act. And now I understand that this political strategy in Washington is all about waiting out until 2012. That's five years away from Medicare insolvency. What's the excuse going to be then? You know, these are hard things to do. They are hard things to do, but they're not impossible to do and here's what politicians fear. What politicians fear is you do these things, like say what I just said, and you'll be vaporized into the carpet politically. That's what they're afraid of.

But look at what's happened again in New Jersey and New York. I was elected with 49 percent of the vote, in a three-way race in November of 2009. The first Republican elected to statewide office in twelve years in New Jersey, but not with a majority. Forty-nine percent of the vote, and when I started to say we were going to cut K–12 education funding by more than a billion dollars, we're going to cut municipal aid by more than half a billion dollars, we're going to cut every program that we can find in government and balance without raising taxes—I had everybody telling me, Governor, you can't do it. Your approval ratings will go in the toilet. People love these programs. And what I said to people was, you know what, I'm going to try an experiment here. Let's start treating the people of New Jersey like adults. Because if you think they don't know that we are in deep trouble, than these are not the people I knew growing up. These are tough, smart, self-aware people who understand that we've dug ourselves a hole for more than a decade and we're only going to get out by climbing, and climbing is hard, really hard. But it's time to do it. And what's happened? After thirteen months of fighting and arguing and pushing and impatience, my approval rating is at 54 percent. No disaster—in fact—more popular today than I was the day I was elected, and that's in a state that is as Democratic as any state in America for a Republican governor. But if you really want to see eye-popping numbers, look across the river. At the person who was recently characterized as my soul mate—I wonder how he feels about that. Governor Andrew Cuomo—in a poll that just came out two days ago—his job approval is at 77 percent. Seventy-seven percent. And all he's talked about is cutting spending, not raising taxes, addressing entitlement programs, Medicaid, pensions, taking on public sector unions, capping school superintendent pay, the hard things. The things that people tell you will lead to political ruin, they don't. Politicians make this mistake all the time. They run last election next time. They think that what happened before will happen again. And they don't look around them to see that the times have changed. Our country and our states are weighed down by an albatross of irresponsibility. That we have foisted upon ourselves as leaders, and that you as citizens have permitted us to get away with.

The last example of that is education reform, and all I'll say about this is that in my state, where we spend $17,620 per pupil per year—the highest in America, $24,000 dollars per pupil in [the] city of Newark, $28,000 dollars in Asbury Park—and we have 104,000 students trapped in 200 failing schools across New Jersey. And the education establishment says, don't worry, help is on the way. And the help that's on the way is more money, more money. Well, more money is not going to solve this problem until we take on the issues that are really causing the problem. And until we as Americans are willing to do that final tough thing, which is to look the teachers' union across America in the eye and say to them, you do not represent the best the teachers have to offer, you often represent the worst. And it's time for us to honestly say that we can separate the teachers from the union. We have great teachers in New Jersey, working hard and making a huge difference in the lives of many children, but we don't have enough of them. And one of the reasons why we don't have enough of them is because the bad teachers who remain with lifetime tenure are crowding out opportunity for the good ones, and then when you have reductions, the last ones in are the first ones out because all that matters is seniority and not talent. And so we send a new generation of teachers, good enthusiastic teachers, away because we have built a system—as Michelle Rhee put better than I could—that cares more about the feelings of adults than it cares about the future of our children. I will not take responsibility for that approach. I will not take responsibility for leaving a generation of children behind in America.

I won't do it. And we need to speak out and say it's time to fix that system. Tell me where else in America—well really there's two places—left in America where there's a profession where there is no reward for excellence and no consequence for failure. Of course we all know the first one is weathermen. It doesn't matter, it's going to snow six inches, it snows eighteen. Well, I said it was going to snow, what's the difference? And they're right back on TV the next night. Unfortunately, the second one is teaching. Because the great teacher, the only reward they get is the psychic reward of knowing that they've done a great job for the children in their classroom. And the teacher next door, who's a lousy teacher who doesn't care, gets paid the same as the teacher who stays late and comes early, the same as the teacher who communicates with parents, the same as the teacher who feels it's his or her personal responsibility to lift each child up to the next grade. That's not what America is. America is built on rewarding excellence and having consequence for failure. So we need to deal with that issue as well, not only in every state but in America.

You know, there's a lot of talk now about partisanship and the negative, angry tone in some of our political debates. And there is a time and a place for partisanship, I absolutely believe in that. And so did our founding fathers, they believed in partisanship. They believed in vigorous debate and so do I. You know, it's the nature of our country, based on our founding, to have principled disagreements among people of good will, and I'm not disagreeing with folks just for the sake of disagreeing. And I'm not fighting for the sake of fighting. I fight for the things that matter. I save my energy for the fights of consequence. And as a result, some people say I'm too combative. Some people say I'm too much of a fighter. Well, I'll tell you I'm fighting now because now is the time that matters most for New Jersey's future and for America's future. We are teetering on the edge of disaster. And I love when people talk about American exceptionalism, but American exceptionalism has to include the courage to do the right thing. It cannot just be a belief that, because we are exceptional, everything will work out OK. Part of truly being exceptional is being willing to do the difficult things, is to stop playing the political games, stop looking at the bumper pool of politics and to step up and start doing the right thing. This is the new era that we newly elected officials have inherited. Whether we like it or not, that's the story and we have two choices: to either stand up and do the right thing, to speak the truth and speak it bluntly and directly, or to join the long parade of leaders who have come before us and failed. And maybe people won't remember us, maybe they won't pin the responsibility for failure on us because there's been so much failure around us, but I did not run for this job for failure. I ran for this job for success. For success, not just for me personally and my children, but success for my state. And hopefully, to provide an example for the rest of the country that you can do the difficult things. See, it seems to me that what America is really all about is about a group of people who came from every corner of this Earth because they wanted a chance for greatness. That's what has made us the greatest country on Earth. Our calling for greatness at this time is to confront these issues, to say them out loud, and to stop playing around and to not waste another minute.

You know, the World War II generation was called "the greatest generation," and they were because they put their lives on the line to protect our way of life. And they're called the greatest generation because we judged them. We judged them in the aftermath and we found them to be great, by any objective measure. Let me guarantee you one thing: we will be judged too. We will be judged by our children and our grandchildren—that at this moment of crisis, what did we do? Did we bury our heads in the sand? Did we surround ourselves with our creature comforts and believe that just because we're America everything's going to be OK? Or will our children and grandchildren be able to say that at this moment of crisis, we stood up and did the hard things that made a future of greatness possible for them? Believe me, we will be judged. I know the way I want that judgment to turn out for me, and I know in the hearts and the minds of most New Jerseyans and Americans, I know how they want that judgment to turn out for them. So it's time for us to get to work, to find our greatness again. And I believe we will find our greatness through doing the big things, the really big things that will lead America to another century of exceptionalism and not a century of settling for second best. That's what this fight is about. If you're willing to join me, I'm willing to join you and that's what I came down here today to talk to you. Thank you all very much.

"If We Don't Believe in Americans, Who Will?"*

Mitch Daniels

Governor (R) of Indiana, 2005– ; born Monongahela, PA, April 7, 1949; B.A., Princeton University, 1971; J.D., Georgetown University, 1979; chief of staff to Indianapolis mayor Richard Lugar, 1977–1982; executive director, National Republican Senatorial Committee (NRSC), 1983–84; chief political advisor and liaison to President Ronald Reagan, 1985–87; president and chief executive officer (CEO), Hudson Institute, 1987–1990; executive, 1990–2001, president, North American operations, 1993–97, senior vice president, corporate strategy and policy, 1997–2001, Eli Lilly & Co.; director, White House Office of Management and Budget (OMB), 2001–03.

Editor's introduction: Conservative commentator David Brooks, writing in *The New York Times* on February 24, 2011, described the following presentation by Indiana governor Mitch Daniels as "one of the best Republican speeches in recent decades." In the address, delivered at the Conservative Political Action Conference (CPAC)'s Ronald Reagan Centennial Dinner, Daniels discusses his fellow Indianans, declaring that Hoosiers "cling" to their core beliefs—a pointed reference to a notorious gaffe by Barack Obama from the 2008 campaign, when he characterized some Americans as "clinging to guns or religion . . . as a way to explain their frustrations." One core belief, as Daniels describes it, is that government must spend less than it takes in. He goes on to characterize the national debt as a new Red Menace and laments today's "venomous, petty, often ad hominem political discourse." He also warns against relying on the good faith of Democrats, asserting that to them, "power . . . is everything, so there's nothing they won't say to get it."

Mitch Daniels's speech: Phyllis Schlafly, David Keene, George Will, good friends, thank you for the enormous privilege of this podium. Even a casual observer of American public life knows how many great ideas have been born here, how many important debates joined here, how many giants of our democracy appeared on this platform. When David broached the invitation, my first reaction was one I often have: "Who cancelled?" But first choice or fifteenth, the honor, and the respon-

---

* Delivered on February 11, 2011, at Washington, D.C.

sibility to do the occasion justice, is the same. I am seized with the sentiment best expressed by Hizzoner, the original Mayor Richard Daley, who once proclaimed a similar honor the "pinochle of success."

We are all grateful to our co-sponsors, the Reagan Foundation and the Reagan Ranch. How fitting that we convene under their auspices, as we close this first week of the centennial. Those of us who served President Reagan were taught to show constant respect for the presidency and whoever occupies it. But, among us alums, the term "the President" tends to connote just one of those 44 men, that great man with whom God blessed America 100 years ago this week.

The prefix in "co-sponsor" is meaningful tonight. It is no state secret that the two foundations have not always been co-operative, or co-llaborative, or co-llegial. So it is a tribute to the stature and diplomacy of David Keene that they have come together to produce so warm a moment as this. I am now converted to the view that yes, the Israeli-Palestinian conflict will be solved.

Well done, David; Nobel Peace Prizes have been awarded for far less.

I bring greetings from a place called Indiana. The coastal types present may think of it as a "flyover" state, or one of those "I" states. Perhaps a quick anthropological summary would help. We Hoosiers hold to some quaint notions. Some might say we "cling" to them, though not out of fear or ignorance. We believe in paying our bills. We have kept our state in the black throughout the recent unpleasantness, while cutting rather than raising taxes, by practicing an old tribal ritual—we spend less money than we take in.

We believe it wrong ever to take a dollar from a free citizen without a very necessary public purpose, because each such taking diminishes the freedom to spend that dollar as its owner would prefer. When we do find it necessary, we feel a profound duty to use that dollar as carefully and effectively as possible, else we should never have taken it at all. Before our General Assembly now is my proposal for an automatic refund of tax dollars beyond a specified level of state reserves. We say that anytime budgets are balanced and an ample savings account has been set aside, government should just stop collecting taxes. Better to leave that money in the pockets of those who earned it than to let it burn a hole, as it always does, in the pockets of government.

We believe that government works for the benefit of private life, and not the other way around.

We see government's mission as fostering and enabling the important realms— our businesses, service clubs, little leagues, churches—to flourish. Our first thought is always for those on life's first rung, and how we might increase their chances of climbing. Every day, we work to lower the costs and barriers to free men and women creating wealth for each other. We build roads, and bridges, and new sources of homegrown energy at record rates, in order to have the strongest possible backbone to which people of enterprise can attach their investments and build their dreams. When business leaders ask me what they can do for Indiana, I always reply: "Make money. Go make money. That's the first act of 'corporate citizenship.' If you do that, you'll have to hire someone else, and you'll have enough profit to help one of those non-profits we're so proud of."

We place our trust in average people. We are confident in their ability to decide wisely for themselves, on the important matters of their lives. So when we cut property taxes, to the lowest level in America, we left flexibility for localities to raise them, but only by securing the permission of their taxpayers, voting in referendum. We designed both our state employee health plans and the one we created for low-income Hoosiers as Health Savings Accounts, and now in the tens of thousands these citizens are proving that they are fully capable of making smart, consumerist choices about their own health care.

We have broadened the right of parents to select the best place for their children's education to include every public school, traditional or charter, regardless of geography, tuition-free. And before our current legislature adjourns, we intend to become the first state of full and true choice by saying to every low and middle-income Hoosier family, if you think a non-government school is the right one for your child, you're as entitled to that option as any wealthy family; here's a voucher, go sign up.

Lastly, speaking now for my administration colleagues, we believe in government that is limited but active. Within that narrow sphere of legitimate collective action, we choose to be the initiators of new ideas or, as we have labeled ourselves, the Party of Purpose. In President Reagan's phrase, "We are the change." On election nights, we remind each other that victory is not a vindication, it is an instruction, not an endorsement, but an assignment. The national elections of 2010 carried an instruction. In our nation, in our time, the friends of freedom have an assignment, as great as those of the 1860s, or the 1940s, or the long twilight of the Cold War. As in those days, the American project is menaced by a survival-level threat. We face an enemy, lethal to liberty, and even more implacable than those America has defeated before. We cannot deter it; there is no countervailing danger we can pose. We cannot negotiate with it, any more than with an iceberg or a Great White.

I refer, of course, to the debts our nation has amassed for itself over decades of indulgence. It is the new Red Menace, this time consisting of ink. We can debate its origins endlessly and search for villains on ideological grounds, but the reality is pure arithmetic. No enterprise, small or large, public or private, can remain self-governing, let alone successful, so deeply in hock to others as we are about to be.

Need I illustrate? Surely the consequences, to prosperity, world influence, and personal freedom itself are as clear to this audience as to anyone could appear before. Do I exaggerate? I'd love to be shown that I do. Any who think so please see me in the hallway afterward, and bring your third grade math books.

If a foreign power advanced an army to the border of our land, everyone in this room would drop everything and look for a way to help. We would set aside all other agendas and disputes as secondary, and go to the ramparts until the threat was repelled. That is what those of us here, and every possible ally we can persuade to join us, are now called to do. It is our generational assignment. It is the mission of our era. Forgive the pun when I call it our "raison debt."

Every conflict has its draft dodgers. There are those who will not enlist with us. Some who can accept, or even welcome, the ballooning of the state, regardless of the cost in dollars, opportunity, or liberty, and the slippage of the United States into a gray parity with the other nations of this earth. Some who sincerely believe that history has devised a leftward ratchet, moving in fits and starts but always in the direction of a more powerful state. The people who coined the smug and infuriating term—have you heard it?—"the Reagan Interruption."

The task of such people is now a simple one. They need only play good defense. The federal spending commitments now in place will bring about the leviathan state they have always sought. The health care travesty now on the books will engulf private markets and produce a single-payer system or its equivalent, and it won't take long to happen. Our fiscal ruin and resulting loss of world leadership will, in their eyes, be not a tragic event but a desirable one, delivering the multilateral world of which they've dreamed so long.

Fortunately, these folks remain few. They are vastly outnumbered by Americans who sense the presence of the enemy, but are awaiting the call for volunteers, and a credible battle plan for saving our Republic. That call must come from this room, and rooms like it.

But we, too, are relatively few in number, in a nation of 300 million. If freedom's best friends cannot unify around a realistic, actionable program of fundamental change, one that attracts and persuades a broad majority of our fellow citizens, big change will not come. Or rather, big change will come, of the kind that the skeptics of all centuries have predicted for those naïve societies that believed that government of and by the people could long endure.

We know what the basic elements must be. An affectionate thank you to the major social welfare programs of the last century, but their sunsetting when those currently or soon to be enrolled have passed off the scene. The creation of new Social Security and Medicare compacts with the young people who will pay for their elders and who deserve to have a backstop available to them in their own retirement.

These programs should reserve their funds for those most in need of them. They should be updated to catch up to Americans' increasing longevity and good health. They should protect benefits against inflation but not overprotect them. Medicare 2.0 should restore to the next generation the dignity of making their own decisions, by delivering its dollars directly to the individual, based on financial and medical need, entrusting and empowering citizens to choose their own insurance and, inevitably, pay for more of their routine care like the discerning, autonomous consumers we know them to be.

Our morbidly obese federal government needs not just behavior modification but bariatric surgery. The perverse presumption that places the burden of proof on the challenger of spending must be inverted, back to the rule that applies elsewhere in life: "Prove to me why we should."

Lost to history is the fact that, in my OMB assignment, I was the first loud critic of Congressional earmarks. I was also the first to get absolutely nowhere in reducing them: first to rail and first to fail. They are a pernicious practice and should be stopped. But, in the cause of national solvency, they are a trifle. Talking much more about them, or "waste, fraud, and abuse," trivializes what needs to be done, and misleads our fellow citizens to believe that easy answers are available to us. In this room, we all know how hard the answers are, how much change is required.

And that means nothing, not even the first and most important mission of government, our national defense, can get a free pass. I served in two administrations that practiced and validated the policy of peace through strength. It has served America and the world with irrefutable success. But if our nation goes over a financial Niagara, we won't have much strength and, eventually, we won't have peace. We are currently borrowing the entire defense budget from foreign investors. Within a few years, we will be spending more on interest payments than on national security. That is not, as our military friends say, a "robust strategy."

I personally favor restoring impoundment power to the presidency, at least on an emergency basis. Having had this authority the last six years, and used it shall we say with vigor, I can testify to its effectiveness, and to this finding: You'd be amazed how much government you'll never miss.

The nation must be summoned to General Quarters in the cause of economic growth. The friends of freedom always favor a growing economy as the wellspring of individual opportunity and a bulwark against a domineering state. But here, doctrinal debates are unnecessary; the arithmetic tells it all. We don't have a prayer of defeating the Red Threat of our generation without a long boom of almost unprecedented duration. Every other goal, however worthy, must be tested against and often subordinated to actions that spur the faster expansion of the private sector on which all else depends.

A friend of mine attended a recent meeting of the NBA leadership, at which a small-market owner, whom I won't name but will mention is also a member of the U.S. Senate, made an impassioned plea for more sharing of revenue by the more successful teams. At a coffee break, Mr. Prokhorov, the new Russian owner of the New Jersey Nets, murmured to my friend, "We tried that, you know. It doesn't work."

Americans have seen these last two years what doesn't work. The failure of national economic policy is costing us more than jobs; it has begun to weaken that uniquely American spirit of risk-taking, large ambition, and optimism about the future. We must rally them now to bold departures that rebuild our national morale as well as our material prosperity. Here, too, the room abounds with experts and good ideas, and the nation will need every one.

Just to name three: it's time we had, in Bill Simon's words, "a tax system that looks like someone designed it on purpose." And the purpose should be private growth. So lower and flatter, and completely flat is best. Tax compensation but not the savings and investment without which the economy cannot boom.

Second, untie Gulliver. The regulatory rainforest through which our enterprises must hack their way is blighting the future of millions of Americans. Today's EPA should be renamed the "Employment Prevention Agency." After a two-year orgy of new regulation, President Obama's recent executive order was a wonderment, as though the number one producer of rap music had suddenly expressed alarm about obscenity.

In Indiana, where our privatization of a toll road generated billions for reinvestment in infrastructure, we can build in half the time at two-thirds the cost when we use our own money only and are free from the federal rulebook. A moratorium on new regulation is a minimal suggestion; better yet, move at least temporarily to a self-certification regime that lets America build, and expand, and explore now and settle up later in those few instances where someone colors outside the lines.

Finally, treat domestic energy production as the economic necessity it is and the job creator it can be. Drill, and frack, and lease, and license, unleash in every way the jobs potential in the enormous energy resources we have been denying ourselves. And help our fellow citizens to understand that a poorer country will not be a greener country, but its opposite. It is freedom and its fruits that enable the steady progress we have made in preserving and protecting God's kingdom.

If this strikes you as a project of unusual ambition, given the state of modern politics, you are right. If it strikes you as too bold for our fellow Americans to embrace, I believe you are wrong. Seven years as a practitioner in elective politics tells me that history's skeptics are wrong. That Americans, in a vast majority, are still a people born for self-governance. They are ready to summon the discipline to pay down our collective debts as they are now paying down their own; to put the future before the present, their children's interest before their own.

Our proposals will be labeled radical, but this is easy to rebut. Starting a new retirement plan for those below a certain age is something tens of millions of Americans have already been through at work.

Opponents will expect us to be defensive, but they have it backwards. When they call the slightest spending reductions "painful," we will say "If government spending prevents pain, why are we suffering so much of it?" And "If you want to experience real pain, just stay on the track we are on." When they attack us for our social welfare reforms, we will say that the true enemies of Social Security and Medicare are those who defend an imploding status quo, and the arithmetic backs us up.

They will attack our program as the way of despair, but we will say no, America's way forward is brilliant with hope, as soon as we have dealt decisively with the manageable problems before us.

2010 showed that the spirit of liberty and independence is stirring anew, that a growing number of Americans still hear Lincoln's mystic chords of memory. But their number will have to grow, and do so swiftly. Change of the dimension we need requires a coalition of a dimension no one has recently assembled. And, unless you disbelieve what the arithmetic of disaster is telling us, time is very short.

Here I wish to be very plainspoken: It is up to us to show, specifically, the best way back to greatness, and to argue for it with all the passion of our patriotism. But, should the best way be blocked, while the enemy draws nearer, then someone will need to find the second best way. Or the third, because the nation's survival requires it.

Purity in martyrdom is for suicide bombers. King Pyrrhus is remembered, but his nation disappeared. Winston Churchill set aside his lifetime loathing of Communism in order to fight World War II. Challenged as a hypocrite, he said that when the safety of Britain was at stake, his "conscience became a good girl." We are at such a moment. I for one have no interest in standing in the wreckage of our Republic saying "I told you so" or "You should've done it my way."

We must be the vanguard of recovery, but we cannot do it alone. We have learned in Indiana, big change requires big majorities. We will need people who never tune in to Rush or Glenn or Laura or Sean. Who surf past C-SPAN to get to SportsCenter. Who, if they'd ever heard of CPAC, would assume it was a cruise ship accessory.

The second worst outcome I can imagine for next year would be to lose to the current president and subject the nation to what might be a fatal last dose of statism. The worst would be to win the election and then prove ourselves incapable of turning the ship of state before it went on the rocks, with us at the helm.

So we must unify America, or enough of it, to demand and sustain the Big Change we propose.

Here are a few suggestions:

We must display a heart for every American, and a special passion for those still on the first rung of life's ladder. Upward mobility from the bottom is the crux of the American promise, and the stagnation of the middle class is in fact becoming a problem, on any fair reading of the facts.

Our main task is not to see that people of great wealth add to it, but that those without much money have a greater chance to earn some.

We should address ourselves to young America at every opportunity. It is their futures that today's policies endanger, and in their direct interest that we propose a new direction.

We should distinguish carefully skepticism about Big Government from contempt for all government. After all, it is a new government we hope to form, a government we will ask our fellow citizens to trust to make huge changes.

I urge a similar thoughtfulness about the rhetoric we deploy in the great debate ahead. I suspect everyone here regrets and laments the sad, crude coarsening of our popular culture. It has a counterpart in the venomous, petty, often ad hominem political discourse of the day.

When one of us—I confess sometimes it was yours truly—got a little hotheaded, President Reagan would admonish us, "Remember, we have no enemies, only opponents." Good advice, then and now.

And besides, our opponents are better at nastiness than we will ever be. It comes naturally.

Power to them is everything, so there's nothing they won't say to get it. The public is increasingly disgusted with a steady diet of defamation, and prepared to reward those who refrain from it. Am I alone in observing that one of conservatism's best moments this past year was a massive rally that came and went from Washington without leaving any trash, physical or rhetorical, behind?

A more affirmative, "better angels" approach to voters is really less an aesthetic than a practical one: with apologies for the banality, I submit that, as we ask Americans to join us on such a boldly different course, it would help if they liked us, just a bit.

Lastly, critically, I urge great care not to drift into a loss of faith in the American people. In speech after speech, article upon article, we remind each other how many are dependent on government, or how few pay taxes, or how much essential virtues like family formation or civic education have withered. All true. All worrisome. But we must never yield to the self-fulfilling despair that these problems are immutable or insurmountable.

All great enterprises have a pearl of faith at their core, and this must be ours: that Americans are still a people born to liberty. That they retain the capacity for self-government. That, addressed as free-born, autonomous men and women of God-given dignity, they will rise yet again to drive back a mortal enemy.

History's assignment to this generation of freedom fighters is in one way even more profound than the tests of our proud past. We are tasked to rebuild not just a damaged economy, and a debt-ridden balance sheet, but to do so by drawing forth the best that is in our fellow citizens. If we would summon the best from Americans, we must assume the best about them. If we don't believe in Americans, who will?

I do believe. I've seen it in the people of our very typical corner of the nation. I've seen it in the hundred Indiana homes in which I have stayed overnight. I've seen it in Hoosiers' resolute support of limited government, their willingness, even insistence, that government keep within the boundaries our constitutional surveyors mapped out for it.

I've always loved John Adams's diary entry, written en route to Philadelphia, there to put his life, liberty, and sacred honor all at risk. He wrote that it was all well worth it because, he said, "Great things are wanted to be done."

When he and his colleagues arrived, and over the years ahead, they practiced the art of the possible. They made compacts and concessions and, yes, compromises. They made deep sectional and other differences secondary in pursuit of the grand prize of freedom. They each argued passionately for the best answers as they saw them, but they never permitted the perfect to be the enemy of the historic good they did for us, and all mankind. They gave us a Republic, citizen Franklin said, if we can keep it.

Keeping the Republic is the great thing that is wanted to be done, now, in our time, by us. In this room are convened freedom's best friends but, to keep our Republic, freedom needs every friend it can get. Let's go find them, and befriend them, and welcome them to the great thing that is wanted to be done in our day.

God bless this meeting and the liberty which makes it possible.

4

Government Secrecy After WikiLeaks

"Let the Eyes of Vigilance Never Be Closed"*

Ron Paul

U.S. representative (R), Texas, 1997– ; born Pittsburgh, PA, August 20, 1935; B.S., Gettysburg College, 1957; M.D., Duke University, 1967; captain, United States Air Force, 1963–65; flight surgeon, Air National Guard, 1965–68; obstetrician-gynecologist, 1968–1996; candidate for U.S. House of Representatives, 1974; U.S. representative (R), Texas, 1976–77; U.S. representative (R), Texas, 1979–1985; ran for the U.S. Senate, 1984; Libertarian presidential nominee, 1988; candidate for 2008 and 2012 Republican presidential nominations; author, The Case for Gold: A Minority Report of the U.S. Gold Commission *(1982);* Abortion and Liberty *(1983);* Freedom Under Siege: The U.S. Constitution After 200 Years *(1987);* Challenge to Liberty: Coming to Grips with the Abortion Issue *(1990);* A Foreign Policy of Freedom *(2007);* The Revolution: A Manifesto *(2008);* Pillars of Prosperity *(2008);* End the Fed *(2009);* Liberty Defined: 50 Essential Issues that Affect Our Freedom *(2011).*

Editor's introduction: In this speech, delivered on the floor of the U.S. House of Representatives, Congressman Ron Paul questions what he calls hysterical reactions to the release of secret and classified documents by the WikiLeaks Web site. In a series of rhetorical questions, he suggests we ask exactly how we could prosecute WikiLeaks's editor-in-chief Julian Assange, who is not a U.S. citizen, for publishing information he did not steal, and consider whether the media organizations that subsequently disseminated the WikiLeaks material ought to be charged as well. Paul concludes with a number of larger questions about American government, foreign policy, and the nature of patriotism.

Ron Paul's speech: WikiLeaks's release of classified information has generated a lot of attention world-wide in the past few weeks.

The hysterical reaction makes one wonder if this is not an example of killing the messenger for the bad news.

---

* Delivered on December 9, 2010, at Washington, D.C.

Despite what is claimed, information so far released, though classified, has caused no known harm to any individual, but it has caused plenty of embarrassment to our government. Losing a grip on our empire is not welcomed by the neoconservatives in charge.

There is now more information confirming that Saudi Arabia is a principal supporter and financier of al Qaeda and this should set off alarm bells since we guarantee its Sharia-run government.

This emphasizes even more the fact that no al Qaeda existed in Iraq before 9/11, and yet we went to war against Iraq based on the lie that it did.

It has been charged, by self-proclaimed experts, that Julian Assange, the Internet publisher of this information, has committed a heinous crime deserving prosecution for treason and execution or even assassination.

But should we not at least ask how the U.S. government can charge an Australian citizen with treason for publishing U.S. secret information, that he did not steal?

And if WikiLeaks is to be prosecuted for publishing classified documents, why shouldn't the *Washington Post*, *New York Times*, and others that have also published these documents be prosecuted? Actually, some in Congress are threatening this as well.

The New York Times, as a result of a Supreme Court ruling, was not found guilty in 1971 for the publication of the Pentagon Papers. Daniel Ellsberg never served a day in prison for his role in obtaining these secret documents.

The Pentagon Papers were also inserted into the Congressional Record by Senator Mike Gravel with no charges being made of breaking any National Security laws.

Yet the release of this classified information was considered illegal by many, and those who lied us into the Vietnam War and argued for its prolongation were outraged. But the truth gained from the Pentagon Papers revealed that lies were told about the Gulf of Tonkin attack which perpetuated a sad and tragic episode in our history.

Just as with the Vietnam War, the Iraq War was based on lies. We were never threatened by weapons of mass destruction or al Qaeda in Iraq, though the attack on Iraq was based on this false information.

Any information that challenges the official propaganda for the war in the Middle East is unwelcome by the administration and supporters of these unnecessary wars. Few are interested in understanding the relationship of our foreign policy and our presence in the Middle East to the threat of terrorism. Revealing the real nature and goal for our presence in so many Muslim countries is a threat to our empire and any revelation of this truth is highly resented by those in charge.

Questions to consider:

1. Do the American people deserve to know the truth regarding the ongoing war in Iraq, Afghanistan, Pakistan, and Yemen?

2. Could a larger question be: how can an Army Private gain access to so much secret material?

3. Why is the hostility mostly directed at Assange, the publisher, and not our government's failure to protect classified information?

4. Are we getting our money's worth from the $80 billion per year we spend on our intelligence agencies?

5. Which has resulted in the greatest number of deaths: lying us into war, or WikiLeaks' revelations or the release of the Pentagon Papers?

6. If Assange can be convicted of a crime for publishing information, that he did not steal, what does this say about the future of the First Amendment and the independence of the Internet?

7. Could it be that the real reason for the near universal attacks on WikiLeaks is more about secretly maintaining a seriously flawed foreign policy of empire than it is about national security?

8. Is there not a huge difference between releasing secret information to help the enemy in the time of a declared war—which is treason—and the releasing of information to expose our government lies that promote secret wars, death, and corruption?

9. Was it not once considered patriotic to stand up to our government when it's wrong?

Thomas Jefferson had it right when he advised: "Let the eyes of vigilance never be closed."

Secrecy in Our Open Society[*]

Gabriel Schoenfeld

Senior adviser, Romney for President, 2011– ; born New York, NY, November 17, 1955; B.A., Sarah Lawrence College, 1979; Ph.D., Harvard University, 1989; teaching fellow, Department of Government, Harvard University, 1984–88; foreign service officer, U.S. Information Agency, 1986–87; senior fellow, Center for Strategic and International Studies, 1990–94; senior editor, Commentary, *1994–2008; senior fellow, Hudson Institute, 2008–11; resident scholar, Witherspoon Institute, 2008–2011; author,* The Return of Anti-Semitism *(2004),* Necessary Secrets: The Media, National Security, and the Rule of Law *(2010).*

Editor's introduction: In this address, presented to a hearing of the House Committee on the Judiciary on the Espionage Act and the legal and constitutional concerns raised by WikiLeaks, Gabriel Schoenfeld acknowledges that government openness is vital to democracy but contends that secrecy is also essential, especially in times of war. He compares the release of classified information by WikiLeaks to WMD—"weapons of mass disclosure." He offers both recent and historical examples of harmful media revelations of classified information to support his case and issues more general warnings about the possible effects the fear of leaks may have on policymaking. Schoenfeld also discusses self-interest as a possible motive for publicizing secret information and addresses questions relating to the prosecution of leakers and the First Amendment.

Gabriel Schoenfeld's speech: A basic principle of our political order, enshrined in the First Amendment guarantee of freedom of speech and of the press, is that openness is an essential prerequisite of self-governance. Indeed, at the very core of our democratic experiment lies the question of transparency. Secrecy was one of the cornerstones of monarchy, a building block of an unaccountable political system constructed in no small part on what King James the First had called the "mysteries of state." Secrecy was not merely functional, a requirement of an effective monarchy, but intrinsic to the mental scaffolding of autocratic rule.

---

[*] Delivered on December 16, 2010, at Washington, D.C.

Standing in diametrical opposition to that mental scaffolding was an elementary proposition of democratic theory: Legitimate power could rest only on the informed consent of the governed. Along with individuals at liberty to give or to withhold approval to their government, informed consent requires, above all else, information, freely available and freely exchanged. Official secrecy is anathema to this conception. No one has put this proposition more forcefully than James Madison, who tells us that "A popular government, without popular information, or the means of acquiring it, is but a Prologue to a Farce or a Tragedy, or, perhaps both. Knowledge will forever govern ignorance: And a people who mean to be their own Governors must arm themselves with the power which knowledge gives."

Our country has long operated under a broad consensus that secrecy is antithetical to democratic rule and can encourage a variety of political deformations. Secrecy can facilitate renegade governmental activity, as we saw in the Watergate and the Iran-Contra affairs. It can also be a breeding ground for corruption. Egregious recent cases are easy to tick off.

The potential for excessive concealment has grown more acute as the American national security apparatus expanded massively in the decades since World War II, bringing with it a commensurately large extension of secrecy. In 2008 alone, there were a staggering 23 million so-called "derivative classification" decisions, the government's term for any step "incorporating, paraphrasing, restating, or generating in a new form information that is already classified."

With a huge volume of information pertaining to national defense walled off from the public, secrecy almost inevitably has become haphazard. Arresting glimpses of mis- and overclassification are not hard to uncover. The CIA has disclosed, for example, the total government-wide intelligence budget for 1997, 1998, 2007, and 2008, while similar numbers for both intermediate and earlier years remain a state secret. This seems entirely capricious.

Given the massive secrecy, and given our political traditions, it can hardly come as a surprise that leaking is part and parcel of our system of rule. Not a day goes by in Washington without government officials sharing inside information with journalists and lobbyists in off-the-record briefings and in private discussions over lunch. Much of the material changing hands in this fashion winds up getting published. A study by the Senate Intelligence Committee counted 147 separate disclosures of classified information that made their way into the nation's eight leading newspapers in a six-month period alone.

As these high numbers indicate, leaks to the press are a well-established informal practice. They enable policy makers to carry out any one of a number of objectives: to get out a message to domestic and foreign audiences, to gauge public reaction in advance of some contemplated policy initiative, to curry favor with journalists, and to wage inter- or intra-bureaucratic warfare. For better or worse, leaking has become part of the normal functioning of the U.S. government. And for better or worse, leaking is one of the prime ways that we as citizens are informed about the workings of our government.

But if openness is the default position we would all prefer in a self-governing society, it cannot be unlimited. Secrecy, like openness, is also an essential prerequisite of governance. To be effective, even many of the most mundane aspects of democratic rule, from the development of policy alternatives to the selection of personnel, must often take place behind closed doors. To proceed always under the glare of public scrutiny would cripple deliberation and render government impotent.

And when one turns to the most fundamental business of democratic governance, namely, self-preservation, the imperative of secrecy becomes critical, often a matter of survival. Even in times of peace, the formulation of foreign and defense policies is necessarily conducted in secret. But this is not a time of peace. Ever since September 11, the country has been at war. And we are not only at war, we are engaged in a particular kind of war—an intelligence war against a shadowy and determined adversary. The effectiveness of the tools of intelligence—from the recruitment of agents to the capabilities of satellite reconnaissance systems to the interception of terrorist communications—remains overwhelmingly dependent on their clandestine nature. It is not an overstatement to say that secrecy today is one of the most critical tools of national defense.

The leaking of secrets thus can fundamentally impair our ability to protect ourselves. The various WikiLeaks data dumps of the last few months are a vivid case in point. There is a widespread recognition that the massive releases of classified information have injured the security of the United States. Indeed, thanks in part to the march of technology, we have on our hands what might be called WMDs, weapons of mass disclosure, leaks so massive in volume and so indiscriminate in what they convey, that it becomes difficult to assess the overall harm, precisely because there are so many different ways for the harm to occur. Secretary of State Hillary Clinton has condemned WikiLeaks for "endangering innocent people" and "sabotaging the peaceful relations between nations on which our common security depends." Admiral Mike Mullen, chairman of the Joint Chiefs of Staff, has stated that WikiLeaks might already have blood on its hands. Secretary of Defense Robert Gates, responding to the release of classified military field reports this past summer, called the consequences "potentially severe and dangerous" for our troops and Afghan partners.

But the WikiLeaks phenomenon is hardly the only significant and damaging leak of the recent era. To take just one of several examples readily at hand, the 9/11 Commission had singled out the tracking of terrorist finances as one of the weak points in U.S. intelligence that had allowed the Sept. 11 plot to succeed. After 9/11, a top secret joint CIA-Treasury Department program was set in motion to monitor the movement of al Qaeda funds via access to the computerized records of a Belgian financial clearing house known as SWIFT. But In June 2006, the *New York Times* published a front-page story revealing the existence of the intelligence gathering effort.

The *Times* story itself noted that the monitoring had achieved significant successes, including providing information leading to the arrest of Hambali, the top operative in that al Qaeda affiliate in Southeast Asia behind the 2002 bombing of

Bali in Indonesia. By revealing details of the secret program, the *Times* telegraphed to al Qaeda one of our most important means of tracking its plans. Both leading Republicans and Democrats in Congress, and ranking career intelligence officials said that the leak prompted al Qaeda operatives to move funds in ways far less easy for the U.S. government to track. In this connection, it is quite notable that the al Qaeda and the Taliban are now making extensive use of such means of moving money as untraceable money-grams, hawala, and couriers. Our adversaries do pay attention to what we reveal to them.

The *Times* published the SWIFT story against the strenuous objections of government officials, Republican and Democratic alike. It has never offered a convincing justification for doing so. Its own ombudsman and its chief counsel both subsequently disavowed the decision. Eric Lichtblau, one of the two reporters who wrote the SWIFT story, offered his own rationale for its publication, explaining that it was, "above all else, an interesting yarn." It is difficult to imagine a more trivial justification for a step of such gravity.

Sometimes it takes many years for the damage from such interesting yarns to make itself felt. In my recent book, *Necessary Secrets: National Security, the Media, and the Rule of Law,* I explored an older leak—the so called Black Chamber Affair—that contributed significantly to the success of the Japanese surprise attack on Pearl Harbor. In 1931 a retired American cryptographer by the name of Herbert O. Yardley, out of a job in the Great Depression and having fallen on hard times, published a book called *The American Black Chamber* that laid bare the entire history of American codebreaking efforts, including our prior successes in cracking Japanese codes.

Here in the United States, Mr. Yardley's book was praised highly in some quarters of the press. As one leading publication wrote in a typical vein, "Simply as entertainment, this exposé is well worth the price." In Japan, on the other hand, the book caused an uproar about the laxity with which codes had been constructed. One of the consequences of the uproar was that the Japanese military infused new funds into research on cryptographic security. Within three years they had developed a machine-generated cipher, a precursor to the famously complex Purple code machine. Some sensitive Japanese communications were no longer transmitted over the airwaves even in encrypted form. Instead a worldwide courier system was introduced to ensure their secure delivery.

We did not suffer the consequences of any of all this activity for a decade, but in the months before Pearl Harbor, one of the ramifications of Mr. Yardley's book was that the United States was not able to read crucial Japanese military communications, and we missed key warning signs that Pearl Harbor was going to be attacked.

Informing our adversaries of our capabilities is the most direct form of damage caused by leaking. But this hardly exhausts the universe of the kinds of harm that leaks of secret information can cause. Let me mention several others, especially as they impinge today on conduct on the war on terrorism.

For one thing, leaks significantly impact our ability to engage in exchanges of information with allies and adversaries alike. Even routine diplomatic discourse becomes impossible if both foreign and American officials labor in fear that their confidential remarks are to going to end up on the front page of the *New York Times* via an outfit like WikiLeaks. Even more dangerous is the impact on intelligence sharing. In any particular instance in which information gathered by an ally is particularly sensitive, foreign intelligence officials can be quite reluctant to share it with our government if it will result in a headline that might compromise their own sources and methods, and possibly lead to the deaths of informants and agents.

For another thing, leaks tend to cripple our deliberative and decision-making processes. We have vast national-security bureaucracies filled with leading experts on all manner of questions. And yet whenever important decisions are taken, ranking officials almost always conclude that it essential to push their underlings away as far as possible, lest someone in the bowels of the bureaucracy, for whatever motive, places a telephone call to a reporter and torpedoes the policy. American decisionmakers are thus compelled to take crucial decisions while in effect groping in the dark, with results that often times speak for themselves.

And for yet another thing, leaks constrict the arteries by which information is circulated across and within the national-security machinery of the U.S. government. The 9/11 Commission pointed to a dearth of information sharing among government agencies as one of the factors that led to al Qaeda's terrible achievement in penetrating our defenses. Remedial measures taken after September 11 have allowed information to flow more freely to where it needs to go, although bottlenecks still exist. The Pentagon, for its part, has succeeded in pushing raw intelligence down to the war-fighters on the battlefield so that it can actually be used. But with greater access came greater risks. One of those risks turned up in the person of Pfc. Bradley Manning, who seems to be the culprit who turned over vast quantities of information to WikiLeaks. That breach has increased the pressure to tighten the information spigot, undoing some of the important gains in our counterterrorism efforts garnered by post 9/11 reforms.

Finally, leaking is an assault on democratic self-governance itself. We live in a polity that has an elected president and elected representatives. Leaking is a way in which individuals elected by no one and representing no one can use their privileged access to information to foist their own views on a government chosen by the people.

There are two different kinds of perpetrators engaged in this assault and they operate under very different ethical and legal strictures. On one side are so-called whistleblowers, who pass along secrets from within the national-security apparatus to journalists. Somewhere upward of 2.4 million Americans hold security clearances. A population that size will always contain a significant quotient of individuals disaffected for one or another reason. The power to leak on a confidential basis offers any one of the 2.4 million a megaphone into which he or she can speak while wearing a mask. Often acting from partisan motives or to obtain personal advancement, and almost always under the cover of anonymity, such whistleblowers are willing to imperil the nation but not their careers.

The other face of the assault on democratic self-government comes from journalists, who operate in tandem with the whistleblowers, and claim protection to publish whatever they would like under the banner of the First Amendment. In publishing leaked materials, journalists indefatigably demand openness in government and claim to defend the people's "right to know." But along with the public's "right to know," constantly invoked by the press, there is also something rarely spoken about let alone defended: namely the public's right not to know. Yet when it comes to certain sensitive subjects in the realm of security, the American people have voluntarily chosen to keep themselves uninformed about what their elected government is doing in their name. The reason why we choose to keep ourselves uninformed is not an enigma. It is obvious. We entrust our government to generate and to protect secrets, secrets that are kept from us, because what we know about such matters our adversaries will know as well. If we lay our secrets bare and fight the war on terrorism without the tools of intelligence, we will succumb to another attack.

Norman Pearlstine, the chief executive of Time Inc., says that "when gathering and reporting news, journalists act as surrogates for the public." Pearlstine's observation can be true. But when journalists reveal secrets necessary to secure the American people from external enemies, a converse observation can be true. In that event, journalists are not surrogates for the public but usurpers of the public's powers and rights.

Reporters and editors regard themselves as public servants, but they suffer from a tendency to forget that they are private individuals, elected by no one and representing no one. They operate inside private corporations which are themselves not at all transparent. Indeed, the putative watchdogs of the press, ever on the lookout for the covert operations of government, can themselves be covert operators, with agendas hidden from the public. The press plays an indispensable role in our system as a checking force, but its practitioners can and sometimes do wield their power—including the power to disclose government secrets—for political ends of their own choosing.

That is not the only point of conflict between the press and the public, for newspapers are also profit-seeking institutions. Every day of the year, journalists delve into the potential and real financial misdeeds and conflicts of interest besetting corporate America. But newspapers, curiously, seldom if ever delve into the potential and real conflicts of interest besetting journalism, particularly in the area of publishing sensitive government secrets. Or perhaps it is not so curious. For journalists operate inside a market economy in which financial rewards accrue not just to news corporations and their shareholders but also to they themselves. A Pulitzer Prize brings immense prestige in the profession, and a $10,000 check, a sum almost always matched by news organizations with generous raises and/or bonuses. And then of course there is a book market in which discussion of secret programs can generate hundreds of thousands of dollars in royalties. Lecture fees can add tens of thousands of dollars more. The incentives to cast aside scruples about injury to national security, injury that is seldom immediately apparent, and lay bare vital secrets can be powerful, indeed, irresistible.

At the end of the day, we are presented with two conflicting positions: on the one hand, leaking is a necessary and widespread practice inside our democracy. On the other hand, it is fundamentally anti-democratic and it can cause great harm. Both views are right and we are faced with a contradiction. How can the tension between these two very different faces of the phenomenon be reconciled?

One pathway through the contradiction is by looking at the legal framework in which the leaking occurs. For law is not just a mechanical set of rules and sanctions, but also a moral code by which conduct can be considered and judged.

There are two classes that have to be considered here: leakers and those who disseminate information provided by the leakers to a mass audience.

Leakers are almost in every instance, except when they possess the actual legal authority to declassify information, breaking the law. Everyone who works with classified information is in effect being entrusted by the public to safeguard the secrets they encounter. As a condition of employment, they are asked to sign an agreement pledging to observe the laws protecting those secrets. The agreement reads in part:

> I have been advised that the unauthorized disclosure, unauthorized retention, or negligent handling of classified information by me could cause damage or irreparable injury to the United States or could be used to advantage by a foreign nation. I hereby agree that I will never divulge classified information to anyone unless: (a) I have officially verified that the recipient has been properly authorized by the United States Government to receive it; or (b) I have been given prior written notice of authorization from the United States Government Department or Agency (hereinafter Department or Agency) responsible for the classification of the information or last granting me a security clearance that such disclosure is permitted. I understand that if I am uncertain about the classification status of information, I am required to confirm from an authorized official that the information is unclassified before I may disclose it, except to a person as provided in (a) or (b), above. I further understand that I am obligated to comply with laws and regulations that prohibit the unauthorized disclosure of classified information. . . . I have been advised that any unauthorized disclosure of classified information by me may constitute a violation, or violations, of United States criminal laws.

Nothing about this promise is unclear. No one who affixes his name to this nondisclosure agreement is compelled to do so; government officials sign it of their own free will.

What is more, officials who uncover illegal conduct in the government are by no means bound by their signature to keep silent and permit violations of law to continue. Congress has enacted "whistleblower protection acts" that offer clear and workable procedures for civil servants to report misdeeds and ensure that their complaints will be duly and properly considered. When classified matters are at issue, these procedures include direct appeals to the Justice Department and to members of the intelligence committees in Congress. They emphatically do not include blowing vital secrets by disclosing them to al Qaeda and the rest of the world via WikiLeaks or the news media.

The rules and laws governing leakers are quite clear. The same, alas, cannot be said regarding those who disseminate leaked information in the media. Here there are two radically opposing views.

On one side there is the position put forward by journalists, who maintain that the First Amendment gives the press an absolute right to publish whatever government secrets it wants to publish. Bill Keller, executive editor of the *Times*, says that the Founding Fathers, in opening the Bill of Rights with the First Amendment, "rejected the idea that it is wise, or patriotic to surrender to the government important decisions about what to publish." This absolutist view of the First Amendment is widespread among journalists. They say that the words of the First Amendment are unequivocal: "Congress shall make no law . . . abridging the freedom of speech, or of the press." "No law" means "no law," are what journalists and their defenders repeat over and over again.

But the framers were hardly the apostles of libertarianism that they are today made out to be by Mr. Keller and many others. More than anything else, the First Amendment was conceived of by the framers as a continuation of the Blackstonian understanding embedded in British common law, as a prohibition on prior restraint on the press. Censorship was what the framers aimed to forbid. But laws punishing the publication of certain kinds of material after the fact were something else again. Joseph Story, the preeminent 19th century interpreter of the Constitution put this understanding most forcefully when he wrote that the idea that the First Amendment was "intended to secure to every citizen an absolute right to speak, or write, or print, whatever he might please is a supposition too wild to be indulged by any rational man."

And indeed our courts have long held, and the press itself has long readily accepted, that the sweeping words of the First Amendment are fully compatible with legal restrictions on what journalists can and cannot say in print. Statutes forbidding certain kinds of commercial speech and punishing libel, to which virtually no one inside the media ever objects, have long been held to be fully constitutional abridgements of freedom of the press.

But in the vital area of national security, journalists nevertheless insist that they and they alone are the final arbiters of what can and cannot be published. And they act upon this insistence, publishing national-security secrets on some occasions with little or no regard for the consequences. As Dean Baquet, the Washington bureau chief of the *New York Times*, has put it, the press is free to publish whatever it wishes "no matter the cost."

But Mr. Baquet's understanding is not in line with either our Constitution or our laws. Congress—that is, the American people, acting through their elected representatives—has enacted a number of different statutes that prohibit the publication of certain kinds of national-security secrets. Thanks to the Valery Plame-Judith Miller affair, we are most familiar these days with a 1982 law, the Intelligence Identities Protection Act, that makes it a felony to disclose the identity of undercover operatives working for the CIA or other U.S. intelligence agencies. Congress has also carved out special protection for secrets concerning atomic weapons and communications intelligence. The 1917 Espionage Act offers a more general blanket protection to all closely held information pertaining to national defense.

These laws are on the books, and they have been upheld by the Supreme Court. But the stark fact is that they are not being enforced. Remarkably enough, despite how ubiquitous leaking is in our system, there have been only three successful prosecutions of leakers in our entire history. The prosecution of leakers is rare because they are exceptionally difficult to catch. Almost every president beginning with Richard Nixon has launched investigations designed to ferret out leakers, but law enforcement almost always comes up empty. The simple fact is that typically with respect to any given leaked secret, too many people, sometimes hundreds, have had access to it, and the tools of investigation, including polygraph interviews, simply do not yield results. The problem of controlling the illicit flow of information out of the bureaucracies remains unresolved.

As for prosecutions of the press, they have been rarer still than the prosecution of leakers. Indeed, there have been no successful convictions in our entire history and only one attempted prosecution. That attempted prosecution occurred during World War II, and is highly relevant today. It was directed against the *Chicago Tribune*, then published by Colonel Robert McCormick, an ardent isolationist, who seemed to hate Roosevelt far more than he hated either Hitler or Hirohito.

In 1942, in the immediate aftermath of the Battle of Midway, the *Chicago Tribune* published a story strongly suggesting that the decisive American naval victory at Midway owed to the fact that the United States had been successfully reading Japanese codes. Shocked officials in the War Department in Washington sought to throw the book at Col. McCormick and a grand jury was empanelled to hear evidence and bring charges. When it turned out that the Japanese had not changed their codes in reaction to the news story, the War Department asked the Justice Department to drop the proceedings lest further attention be called to a story the Japanese had seemingly ignored.

But there can be no blinking the gravity of that breach. If the United States, thanks to the *Chicago Tribune*, had lost its window into Japanese military communications, the war in the Pacific would still have ended in certain Japanese defeat. That outcome was all but assured by the atomic bomb. But three years were to elapse before the atomic bomb was ready for use. In the interim, without the priceless advantage of knowing Tokyo's every next move in advance, thousands—tens of thousands—of American soldiers and sailors would have needlessly died.

Since 1942, we have never had a subsequent prosecution. Perhaps the major reason is that the press has for the most part, until quite recently, been fairly restrained and responsible. Consider, for example, the *New York Times*'s decision in 1971 to publish excerpts of the top-secret collection of documents provided to it by Rand Corporation researcher Daniel Ellsberg. By any measure, that was the most sensational leak in all of American history up to its time. But the Pentagon Papers case was sensational not so much because of the sensitive nature of the secrets disclosed but primarily because Richard Nixon tried, unsuccessfully, to get a prior restraint from the courts to stop the presses.

In the Pentagon Papers case, the secrets at issue were nothing at all like the ultra-sensitive material published by the *Chicago Tribune*. The Pentagon Papers became public during the Nixon administration, but they had been compiled during the Johnson administration. By 1971, when Mr. Ellsberg turned the Pentagon Papers over to Neil Sheehan of the *New York Times*, not one of the documents in the Pentagon Papers case was less than three years old. Though the documents bore a top-secret stamp, the passage of time had rendered them nearly innocuous. No ongoing intelligence operations or war plans were disclosed.

This brings us back to our current dilemmas. For the fact is that the material being published today by WikiLeaks and by our leading newspaper is closer to what the *Chicago Tribune* published during World War II than to what was contained in the Pentagon Papers. The secrets that are being revealed today are not historical in nature; they involve ongoing diplomatic, military and intelligence programs.

Such conduct brings urgently to the fore a fundamental question raised by the phenomenon of leaking: namely, who in the final analysis gets to decide what can be kept secret and what cannot?

It is not question susceptible to a glib answer or an easily formulated rule, for the crux of the matter is that the public interest in transparency, and a vigorous press that ensures transparency, is diametrically opposed to the public interest in secrecy.

On the one hand, we live now in a world in which small groups of remorseless men are plotting to strike our buildings, bridges, tunnels, and subways, and seeking to acquire weapons of mass destruction that they would not hesitate to use against our cities, taking the lives of hundreds of thousands or more. To contend with that grim reality, our national-security apparatus inexorably generates more secrets, and more sensitive secrets, and seemingly exercises weaker control over those same vital secrets than ever before.

Yet on the other hand, we cannot lose sight of facts that I noted at the outset, namely, that our national security system is saddled with pervasive mis- and over-classification that remains entrenched despite universal recognition of its existence and numerous attempts at reform.

With the two desiderata of set in extreme tension, it would hardly make sense for the Justice Department to prosecute the press on each and every occasion when it drops classified information into the public domain. Such an approach would be absurd, a cure that would drain the lifeblood from democratic discourse and kill the patient.

A much more reasonable approach would be to continue to live with the ambiguities of our current practices and laws. Vigorously prosecuting and punishing leakers is an obvious place to begin. It is an irony that it is Barack Obama, the President who came into office pledging maximum transparency in government, who is now carrying out such a policy. His administration has thus far launched four leak prosecutions, more than all preceding American presidents combined.

As for the press, a first step is to try to alter the political climate in which irresponsible tell-all-and-damn-the-consequences journalism flourishes. The WikiLeaks case, in which documents have been released wholesale with consequences that cannot yet even be imagined, has already caused a change in attitudes, making it clear to the public that not all so-called whistle-blowing is commendable, and that in extreme cases, the dissemination of secrets can merit prosecution.

The press does and should have an essential checking role on the government in the realm of foreign affairs, national defense, and intelligence. And that checking role, if it is to be more than a charade, must extend, as it now does, into the inner workings of the U.S. national security apparatus where secrecy is the coin of the realm. But in ferreting out and choosing to report secrets, the press has to exercise discretion.

Newspaper editors are fully capable of exercising discretion about sensitive matters when they so choose. A dramatic example came to light in 2009 when the *New York Times* revealed that it had succeeded for a period of six months in suppressing news that one of its reporters, David Rohde, had been kidnapped in Afghanistan by the Taliban. Indeed, the editors seemed to exercise the art of concealment with greater success than the U.S. government's own secrecy apparatus is often capable of achieving. Neither the *Times* nor its industry competitors, who readily agreed to gag themselves at the *Times*'s request, published a word about the missing journalist until Mr. Rohde escaped his captors and made his way to safety. Bill Keller's explanation was: "We hate sitting on a story, but sometimes we do. I mean, sometimes we do it because a military or another government agency convinces us that, if we publish information, it will put lives at risk."

Mr. Keller deserves some measure of praise for that. But such discretion cannot be—and under our current laws is not—a strictly voluntary affair. Despite Mr. Keller's claims, the *Times* and other leading newspapers have been far from responsible in their handling of secrets. But even if they were models of rectitude, the public would still be left without recourse in the face of other lesser publications that are not such models, or outfits like WikiLeaks.

Thus, even as the press strives to carry the invaluable function of delving into government secrets, this does not mean it should be exempt from the strictures of law. What it does mean is that in enforcing the law, the executive must also exercise judgment and seek to punish only the publication of those secrets that truly endanger national security while giving a pass to all lesser infringements.

Just as there must be editorial discretion, so too must there be prosecutorial discretion. It is right and proper that jaywalkers are not ticketed for crossing little-trafficked roads. It is also right and proper that they are arrested for wandering onto interstate highways. When newspaper editors publish secrets whose disclosure is arguably harmless—say, for example, the still-classified CIA budget for fiscal year 1964—or secrets that conceal abuses or violations of the law, they should trust that, if indicted by a wayward government, a jury of twelve citizens would evaluate the government's ill-conceived prosecution and vote to acquit. On the other hand, if newspapers editors or an organization like WikiLeaks disclose a secret vital to our national security—and have no justification for doing so beyond a desire to expose for exposure's sake—they should also be prepared to face the judgment of a jury of twelve citizens and the full wrath of the law. Journalists and their defenders, and WikiLeaks and its defenders, find that view anathema. They want unlimited freedom and accountability to no one but themselves. Their behavior raises the fundamental question of whether the free society built by the Founding Founders can defend itself from those who would subvert democracy by placing themselves above or outside the law.

I thank the members of the Committee for addressing the difficult and important issues involved in maintaining secrets in an our open society.

Dissecting the "WikiMyths"[*]

Thomas Blanton

*Director, National Security Archive, George Washington University, 1992– ; gradu-
ate, Harvard University; director of Planning & Research, 1986–89, deputy director, 1989–1992, National Security Archive, George Washington University; author
of books, including* The Chronology *(1987);* White House E-Mail: The Top Secret
Computer Messages the Reagan-Bush White House Tried to Destroy *(1995);* Mas-
terpieces of History: The Peaceful End of the Cold War in Europe, 1989 *(2010,
with Svetlana Savranskaya and Vladislav Zubok); contributing author, three editions
of the ACLU's* Litigation Under the Federal Open Government Laws; Atomic Au-
dit: The Costs and Consequences of U.S. Nuclear Weapons Since 1940 *(1998); his
articles have appeared in* The International Herald-Tribune, The New York Times,
The Washington Post, Los Angeles Times, The Wall Street Journal, The Boston
Globe, Slate, *and the* Wilson Quarterly.

Editor's introduction: Speaking before the same House Judiciary Committee
hearing as Gabriel Schoenfeld, Thomas Blanton warns against what he describes as
government overreaction to the WikiLeaks disclosures. Rather than invoking the
Espionage Act to prosecute the culprits, Blanton urges government restraint. He
outlines the work and the successes of his own organization before suggesting that
overclassification—too much secrecy—is a greater problem than leaks. He goes on
to enumerate a series of "WikiMyths," or popular misconceptions about the leaked
diplomatic cables. Finally, Blanton contends that the best way to combat damaging leaks is through greater government openness.

Thomas Blanton's speech: Mr. Chairman, Ranking Member Smith, and members
of the Committee, thank you for your invitation to testify today on the implications of the WikiLeaks controversy. I am reminded of the ancient Chinese curse,
"May you live in interesting times."

---

[*] Delivered on December 16, 2010, at Washington, D.C.

This extraordinary panel has the expertise to address the Espionage Act and the Constitution, so I want to focus just on our secrecy system, which is my own specialty. I have three main points to make today:

First, the government always overreacts to leaks, and history shows we end up doing more damage from the overreaction than from the original leak. Second, the government's national security classification system is broken, overwhelmed with too much secrecy, which actually prevents the system from protecting the real secrets on the one hand, and on the other keeps us from being able to protect ourselves from tragedies like the 9/11 attacks. Third, we are well into a syndrome that one senior government official called "Wikimania," where WikiMyths are common and there is far more heat than light. That heat will actually produce more leaks, more crackdowns, less accountable government, and diminished security. So my recommendation to you today, and to those prosecutors over at the Justice Department who are chomping at the bit, is to leave the Espionage Act in mothballs where it belongs. It's not often that you have a witness who recommends that we all go take a nap, but here in sleep-deprived Washington, it would be wise to show some restraint. I should note that the media organizations including WikiLeaks that have the leaked cables are showing a great deal of restraint, which we should encourage, not prosecute. By way of background, I should say right up front that my organization, the National Security Archive, has not gotten any 1.6 gigabyte thumb drives in the mail in response to our many Freedom of Information Act requests, nor have we found any Bradley Mannings among the many highly professional FOIA officers who handle our cases. It's a lot more work to pry loose national security documents the way we do it, but then it's a lot of work worth doing to make the rule of law a reality and give real force to the Freedom of Information Act.

It takes us years of research and interviews and combing the archives and the memoirs and the press accounts, even reading the agency phone books, to design and file focused requests that don't waste the government's time or our time but home in on key documents and key decision points, then to follow up with the agencies, negotiate the search process, appeal the denials, even go to court when the stonewalling gets out of hand. Changing the iron laws of bureaucracy is a tall order, but we have allies and like-minded openness advocates in more than 50 countries now, passing access laws and opening Politburo and military dictators' files, poring through Communist Party records and secret police archives and death squad diaries, rewriting history, recovering memory, and bringing human rights abusers to trial. Our more than 40,000 Freedom of Information requests have opened up millions of pages that were previously classified; we've published more than a million pages of documents on the Web and other formats; our staff and fellows have authored more than 60 books, one of which won the Pulitzer. Our Freedom of Information lawsuits have saved tens of millions of White House e-mail spanning from Reagan to Obama, whose Blackberry messages are now saved for posterity.

The George Foster Peabody Award in 1998 recognized our documentary contributions to CNN's Cold War series both from the Freedom of Information Act and from the Soviet archives; the Emmy Award in 2005 recognized our "outstanding achievement in news and documentary research"; and the George Polk Award citation (April 2000) called us "a FOIL'ers best friend" and used a wonderful phrase to describe what we do: "piercing the self-serving veils of government secrecy, guiding journalists in search for the truth, and informing us all."

Most pertinent to our discussion here today is our experience with the massive overclassification of the U.S. government's national security information. Later in this testimony I include some of the expert assessments by current and former officials who have grappled with the secrecy system and who estimate that between 50 percent to 90 percent of what is classified is either overclassified or should not be classified at all. That reality should restrain us from encouraging government prosecutors to go after anybody who has unauthorized possession of classified information: such encouragement is an invitation for prosecutorial abuse and overreach—exactly as we have seen in the case of the lobbyists for the American Israel Public Affairs Committee.

The reality of massive overclassification also points us towards remedies for leaks that are the opposite of those on the front burners such as criminalizing leaks. The only remedies that will genuinely curb leaks are ones that force the government to disgorge most of the information it holds rather than hold more information more tightly.

But a rational response to excessive government secrecy will be even more difficult to achieve in the current atmosphere of Wikimania. The heated calls for targeted assassinations of leakers and publishers remind me of the Nixon White House discussions of firebombing the Brookings Institution on suspicion of housing a copy of the Pentagon Papers. It was the earlier leak of the secret bombing of Cambodia that started President Nixon down the path to the Watergate plumbers, who began with righteous indignation about leaks, then moved to black bag jobs and break-ins and dirty tricks, and brought down the presidency. All the while, as the Doonesbury cartoon pointed out, only the American people and Congress were in the dark. One famous strip showed a Cambodian couple standing amid bomb wreckage, and the interviewer asks, was this from the secret bombing? Oh, no, not a secret at all, "I said, look Martha, here come the bombs."

Few have gone as far as Nixon, but overreaction to leaks has been a constant in recent American history. Almost every president has tied his White House in knots over embarrassing internal leaks; for example, the moment of greatest conflict between President Reagan and his Secretary of State George Shultz was not over the Iran-contra affair, but over the idea of subjecting Shultz and other high officials to the polygraph as part of a leak prevention campaign. President Ford went from supporting to vetoing the Freedom of Information Act amendments of 1974 because of his reaction to leaks (only to be overridden by Congress). President George W. Bush was so concerned about leaks, and about aggrandizing presidential power, that his and Vice President Cheney's top staff kept the Deputy Attorney General, number two at Justice, out of the loop on the warrantless wiretapping program, and didn't even share legal opinions about the program with the top lawyers of the National Security Agency that was implementing the intercepts.

But even with this background, I have been astonished at the developments of the last week, with the Air Force and the Library of Congress blocking the WikiLeaks web site, and warning their staff not to even peek. I should have known the Air Force would come up with something like this. The Archive's own Freedom of Information Act lawsuit over the last 5 years had already established that the Air Force created probably the worst FOIA processing system in the entire federal government—the federal judge in our case ruled the Air Force had "miserably failed" to meet the law's requirements. But now, apparently, the worst FOIA system has found a mate in the worst open-source information system? This policy is completely self-defeating and foolish. If Air Force personnel do not look at the leaked cables, then they are not doing their job as national security professionals.

Comes now the Library of Congress, built on Thomas Jefferson's books, also blocking access to the WikiLeaks site. On the LC blog, a repeated question has been when exactly are you going to cut off the *New York Times* site too? One might also ask, when will you remove Bob Woodward's books from the shelves?

Official reactions like these show how we are suffering from "Wikimania." Almost all of the proposed cures for Bradley Manning's leak of the diplomatic cables are worse than the disease. The real danger of Wikimania is that we could revert to Cold War notions of secrecy, to the kind of stovepipes and compartments that left us blind before 9/11, to mounting prosecutions under the Espionage Act that just waste taxpayers' money and ultimately get dropped, and to censorship pressure on Internet providers that emulates the Chinese model of state control rather than the First Amendment. So perhaps a first order of business should be to dissect some of what I call the "WikiMyths."

1. A document dump.

So far there has been no dump of the diplomatic cables. As of yesterday, there were fewer than 2,000 cables posted on the Web in the WikiLeaks and media sites combined, and another 100 or so uploaded each day, not the 251,000 that apparently exist in the overall database as downloaded by Bradley Manning. And even that set of a quarter-million cables represents only a fraction of the total flow of cable traffic to and from the State Department, simply the ones that State staff considered "reporting and other informational messages deemed appropriate for release to the US government interagency community" (the Foreign Affairs Manual explanation of the SIPDIS tag). According to the editors of *Le Monde* and *The Guardian*, WikiLeaks is following the lead of the media organizations on which documents to post, when to do so, and what to redact from the cables in terms of source identities that might put someone at risk. Such behavior is the opposite of a dump. At the same time, an "insurance" file presumably containing the entire database in encrypted form is in the hands of thousands, and WikiLeaks founder Julian Assange has threatened to send out the decrypt key, if and when his back is against the wall. So a dump could yet happen of the cables, and the prior record is mixed. A dump did begin of the Iraq and Afghan war logs, but once reporters pointed out the danger to local cooperators from being named in the logs, WikiLeaks halted the dump and withheld some 15,000 items out of 91,000 Afghan records.

2. An epidemic of leaks.

While the quantity of documents seems huge (hundreds of thousands including the Iraq and Afghan materials), from everything we know to date, all four tranches of WikiLeaks publicity this year have come from a single leaker, the Army private Bradley Manning, who is now behind bars. First, in April, was the helicopter video of the 2007 shooting of the Reuters cameramen. Then came the Iraq and Afghan war logs (highly granular situation reports for the most part) in July and October. Now we see the diplomatic cables from the SIPRNet. Between 500,000 and 600,000 U.S. military and diplomatic personnel were cleared for SIPRNet access, so a security official looking for a glass half full would point out that a human-designed security system with half a million potential error points ended up only with one.

A better contrast would be to compare the proposals for dramatic expansion of the Espionage Act into arresting foreigners, to the simple operational security change that the Defense Department has already implemented. The latter would have prevented Manning from doing his solo downloads onto CD, and we should ask which approach would be more likely to deter future Mannings. State Department officials were gloating last week that no embassy personnel could pull a Manning because State's version of the SIPRNet wouldn't allow downloads onto walk-away media like thumb drives or CDs. Defense's rejoinder was that its wide range of forward operating bases, equipment crashes from dust storms and incoming fire, and often tenuous Internet connections—certainly compared to the usually cushy conditions inside embassies—meant some download capacity was essential. Now, just as nuclear missile launch requires two operators' keys, and the handling of sensitive communications intelligence manuals requires "two person integrity," and the Mormons send their missionaries out in pairs, a SIPRNet download would take two to tango.

3. A diplomatic meltdown.

Headline writers loved this phrase, aided and abetted by official statements like Secretary of State Hillary Clinton's characterization of the cables' release as an "attack on America" "sabotaging peaceful relations between nations." In contrast, the Secretary of Defense Robert Gates played down the heat, in a much more realistic assessment that bears repeating. Gates told reporters two weeks ago, "I've heard the impact of these releases on our foreign policy described as a meltdown, as a game-changer and so on. I think these descriptions are fairly significantly overwrought. . . . Is this embarrassing? Yes. Is it awkward? Yes. Consequences for U.S. foreign policy? I think fairly modest." I should point out that most international affairs scholars are calling the cables fascinating and useful, especially for students of bi-lateral relations. But at least so far, we have really seen nothing in the diplomatic cables that compares to the impact on public policy and the public debate in 2004 from the leak of the Abu Ghraib photographs, or other recent leaks of the existence of the secret prisons, or the torture memos, or the fact of warrantless wiretapping, or even the Pentagon Papers' contribution to the end of the Vietnam war.

4. Alternatively, no news here.

WikiLeaks critics who are not bemoaning a global diplomatic meltdown often go to the opposite extreme, that is to say there was nothing really new in the Bradley Manning cables. The past two weeks' worth of front-page headlines in the leading newspapers and broadcasts around the world should lay this myth to rest. Folks with more news judgment than we have in this room are continuing to assign stories from the cables, and foreign media in particular are getting an education perhaps more valuable for their understanding of their own countries than of the U.S. Likewise, the blogs are full of lists of stories showing all the things we didn't know before the cables emerged. The real problem with the modern news media is evident from the fact that there are many more reporters clustered around the British jail holding Julian Assange, than there are reporters in newsrooms actually reading through the cables for their reporting. Celebrity over substance every time.

5. Wikiterrorists.

I wish all terrorist groups would write the local U.S. ambassador a few days before they are launching anything—the way Julian Assange wrote Ambassador Louis Susman in London on November 26—to ask for suggestions on how to make sure nobody gets hurt. I can certainly understand the State Department's hostile response and refusal to engage with Assange in the kind of dialogue U.S. government officials routinely have with mainstream media, and were already having with the New York Times over these particular cables. Given WikiLeaks's prior stance, who in State could possibly have taken at face value the phrase in the November 26 letter which says "WikiLeaks will respect the confidentiality of the advice provided by the United States Government" about risk to individuals? But I wish all terrorist groups would partner up with *Le Monde* and *El Pais* and *Der Spiegel* and *The Guardian*, and *The New York Times*, and take the guidance of those professional journalists on what bombs go off and when and with what regulators. Even to make the comparison tells the story—WikiLeaks is not acting as an anarchist group, even remotely as terrorists, but as a part of the media, as publishers of information, and even more than that—the evidence so far shows them trying to rise to the standards of professional journalism.

I was quoted in Sunday's *New York Times* as saying "I'm watching WikiLeaks grow up" as they embrace the mainstream media which "they used to treat as a cuss word." So far, with only a few mistakes to date, the treatment of the cables by the media and by WikiLeaks has been very responsible, incorporating governmental feedback on potential damage, redacting names of sources, and even withholding whole documents at the government's request. Of course, Assange and his colleagues could revert to more adolescent behavior, since there is the threat out there of the encrypted "insurance" file that would be dropped like a piñata if the organization reaches dire straits. But even then, even if all the cables went online, most of us would condemn the recklessness of such an action, but the fundamental media and publisher function WikiLeaks is serving would not change.

6. When the government says it's classified, our job as citizens is to salute.

Actually our job as citizens is to ask questions. I have mentioned that experts believe 50 percent to 90 percent of our national security secrets could be public with little or no damage to real security. A few years back, when Rep. Christopher Shays (R-CT) asked Secretary of Defense Donald Rumsfeld's deputy for counter-intelligence and security how much government information was overclassified, her answer was 50 percent. After the 9/11 Commission reviewed the government's most sensitive records about Osama bin Laden and al Qaeda, the co-chair of that commission, former Governor of New Jersey Tom Kean, commented that "three-quarters of what I read that was classified shouldn't have been"—a 75 percent judgment. President Reagan's National Security Council secretary Rodney McDaniel estimated in 1991 that only 10 percent of classification was for "legitimate protection of secrets"—so 90 percent unwarranted. Another data point comes from the Interagency Security Classification Appeals Panel, over the past 15 years, has overruled agency secrecy claims in whole or in part in some 65 percent of its cases.

When two of the CIA's top officers retired and went into business, the *Washington Post*'s Dana Hedgpeth asked them what was most surprising about being in the private sector. Cofer Black and Robert Richer responded that "much of the information they once considered top secret is publicly available. The trick, Richer said, is knowing where to look. 'In a classified area, there's an assumption that if it is open, it can't be as good as if you stole it,' Richer said. 'I'm seeing that at least 80 percent of what we stole was open.'" ("Blackwater's Owner Has Spies for Hire," by Dana Hedgpeth, *Washington Post*, November 3, 2007). And this was before the Bradley Manning leaks.

In the National Security Archive's collections, we have dozens of examples of documents that are classified and unclassified at the same time, sometimes with different versions from different agencies or different reviewers, all because the secrecy is so subjective and overdone. My own favorite example is a piece of White House e-mail from the Reagan years when top officials were debating how best to help out Saddam Hussein against the Iranians. The first version that came back from our Freedom of Information lawsuit had large chunks of the middle section blacked out on national security grounds, classified at the secret level as doing serious damage to our national security if released. But the second version, only a week or so later, had almost no black in the middle, but censored much of the top and the bottom sections as secret. Slide the two versions together and you could read practically the entire document. The punch line is: This was the same reviewer both times, just with almost completely contradictory notions of what needed to stay secret.

The Associated Press reported last week (December 9, 2010) that reporter Matt Apuzzo's review of the Bradley Manning cables "unmasked another closely guarded fact: Much of what the government says is classified isn't much of a secret at all. Sometimes, classified documents contained little more than summaries of press reports. Political banter was treated as confidential government intelligence. Information that's available to anyone with an Internet connection was ordered held under wraps for years." The first example AP cited was a cable from the U.S. Embassy in Ottawa briefing President Obama in early 2009 for an upcoming trip to Canada, a cable which "included this sensitive bit of information, marked confidential: 'No matter which political party forms the Canadian government during your Administration, Canada will remain one of our staunchest and most like-minded of allies, our largest trading and energy partner, and our most reliable neighbor and friend.' The document could not be made public until 2019, for national security reasons," the AP reported.

Among other issues raised by the AP reporting is the fact that more than half of the Bradley Manning cables are themselves unclassified to begin with. Why did these items need to be buried inside a system that went up to the secret level? Why couldn't those unclassified cables go up on the State Department's own public Web site? Are they really all press summaries and administrivia? Do they need any further review such as for privacy or law enforcement issues? What objection would the government have to preempting WikiLeaks by posting these—that somehow it would be rewarding illicit behavior?

Bringing the reality of overclassification to the subject of leaks, Harvard law professor Jack Goldsmith, who served President George W. Bush as head of the controversial Office of Legal Counsel at the Justice Department, has written, "A root cause of the perception of illegitimacy inside the government that led to leaking (and then to occasional irresponsible reporting) is, ironically, excessive government secrecy." Goldsmith went on, in what was otherwise a highly critical review of the *New York Times*' coverage of wiretapping during the George W. Bush years ("Secrecy and Safety," by Jack Goldsmith, *The New Republic*, August 13, 2008), to point out, "The secrecy of the Bush administration was genuinely excessive, and so it was self-defeating. One lesson of the last seven years is that the way for the government to keep important secrets is not to draw the normal circle of secrecy tighter. Instead the government should be as open as possible. . . ."

Goldsmith's analysis draws on the famous dicta of Justice Potter Stewart in the Pentagon Papers case: "When everything is classified, then nothing is classified, and the system becomes one to be disregarded by the cynical or the careless, and to be manipulated by those intent on self-protection or self-promotion." In fact, Stewart observed, "the hallmark of a truly effective internal security system would be the maximum possible disclosure" since "secrecy can best be preserved only when credibility is truly maintained." Between Goldsmith and Stewart, then, Mr. Chairman, we have a pretty good guide with which to assess any of the proposals that may come before you in the guise of dealing with WikiLeaks in these next months. We have to ask, will the proposal draw the circle of secrecy tighter, or move us towards maximum possible disclosure? We have to recognize that right now, we have low fences around vast prairies of government secrets, when what we need are high fences around small graveyards of the real secrets. We need to clear out our backlog of historic secrets that should long since have appeared on the public shelves, and slow the creation of new secrets. And those voices who argue for a crackdown on leakers and publishers need to face the reality that their approach is fundamentally self-defeating because it will increase government secrecy, reduce our security, and actually encourage more leaks from the continued legitimacy crisis of the classification system. Thank you for your consideration of these views, and I look forward to your questions.

5

Feminism in the 21st Century

Seattle Inspire Luncheon[*]

Keynote Address

Gloria Steinem

*Social activist, writer, editor, and lecturer; born Toledo, OH, March 25, 1934; B.A.,
Smith College, 1956; journalist, 1960–1972; co-founder,* Ms. *magazine, 1972– ;
founder or co-founder of numerous groups devoted to equal rights for women; author,*
The Thousand Indias *(1957);* The Beach Book *(1963);* Outrageous Acts and Everyday Rebellions *(1983);* Marilyn: Norma Jean *(1986);* Revolution from Within
(1992); Moving Beyond Words *(1993);* Doing Sixty & Seventy *(2006).*

Editor's introduction: Speaking at the Seattle Inspire Luncheon at the Seattle
YWCA, the feminist icon Gloria Steinem pays tribute to the institution as a supporter of the feminist program and its mission of gaining for women "legal and
social equality as human beings." She imagines the country as if it were run by the
YWCA, envisioning positive implications for job opportunities and the understanding of beauty. She contends that family is the place where democratic society
must begin and describes the intertwining of racism and sexism. Claiming a direct
correlation between violence in the home and violence in society, Steinem reasons
that the former must be rooted out if we are to defeat the latter, positing that domestic or "original" violence breaks a vital bond of empathy.

Gloria Steinem's speech: Thank you so much for allowing me to be a part of this
great gathering of good minds and great hearts. Thank you for allowing me to
be here to listen to those life stories. There could be no greater reward than that.
Thank you for inviting me to come back to what I feel now is my second home—
Seattle. Because I am the lucky person who's able to come back and back and
back and back again to Hedgebrook, the Women Writers Retreat on Whidbey. I
note that because I've discovered that sometimes it's better known in the rest of
the world than it is here; do you know you have this international treasure here?
They're quiet out there because they're writing.

---

* Delivered on April 22, 2010, at Seattle, Washington. Reprinted by permission.

And thank you for allowing me to come and celebrate one of this country's—and other countries'—greatest and most humane institutions, which is the YWCA. If I think about the two great waves of social change that we count in this country—I say that "we count" because we unfortunately tend to start the history of this country when the first Europeans showed up—we had the abolitionist and the suffragist era, which established a legal identity as human beings for women of all races and men of color who had been treated and legally defined as chattel, so that was huge, you know, to spend more than a century gaining a legal identity as human beings. And now we have an effort in the civil rights and the feminist movements to gain a legal and social equality as human beings.

And what is the one institution that has carried the heart, and the meaning, and been true to these great missions between those two waves and continued? It is the YWCA. They—really, a lot of people—fell into apathy and kind of disrepair during the 1950's and so on, but not the YWCA. It really kept to its mission.

So, if we think about what we need in this country, it seems to me to be in the purpose and the culture of the YWCA. It continues to understand that in order to solve problems, just as in order to build a house, you have to start at the bottom, not at the top. It continues to understand that the least powerful among us are the place where empowerment must start, and therefore has always, from the very beginning, been opposed to the caste systems based on sex and based on race.

And it understands the best kind of leadership, which is one that creates independence, not dependence. And as I say that phrase, I'd like to bring the spirit of Dorothy Height into this room as well as to bring the spirit of Wilma Mankiller—a great leader of Indian country, who also deeply understood the punishment of dependence from the history of her own culture, and knew how to create independence.

So, in thinking about what I wanted to say to you today, I thought, "Well, I guess what I want to say is that the world should be run by the YWCA."

And so I had this thought as I was walking through New York, and I was going through Central Park, and I thought, "Well, how would the world be different?" And I could see women of color who were nannies wheeling white babies, understanding that those women might or might not be being properly paid, and I thought, "Well, if the YWCA ran the world, there would be white guys—well paid—wheeling babies of color"—No, I'm not kidding! Raising baby humans is really interesting! It's one of the most interesting things you can do, right? Men are being deprived if they are not able to do this.

I passed a newsstand and I thought, "Well, if the YWCA was in power, there would be a lot more erotica and a lot less pornography." You know, the difference is contained in the words. Porn means "female slavery." So it means the depiction of female slavery, or that of an unequal relationship. Eros means love—it has some idea of free choice and mutual pleasure. So there's really a big-time difference.

I thought I would turn on Oprah and see a show about men trying to combine home and career.

I thought, "Well, probably the schools, the national system of childcare"—which, of course we would have; we are now the only modern democracy in the world without a national system of childcare—so, the schools and the system of childcare would have the military budget, and the military would have the school budget, and—as you can see, it's really fun to think about this—I recommend it to you, because you'll think of many more things.

We would know that beauty, whether male or female, was individual and authentic, not collective and conformist—especially when it comes to female human beings. We would have figured out that it is about politics, not aesthetics. That is, rich countries value skinny women and poor cultures value fat women; but all cultures that are patriarchal or male-dominant value weakness in women; therefore the sports and the strength and the fitness programs that we have are much more revolutionary than we think. Right?

And when the culture wants us to have a lot of children, as after World War Two, we have ideals of beauty that are breasts and hips and very voluptuous and so on (like Marilyn Monroe)—and then when we've had enough children, the ideal becomes very, very skinny—you know. So it is about behavior and not about beauty as a—as a permanent aesthetic. Therefore we would be able, finally, to celebrate however we look individually, and understand that in itself is a glory.

Certainly we would understand that it's not possible to fight racism and sexism separately. They are intertwined; it is impossible to fight them except together. Part of that is at a kind of simple level, because the family is the first place we learn that people are born into groups—and group labels—so it's okay if one group cooks and the other one eats; it's okay if one group lives in the house and the other group cleans it and takes care of it; it's okay if one group has more freedom, or more education money, and the other one has less; and that digs a kind of trench in our brains and we come to deeply believe and expect that people will be divided into groups.

It makes it okay. It normalizes our experience of race and of class and of differences based on sexuality and other born differences as we progress through life. If we are ever going to have a democratic society, we have to have democratic families. Because that is where our expectations are normalized.

And of course, the truth is that there are more differences between two individual women or two individual men—or two individual people of one race, or another race, or another ethnicity—than there are between males and females or people as groups. It is that individual difference that we are trying to let flower, and it is the group restriction that we are trying to humanize and free ourselves from.

There is a deeper reason for the intertwining of race and sex I want us to remember, because this past election—or at least the coverage of this past election—took two people who were virtually the same on the issues, Hillary Clinton and Barack Obama, and kept behaving as if sex and race were opposed. Which left women of color nowhere, or with Solomon's sword, and made an opposition that was artificial.

I hope that we remember the deep reason that sex and race are intertwined, and that you can't maintain racism or visible differences without restricting the freedom of women is because women are the most basic means of production—the means of reproduction. Wherever you find racism you will find that women of the so-called "superior" or "more powerful" group are restricted—very restricted, very dehumanized; as a black suffragist said to her white suffragist sisters, "A pedestal is as much a prison as any other small space"—and the women of color are exploited and used to produce more people marked on their skins as cheap labor. Wherever one group is restricted, the other is exploited; it's not possible to continue a racial hierarchy into many, many future generations without restricting females.

That—what I just said—in a paragraph, if you poured water on it, would probably become a volume, but I hope that we remember it so that we always understand it's not possible to be a feminist or a womanist or a women's liberationist or a mujerista without also being an anti-racist. And it's not possible to be an anti-racist without also being a feminist, a mujerista, a womanist—and that's what the YWCA stands for, has always stood for, and now with its new slogan stands for even more.

And I hope we understand how important the work against violence in the home (that the YWCA is on the forefront of)—how important that is. When we first in this wave of feminism began to understand—because people began to tell the truth, women had circles in which they could tell the truth—how prevalent violence against women in the home, so-called "domestic violence" really is, it was the YWCA in my experience, in my travels, who started the very first shelters. Who really first understood that this thing that in my childhood, in my factory-working neighborhood in Toledo, Ohio was just called "life"—there was no word for domestic violence—that this was societal-wide and deep and important, and programs had to be constructed around it.

It is, after all, in the family that violence also is normalized. If we see it as inevitable or even an okay way of solving conflict as we are growing up, then it is normalized everywhere else. You can exactly predict the violence in public life, and the militarism in a society, by the degree of violence against children especially, and domestic violence in general. You can exactly predict it. If we are ever going to uproot it, it has to be in the home first.

And, conversely, if you look at the ways in which systems of exploitation have been perpetuated, you understand that they had to—children had to be trained for it. For colonial powers, for instance, to maintain centuries of injustice and taking over other peoples' land, they had to take children young—boys young—and break the natural leap of empathy that exists between one human being and another by (think about England) taking them away from their parents at the age of five, putting them in cruel, taunting boarding schools, convincing them deeply that there were only two choices: to be the victim or the victimizer.

If we think about where it comes from—where violence comes from—where that leap of empathy is interrupted, we begin to understand the profound, deep importance of domestic violence. Maybe "domestic violence" is too small-sound-ing a term. Maybe we should call it "original violence." Because it is so clearly what everything comes from.

For instance, when there were Good Samaritans during World War Two—that is, people who were not themselves Jewish but helped Jews at great peril to their own lives—the many studies of those Good Samaritans after the war (because of course we all wanted to replicate the goodness of these people), the many studies looked to see whether it was education or religion or family structure . . . what was it that enabled these people to make this brave, brave, brave gesture? What was remarkable about it is that they generally described it in the same way: "I don't know why I did it, I just did it. I'm not a hero—I just did it."

And what was concluded was that probably the most shared characteristic of these Good Samaritans was that they had not been abused as children. So the natural leap of empathy from one human being to another—which is part of our evolutionary equipment! The species could not have survived if we did not instinctively, as they did, said, "I don't know why I did it. I just did it"; help a member of our species who's in trouble.

But vast systems of hierarchy and patriarchy and racism and nationalism have been set up to break that bond, that natural leap of empathy. And that is what we are trying to restore.

I find it kind of comforting, don't you? To think that it's not so much what we have to learn, but what we have to unlearn? It's actually in us! It is part of our humanity, that we feel this leap of empathy. And I think in a lot of ways it is also part of our natural humanity that we understand equality, you know? We understand that we're not more important than anybody else, but we're not less important either.

Think of all the little children who, out of nowhere, say, "It's not fair." Where does that come from? What about all the kids who say, "You are not the boss of me!"?

What we need to do is preserve that. Preserve the sense of fairness and preserve the empathy.

I think, also, while I was thinking what happens if the YWCA runs the world, I thought, "Well, all adults could get married as long as they don't hit each other."

I think that that's a pretty good standard, and when we're thinking of ourselves, of how to solve a problem or how to judge a candidate or what we want Congress to do: "What would the YWCA do?"

That's not bad.

And I mean that very seriously at this particular time in history as well. Because as I'm sure we all know, in corners of our brains and hearts in this room full of good folks, there's a lot of danger out there right now. The membership of very, very authoritarian and even fascist and Nazi groups is very much up, as the organizations that monitor those groups can tell us. The purchases of guns—even the ones we know about, even the legal purchases—is very much up.

We see the rhetoric of hostility and division that has greatly increased.

We see that for the first time since the Clinton administration—which was the last time that the extremist right wing lost control of the White House and Congress—for the first time since then, an abortion doctor has been murdered; Dr. Tiller, who was murdered in his own church. There are all kinds of ways in which I suspect that each of us here is concerned about how we can go forward respecting differences, feeling empathy for each other, understanding and sharing the kind of community that we feel in this room right now.

And I think, once again, we can learn from the seed of violence, which is the family. If we understand it there, we understand it everywhere. For instance, the most dangerous time for a woman who is escaping violence in the home—from a partner, from a family member—the most dangerous time is when, at the moment she's escaping or right afterwards. That is when murders take place. Why? Because for the violent person (who is not always a man, but 90 percent of the time is a man, and certainly does not represent all men in any way, but is a person who got born into this cult of masculinity and for a certain set of reasons got hooked on it, hooked on control, on superiority), it is the moment at which he is losing control, and usually the woman is going to be free. That's when she's in danger, that's when she's most likely to get killed.

I think in a way it's true of us as a country. What's happening is that we have turned against two wars in the majority much more quickly than we did in the case of Vietnam; we are about to become—on the verge of becoming a minority European-American country and a majority Americans of color country; we have a proud African-American family in the White House; we have an economy that has punished well-paying men's jobs more than poorly-paying women's jobs, so there are more women struggling very hard to support children and to support a whole family, and somewhat more men who are out of work.

There are all kinds of ways in which the hierarchical structure that we are supposed to think of as normal is slipping away. The country is trying to be free. And therefore, we are at the time of maximum danger—because those whose identity depends on control are feeling out of control. We must learn from that and protect each other, and be careful and look after each other, and understand the danger. That's the first thing.

And the second thing is: we can't stop.

Because we would never tell a woman that is in a dangerous house not to escape. We must continue to escape, and be free, and finally have societies in which entire human futures are never again determined by a single element of sex or of race or of ethnicity or sexuality—that we can each be, begin to be the unique individuals we truly are.

Each of us in this room is a combination of millennia upon millennia of environment and heredity combined in a way that could never have happened before and could never happen again. I never understood the "nature vs. nurture" argument, did you? Because obviously it's both.

The question is, how can we set that uniqueness free on the one hand, and on the other have a community that supports it?

On the principle that the means are the ends—the means we choose are the ends we get; I mean, Marx was right about a lot of things, but one of the big things he was wrong about was that the ends justify the means, right? Not true. The means create the ends. I hope that now, today and in the future, you will reach out to each other, tell each other stories—we're in a very big room here. Many of us have been—part of the reason I feel so at home here in Seattle is that I know many people here that I've been in smaller rooms with, so our challenge is to make sure that we see three or four people we don't know, introduce ourselves, say what we care about, tell part of our stories.

Use this moment in time as a way of creating a community, and remember that if we want love and empathy and humor and joy and music at the end of the revolution, we have to have love and empathy and joy and music in everything we do, including, as much as we possibly can, today and in every day of our lives.

I thank you for letting me be part of this huge, huge event here—the biggest ever, and I look forward to hearing what is happening, what the results are, and I just want to say that from now on, whenever I contemplate an act of any kind, I'm going to say to myself, "Would the YWCA approve?"

Thank you.

Reinventing Feminism*

Courtney Martin

Author and activist; born Colorado Springs, CO, December 31, 1979; B.A., Barnard College, 2002; M.A., Gallatin School, New York University (NYU), 2004; adjunct professor, Brooklyn College and Hunter College, 2004–07; lead facilitator, The Op-Ed Project, 2008– ; author, Perfect Girls, Starving Daughters: How the Quest for Perfection Is Harming Young Women *(2007);* The Naked Truth: Young, Beautiful, and (HIV) Positive *(2008);* Click: When We Knew We Were Feminists *(2010);* Do It Anyway: The New Generation of Activists *(2010);* Rebirth: Survival and the Strength of the Human Spirit from 9/11 Survivors *(2011).*

Editor's introduction: Aiming to define feminism for the 21st century and distinguish her feminism from that of her mother, Courtney Martin, in this speech presented at a 2010 TEDWomen conference, suggests that for her generation online organizing and blogging are today's equivalent of protest marches, and that immigration is as much a feminist issue as pay equality. For today's feminists, she says, the world's problems are overwhelming and their goals too lofty to be achieved, but we can celebrate failing well in the face of such enormous odds.

Courtney Martin's speech: So I was born on the last day of the last year of the '70s. I was raised on "Free to be you and me"—(cheering) hip hop—not as many woohoos for hip hop in the house. Thank you. Thank you for hip hop—and Anita Hill. (Cheering) My parents were radicals—(Laughter) who became, well, grown-ups. My dad facetiously says, "We wanted to save the world, and instead we just got rich." We actually just got middle class in Colorado Springs, Colorado, but you get the picture. I was raised with a very heavy sense of unfinished legacy.

At this ripe old age of 30, I've been thinking a lot about what it means to grow up in this horrible, beautiful time. And I've decided, for me, it's been a real journey and paradox. The first paradox is that growing up is about rejecting the past and then promptly reclaiming it. Feminism was the water I grew up in. When I was just a little girl, my mom started what is now the longest running women's film

---

* Delivered on December 7, 2010, at Washington, D.C. Reprinted by permission.

festival in the world. So while other kids were watching sitcoms and cartoons, I was watching very esoteric documentaries made by and about women. You can see how this had an influence. But she was not the only feminist in the house.

My dad actually resigned from the male-only business club in my hometown because he said he would never be part of an organization that would one day welcome his son, but not his daughter. (Applause) He's actually here today. (Applause) The trick here is my brother would become an experimental poet, not a businessman, but the intention was really good.

(Laughter)

In any case, I didn't readily claim the feminist label, even though it was all around me, because I associated it with my mom's women's groups, her swishy skirts and her shoulder pads—none of which had much cachet in the hallways of Palmer High School where I was trying to be cool at the time. But I suspected there was something really important about this whole feminism thing, so I started covertly tiptoeing into my mom's bookshelves and picking books off and reading them—never, of course, admitting that I was doing so. I didn't actually claim the feminist label until I went to Barnard College and I heard Amy Richards and Jennifer Baumgardner speak for the first time. They were the co-authors of a book called "Manifesta." So what very profound epiphany, you might ask, was responsible for my feminist click moment? Fishnet stockings. Jennifer Baumgardner was wearing them. I thought they were really hot. I decided, okay, I can claim the feminist label. Now I tell you this—I tell you this at the risk of embarrassing myself, because I think part of the work of feminism is to admit that aesthetics, that beauty, that fun do matter. There are lots of very modern political movements that have caught fire in no small part because of cultural hipness [showing a slide of Barack Obama with Jon Stewart on *The Daily Show*]. Anyone heard of these two guys as an example?

So my feminism is very indebted to my mom's, but it looks very different. My mom says, "Patriarchy." I say, "intersectionality." So race, class, gender, ability, all of these things go into our experiences of what it means to be a woman. Pay equity? Yes. Absolutely a feminist issue. But for me, so is immigration. Thank you. My mom says, "Protest march." I say, "Online organizing." I co-edit, along with a collective of other super-smart, amazing women, a site called Feministing.com. We are the most widely read feminist publication ever. And I tell you this because I think it's really important to see that there's a continuum.

Feminist blogging is basically the 21st-century version of consciousness raising. But we also have a straightforward political impact. Feministing has been able to get merchandise pulled off the shelves of Walmart. We got a misogynist administrator sending us hate mail fired from a Big 10 school. And one of our biggest successes is we get mail from teenage girls in the middle of Iowa who say, "I Googled Jessica Simpson and stumbled on your site. I realized feminism wasn't about man-hating and Birkenstocks." So we're able to pull in the next generation in a totally new way.

My mom says, "Gloria Steinem." I say, "Samhita Mukhopadhyay, Miriam Perez, Ann Friedman, Jessica Valenti, Vanessa Valenti, and on and on and on and on."

We don't want one hero. We don't want one icon. We don't want one face. We are thousands of women and men across this country doing online writing, community organizing, changing institutions from the inside out—all continuing the incredible work that our mothers and grandmothers started. Thank you.

(Applause)

Which brings me to the second paradox: sobering up about our smallness and maintaining faith in our greatness all at once. Many of my generation—because of well-intentioned parenting and self-esteem education—were socialized to believe that we were special little snowflakes—(Laughter) who were going to go out and save the world. These are three words many of us were raised with. We walk across graduation stages, high on our overblown expectations, and when we float back down to earth, we realize we don't know what the heck it means to actually save the world anyway. The mainstream media often paints my generation as apathetic. And I think it's much more accurate to say we are deeply overwhelmed. And there's a lot to be overwhelmed about, to be fair—an environmental crisis, wealth disparity in this country unlike we've seen since 1928, and globally, a totally immoral and ongoing wealth disparity. Xenophobia's on the rise—the trafficking of women and girls. It's enough to make you feel very overwhelmed.

I experienced this firsthand myself when I graduated from Barnard College in 2002. I was fired up, I was ready to make a difference. I went out and I worked at a non-profit, I went to grad school, I phone-banked, I protested, I volunteered, and none of it seemed to matter. And on a particularly dark night of December of 2004, I sat down with my family, and I said that I had become very disillusioned. I admitted that I'd actually had a fantasy—kind of a dark fantasy—of writing a letter about everything that was wrong with the world and then lighting myself on fire on the White House steps. My mom took a drink of her signature sea breeze, her eyes really welled with tears, and she looked right at me and she said, "I will not stand for your desperation." She said, "You are smarter, more creative, and more resilient than that."

Which brings me to my third paradox. Growing up is about aiming to succeed wildly and being fulfilled by failing really well. (Laughter) (Applause) There's a writer I've been deeply influenced by, Parker Palmer, and he writes that many of us are often whiplashed "between arrogant overestimation of ourselves and a servile underestimation of ourselves." You may have guessed by now, I did not light myself on fire. I did what I know to do in desperation, which is write. I wrote the book I needed to read. I wrote a book about eight incredible people all over this country doing social justice work. I wrote about Nia Martin-Robinson, the daughter of Detroit and two civil rights activists, who's dedicating her life to environmental justice. I wrote about Emily Apt, who initially became a caseworker in the welfare system because she decided that was the most noble thing she could do, but quickly learned, not only did she not like it, but she wasn't really good at it. Instead, what she really wanted to do was make films. So she made a film about the welfare system and had a huge impact. I wrote about Maricela Guzman, the daughter of Mexican immigrants, who joined the military so she could afford college. She was actually sexually assaulted in boot camp and went on to co-organize a group called the Service Women's Action Network.

What I learned from these people and others was that I couldn't judge them based on their failure to meet their very lofty goals. Many of them are working in deeply intractable systems—the military, congress, the education system, etc. But what they managed to do within those systems was be a humanizing force. And at the end of the day, what could possibly be more important than that? Cornel West says, "Of course it's a failure. But how good a failure is it?" This isn't to say we give up our wildest, biggest dreams. It's to say we operate on two levels. On one, we really go after these broken systems of which we find ourselves a part. But on the other, we root our self-esteem in the daily acts of trying to make one person's day more kind, more just, etc.

So when I was a little girl, I had a couple of very strange habits. One of them was I used to lie on the kitchen floor of my childhood home, and I would suck the thumb of my left hand and hold my mom's cold toes with my right hand. (Laughter) I was listening to her talk on the phone, which she did a lot. She was talking about board meetings, she was founding peace organizations, she was coordinating carpools, she was consoling friends—all these daily acts of care and creativity. And surely, at three and four years old, I was listening to the soothing sound of her voice. But I think I was also getting my first lesson in activist work.

The activists I interviewed had nothing in common, literally, except for one thing, which was that they all cited their mothers as their most looming and important activist influences. So often, particularly at a young age, we look far afield for our models of the meaningful life, and sometimes they're in our own kitchens, talking on the phone, making us dinner, doing all that keeps the world going around and around. My mom and so many women like her have taught me that life is not about glory, or certainty, or security even. It's about embracing the paradox. It's about acting in the face of overwhelm. And it's about loving people really well. And at the end of the day, these things make for a lifetime of challenge and reward.

Thank you.

(Applause)

New Data on the Rise of Women[*]

Hanna Rosin

Senior editor, The Atlantic, *senior editor,* Slate, *2008– ; born Tel Aviv, Israel, April 10, 1970; B.A., Stanford University, 1991; senior editor,* The New Republic, *1993–97; columnist,* New York, *1997; reporter,* Washington Post, *1997–2007; author,* God's Harvard: A Christian College on a Mission to Save America *(2007).*

Editor's introduction: In a talk at a 2010 TEDWomen conference, editor Hanna Rosin points out that women are more successful in the workplace now than ever before—even more than men. Not only that, she explains, but even in patriarchal societies worldwide, daughters are becoming more desired than sons. Unlike in the 1920s and the 1960s, this change is not driven by a feminist movement. The shift has resulted from a change in the broader economy, with higher-paying jobs requiring skills more often found in women: rather than strength, intelligence; rather than power, an ability to listen. Furthermore, men may be ill-suited to the demands made on them to re-tool in the current environment, such as going back to college.

Hanna Rosin's speech: We are now going through an amazing and unprecedented moment where the power dynamics between men and women are shifting very rapidly. And in many of the places where it counts the most, women are, in fact, taking control of everything. In my mother's day, she didn't go to college. Not a lot of women did. And now, for every two men who get a college degree, three women will do the same. Women, for the first time this year, became the majority of the American workforce. And they're starting to dominate lots of professions—doctors, lawyers, bankers, accountants. Over 50 percent of managers are women these days. And in the 15 professions projected to grow the most in the next decade, all but two of them are dominated by women. So the global economy is becoming a place where women are more successful than men, believe it or not, and these economic changes are starting to rapidly affect our culture—what our romantic

---

[*] Delivered on December 7, 2010, at Washington, D.C. Reprinted by permission.

comedies look like, what our marriages look like, what our dating lives look like, and our new set of superheroes.

For a long time [showing a slide of the Marlboro Man], this is the image of American manhood that dominated—tough, rugged, in control of his own environment. A few years ago, the Marlboro Man was retired and replaced by [showing a slide of the Old Spice guy] this much less impressive specimen, who is a parody of American manhood. And that's what we have in our commercials today. The phrase first-born son is so deeply ingrained in our consciousness that this statistic alone shocked me. In American fertility clinics, 75 percent of couples are requesting girls and not boys. And in places where you wouldn't think, such as South Korea, India and China, the very strict patriarchal societies are starting to break down a little, and families are no longer strongly preferring first-born sons.

If you think about this, if you just open your eyes to this possibility and start to connect the dots, you can see the evidence everywhere. You can see it in college graduation patterns, in job projections, in our marriage statistics, you can see it in the Icelandic elections, which you'll hear about later, and you can see it on South Korean surveys on son preference, that something amazing and unprecedented is happening with women. Certainly this is not the first time that we've had great progress with women. The '20s and the '60s also come to mind. But the difference is that, back then, it was driven by a very passionate feminist movement that was trying to project its own desires, whereas this time, it's not about passion, and it's not about any kind of movement. This is really just about the facts of this economic moment that we live in. The 200,000-year period in which men have been top dog is truly coming to an end, believe it or not, and that's why I talk about the end of men.

Now all you men out there, this is not the moment where you tune out or throw some tomatoes, because the point is that this is happening to all of us. I myself have a husband and a father and two sons whom I dearly love. And this is why I like to talk about this, because if we don't acknowledge it, then the transition will be pretty painful. But if we do take account of it, then I think it will go much more smoothly. I first started thinking about this about a year and a half ago. I was reading headlines about the recession just like anyone else, and I started to notice a distinct pattern—that the recession was affecting men much more deeply than it was affecting women. And I remembered back to about 10 years ago when I read a book by Susan Faludi called *Stiffed: The Betrayal of the American Man* in which she described how hard the recession had hit men. And I started to think about whether it had gotten worse this time around in this recession. And I realized that two things were different this time around. The first was that these were no longer just temporary hits that the recession was giving men—that this was reflecting a deeper underlying shift in our global economy. And second, that the story was no longer just about the crisis of men, but it was also about what was happening to women.

And now look at this second set of slides. These are headlines about what's been going on with women in the next few years. These are things we never could have imagined a few years ago. Women, a majority of the workplace. And labor statistics: women take up most managerial jobs. This second set of headlines: you can see that families and marriages are starting to shift. And look at that last headline: young women earning more than young men. That particular headline comes to me from a market research firm. They were basically asked by one of their clients who was going to buy houses in that neighborhood in the future. And they expected that it would be young families, or young men, just like it had always been. But in fact, they found something very surprising. It was young, single women who were the major purchasers of houses in the neighborhood. And so they decided, because they were intrigued by this finding, to do a nationwide survey. So they spread out all the census data, and what they found, the guy described to me as a shocker, which is that in 1,997 out of 2,000 communities, women, young women, were making more money than young men. So here you have a generation of young women who grow up thinking of themselves as being more powerful earners than the young men around them.

Now, I've just laid out the picture for you, but I still haven't explained to you why this is happening. And in a moment, I'm going to show you a graph, and what you'll see on this graph—it begins in 1973, just before women start flooding the workforce, and it brings it up to our current day. And basically what you'll see is what economists talk about as the polarization of the economy. Now what does that mean? It means that the economy is dividing into high-skill, high-wage jobs and low-skill, low-wage jobs—and that the middle, the middle-skill jobs, and the middle-earning jobs are starting to drop out of the economy. This has been going on for 40 years now. But this process is affecting men very differently than it's affecting women. You'll see the women in red, and you'll see the men in blue. You'll watch them both drop out of the middle class, but see what happens to women and see what happens to men. There we go. So watch that. You see them both drop out of the middle class. Watch what happens to the women. Watch what happens to the men. The men sort of stagnate there, while the women zoom up in those high-skill jobs. So what's that about? It looks like women got some power boost on a video game, or like they snuck in some secret serum into their birth-control pills that lets them shoot up high. But of course, it's not about that.

What it's about is that the economy has changed a lot. We used to have a manufacturing economy, which was about building goods and products, and now we have a service economy and an information and creative economy. Those two economies require very different skills. And as it happens, women have been much better at acquiring the new set of skills than men have been. It used to be that you were a guy who went to high school who didn't have a college degree, but you had a specific set of skills, and with the help of a union, you could make yourself a pretty good middle-class life. But that really isn't true anymore. This new economy is pretty indifferent to size and strength, which is what's helped men along all these years. What the economy requires now is a whole different set of skills. You basically need intelligence, you need an ability to sit still and focus, to communicate openly, to be able to listen to people and to operate in a workplace that is much more fluid than it used to be. And those are things that women do extremely well, as we're seeing.

If you look at management theory these days, it used to be that our ideal leader sounded something like Gen. Patton, right. You would be issuing orders from above. You would be very hierarchical. You would tell everyone below you what to do. But that's not what an ideal leader is like now. If you read management books now, a leader is somebody who can foster creativity, who can get his—get the employees—see, I still say "his"—who can get the employees to talk to each other, who can basically build teams and get them to be creative. And those are all things that women do very well.

And then on top of that, that's created a kind of cascading effect. Women enter the workplace at the top, and then at the working class, all the new jobs that are created are the kinds of jobs that wives used to do for free at home. So that's child care, elder care and food preparation. So those are all the jobs that are growing, and those are jobs that women tend to do. Now one day it might be that mothers will hire an out-of-work, middle-aged, former steelworker guy to watch their children at home, and that would be good for the men, but that hasn't quite happened yet.

To see what's going to happen, you can't just look at the workforce that is now, you have to look at our future workforce. And here the story is fairly simple. Women are getting college degrees at a faster rate than men. Why? This is a real mystery. People have asked men, why don't they just go back to college, to community college, say, and retool themselves, learn a new set of skills. Well, it turns out that they're just very uncomfortable doing that. They're used to thinking of themselves as providers, and they can't seem to build the social networks that allow them to get through college. So for some reason men just don't end up going back to college. And what's even more disturbing is what's happening with younger boys. There's been about a decade of research about what people are calling the boy crisis. Now the boy crisis is this idea that very young boys, for whatever reason, are doing worse in school than very young girls. And people have theories about that. Is it because we have an excessively verbal curriculum, and little girls are better at that than little boys? Or that we require kids to sit still too much, and so boys initially feel like failures? And some people say it's because, in 9th grade, boys start dropping out of school. Because I'm writing a book about all this, I'm still looking into it, so I don't have the answer. But in the meantime, I'm going to call on the worldwide education expert, who's my 10-year-old daughter, Noah, to talk to you about why the boys in her class do worse.

(Video) Noah: The girls are obviously smarter. I mean they have a much larger vocabulary. They learn much faster. They are more controlled. On the board today for losing recess tomorrow, only boys.

Hanna Rosin: And why is that?

Noah: Why? They were just not listening to the class while the girls sat there very nicely.

HR: So there you go. This whole thesis really came home to me when I went to visit a college in Kansas City—working-class college. Certainly when I was in college, I had certain expectations about my life—that my husband and I would both work, and that we would equally raise the children. But these college girls had a completely different view of their future. Basically, the way they said it to me is, that they would be working 18 hours a day, that their husband would maybe have a job, but that mostly he would be at home taking care of the kiddies. And this was kind of a shocker to me. And then here's my favorite quote from one of the girls: "Men are the new ball and chain."

(Laughter)

Now you laugh, but that quote has kind of a sting to it, right? And I think the reason it has a sting is because thousands of years of history don't reverse themselves without a lot of pain. And that's why I talk about us all going through this together. The night after I talked to these college girls, I also went to a men's group in Kansas. And these were exactly the kind of victims of the manufacturing economy, which I spoke to you about earlier. They were men who had been contractors, or they had been building houses and they had lost their jobs after the housing boom, and they were in this group because they were failing to pay their child support. And the instructor was up there in the class explaining to them all the ways in which they had lost their identity in this new age. He was telling them they no longer had any moral authority, that nobody needed them for emotional support anymore, and they were not really the providers. So who were they? And this was very disheartening for them. And what he did was he wrote down on the board $85,000, and he said, "That's her salary." And then he wrote down $12,000. "That's your salary. So who's the man now?" he asked them. "Who's the damn man? She's the man now." And that really sent a shudder through the room. And that's part of the reason I like to talk about this, because I think it can be pretty painful, and we really have to work through it.

And the other reason it's kind of urgent is because it's not just happening in the U.S. It's happening all over the world. In India, poor women are learning English faster than their male counterparts in order to staff the new call centers that are growing in India. In China, a lot of the opening up of private entrepreneurship is happening because women are starting businesses, small businesses, faster than men. And here's my favorite example, which is in South Korea. Over several decades, South Korea built one of the most patriarchal societies we know about. They basically enshrined the second-class status of women in the civil code. And if women failed to birth male children, they were basically treated like domestic servants. And sometimes family would pray to the spirits to kill off a girl child so they could have a male child. But over the '70s and '80s, the South Korea government decided they wanted to rapidly industrialize, and so what they did was, they started to push women into the workforce. Now they've been asking a question since 1985: "How strongly do you prefer a first-born son?" And now look at the chart. That's from 1985 to 2003. How much do you prefer a first-born son?

So you can see that these economic changes really do have a strong effect on our culture. Now because we haven't fully processed this information, it's kind of coming back to us in our pop culture in these kind of weird and exaggerated ways, where you can see that the stereotypes are changing. And so we have on the male side, what one of my colleagues likes to call the "omega males" popping up, . . . romantically challenged losers who can't find a job. And they come up in lots of different forms. So we have the perpetual adolescent. We have the charmless misanthrope. Then we have our Bud Light guy who's the happy couch potato. And then here's a shocker: even America's most sexiest man alive, the sexiest man alive [showing George Clooney in the film *Up in the Air*] gets romantically played these days in a movie. And then on the female side, you have the opposite, in which you have these crazy superhero women. You've got Lady Gaga. You've got our new James Bond, who's Angelina Jolie. And it's not just for the young, right. Even Helen Mirren can hold a gun these days. And so it feels like we have to move from this place where we've got these über-exaggerated images, into something that feels a little more normal.

So for a long time in the economic sphere, we've lived with the term "glass ceiling." Now I've never really liked this term. For one thing, it puts men and women in a really antagonistic relationship with one another, because the men are these devious tricksters up there who've put up this glass ceiling. And we're always below the glass ceiling, the women. And we have a lot of skill and experience, but it's a trick, so how are you supposed to prepare to get through that glass ceiling? And also, shattering the glass ceiling is a terrible phrase. What crazy person would pop their head through a glass ceiling?

So the image I like to think of, instead of glass ceiling, is the high bridge. It's definitely terrifying to stand at the foot of a high bridge, but it's also pretty exhilarating, because it's beautiful up there, and you're looking out on a beautiful view. And the great thing is there's no trick like with the glass ceiling. There's no man or woman standing in the middle about to cut the cables. There's no hole in the middle that you're going to fall through. And the great thing is that you can take anyone along with you. You can bring your husband along. You can bring your friends, or your colleagues, or your babysitter to walk along with you. And husbands can drag their wives across, if their wives don't feel ready. But the point about the high bridge is that you have to have the confidence to know that you deserve to be on that bridge, that you have all the skills and experience you need in order to walk across the high bridge, but you just have to make the decision to take the first step and do it.

Thanks very much.

(Applause)

Feminism Has Become a Hot Topic[*]

Phyllis Schlafly

Founder and president, Eagle Forum and Eagle Forum Education and Legal Defense Fund, 1972– ; born St. Louis, MO, August 15, 1924; A.B., Washington University, 1944; M.A., Radcliffe College, 1945; J.D., Washington University Law School, 1978; author of books, including A Choice Not an Echo *(1964);* Safe Not Sorry *(1967);* Kissinger on the Couch *(1974);* The Power of the Christian Woman *(1981);* Equal Pay for UNequal Work *(1984);* Pornography's Victims *(1987);* Feminist Fantasies *(2003);* The Supremacists: The Tyranny of Judges and How to Stop It *(2004).*

Editor's introduction: In this speech, presented at the University of Wisconsin at Eau Claire, conservative activist Phyllis Schlafly characterizes feminism as an ideology "wrapped in whines" about perceived persecution by men. She argues that the principal aim of feminism has been to devalue the role of the housewife and propagate the view that women can find fulfillment only in the labor force. Feminism has never been about equal rights for women, she asserts, but rather about gaining power for the female left.

Phyllis Schlafly's speech: It's time that somebody explained what a destructive force feminism has been in American society. The media, college courses in women's studies, and women's magazines are all trying to take young women down this deadend road. But, funny thing, public opinion surveys taken by feminist sources all show that women are not as happy today as they were in the 1960s.

Every couple of years *Time* and *Newsweek* ask "Is Feminism Dead?", and all of a sudden, feminism is being discussed and debated in the Mainstream Media. Feminism is back in vogue as a controversial topic. The blogosphere and newspapers all over the country are debating the meaning of feminism—and what it means to be female and powerful.

The feminist writers—and there are many of them—always picture women as the victims of mean men. The feminists' legislative agenda, from unilateral divorce in the 1960s, to the Equal Rights Amendment in the 1970s, to taxpayer-financed

[*] Delivered on April 7, 2011, at Eau Claire, Wisconsin. Reprinted by permission.

daycare in the 1980s, to the Violence Against Women Act in the 1990s, to the Paycheck Fairness Act in the 2000s, is always wrapped in whines about alleged discrimination against women.

The best definition of feminism was given by a leading modern feminist, Jessica Valenti, writing in the *Washington Post*. She wrote, "Feminism is . . . an ideology based on the notion that patriarchy exists and that it needs to end." In other words, feminists start from the notion that American women are victims of the patriarchy, so the feminist goal is to empower women to put down men and change society into a matriarchy. Another leading current feminist, Linda Hirshman, wrote that "support for abortion rights and ObamaCare are litmus tests for true feminism." That makes it clear that it is ridiculous for any conservative to call herself a feminist, or even some kind of new feminist.

The feminists were the driving force in inflicting our country with unilateral divorce, which means that, after a man and woman stand up and swear before witnesses to be faithful till death do us part, one party can break the contract without the consent of the other as easy as checking a box on a printed form. The spouse who wants out of the marriage contract doesn't have to allege fault by the other spouse, and doesn't even have to give a reason. The majority of divorces are initiated by women.

The feminists have invited, urged, and pressured young women to join the hook-up crowd, promising that it is liberating. The feminists look on our expectation that mothers should care for their own babies as a prime example of the oppression of women, and therefore the feminists demand taxpayer-paid daycare centers to be available to all women.

Harvard Professor Harvey Mansfield courageously made it clear in his book called *Manliness* that the feminist movement is anti-men, anti-masculine, anti-marriage, anti-motherhood, and anti-morality.

The most scholarly book written about the feminist movement is *Domestic Tranquility: A Brief Against Feminism* by Carolyn Graglia. She read all those tiresome books and articles by the feminist leaders, Betty Friedan, Germaine Greer, Kate Millett, Gloria Steinem, and Simone de Beauvoir, and concluded that the principal goal of the feminists since the 1960s has been "the status degradation of the housewife's role."

Mrs. Graglia documented the fact that all branches of feminists are united in the belief that a woman can find identity and fulfillment only in a labor force career. The modern feminist movement was born in the 1960s with the publication of Betty Friedan's book *The Feminine Mystique*. She urged homemakers to leave the home, which she called a "comfortable concentration camp," and join the labor force. Gloria Steinem said that when a woman gets married, she becomes a "semi-non-person," while Simone de Beauvoir and Betty Friedan labeled the housewife a "parasite," wasting her adult capabilities and intelligence.

This devaluing of the role of fulltime homemakers has now become part of our culture. That is what is taught in women's studies courses in colleges and endlessly reiterated on the media. Today, it is simply accepted by most people that the modern woman should be in the workforce because being at home is not enough for a fulfilling life, and caring for her own children is a demeaning lifestyle for an educated woman.

The female left argues for women to be independent of men, self supporting, sexually uninhibited, and liberated from the obligations of marriage and motherhood. That's why the feminists in the 1970s self-labeled themselves as the women's liberation movement. They wanted to be liberated from the duties that accompany home, husband, family and children. Feminists talk endlessly about the need for women to have empowerment and independence from men.

The feminist movement isn't the only factor that has moved wives out of the home into the labor force. Another factor is the invention of so many labor-saving devices that have reduced the time necessary to care for babies and keep the household functioning. Another factor is that women are having fewer children today than they did in the previous generation. Perhaps the most important factor is free trade policies that have shipped millions of well-paying manufacturing jobs overseas so that men today are reduced to taking jobs that don't pay enough to support a fulltime homemaker.

The media feminists gave major publicity to Maria Shriver's Report called "A Woman's Nation Changes Everything," published by the leftwing think tank Center for American Progress. This Shriver Report reproaches Americans for relying on what they call "an outdated model of the American family." The Shriver Report boasts that we are now living in a "woman's world," and that "Emergent economic power gives women a new seat at the table, at the head of the table." That "head of the table" metaphor is one more indication that the feminists believe they are victims of an oppressive patriarchy and want to transform America into a matriarchy. Feminism has never been about equal rights for women. It's about power for the female left. That's what makes feminism the fraud of the century.

But all this independence has not made women happier. All surveys show that feminists are chronically dissatisfied. The National Bureau of Economic Research reports, "As women have gained more freedom, more education, and more power, they have become less happy."

The feminists are not only anti-men; they are especially anti-masculine. They have aggressively used the federal bureaucracy and the courts to force colleges to cancel hundreds of men's college athletic teams, including more than 450 wrestling teams. Wrestling is so masculine, you know. Of course, canceling wrestling doesn't help women in any way; that just hurts men. Canceling wrestling proves that this feminist misuse of the federal law known as Title IX has nothing to do with equalizing funds spent on college sports; wrestling is probably the least expensive college sport.

For the last ten years, the feminists have been whining that women scientists are victims of sex discrimination. The essence of feminism is to complain that an oppressive patriarchy prevents women from earning more money and getting the academic appointments and recognition they think they ought to have.

The feminists got Congress to hold hearings on the fictitious "crisis" of sexism in the sciences, hearing only from feminist witnesses. Congress then created a program (called ADVANCE) that awarded millions of dollars to feminist university professors for anti-bias centers and workshops. The feminists control academia and are skilled in getting grants of taxpayers' money. That was just another feminist racket to get government to pursue their anti-male agenda.

But surprise, surprise, the voice of reason turned up in a prestigious publication that cannot be ignored. *The Proceedings of the National Academy of Sciences* published an objective paper about gender bias in the sciences called "Understanding Current Causes of Women's Underrepresentation in Science." The authors, Cornell University professors Stephen Ceci and Wendy Williams, thoroughly analyzed 20 years of data and the accusations made by the gender-bias movement. The real experts concluded: When it comes to job interviews, hiring, government funding, and publishing, women are treated as well as men and sometimes better. These distinguished professors completely and conclusively demolished feminist claims that women suffer discrimination in science areas.

The ideology of feminism has poisoned the media, most college courses, the judiciary, the bureaucracy, and even daily conversation. Feminism starts with the premise that women are victims of an unjust patriarchy and need government to help them build a career in the workforce. This is especially hurtful to young women because feminism deliberately teaches them to plan their lives to be full time in the workforce, without any space for husband and babies. Many women get to age 40 and bitterly regret that a full life has passed them by because their biological clock has run down.

One of the biggest feminist lies is that, even if feminism is outdated, women owe a debt of gratitude to the feminists of the 1960s and 1970s for creating the education opportunities women have in America today. That's total nonsense. Educational opportunities were available to women long before the modern feminist movement was born. I worked my way through a great coed college, Washington University in St. Louis, competing with all the guys, and got my B.A. degree in 1944. Then I went to Harvard graduate school, where there was no discrimination against women, competed with all the guys, and received my master's degree in 1945. My mother received her college degree at a great university back in 1920. Those opportunities were there for women who wanted to take advantage of them. The fact is, American women are the most fortunate class of people who ever lived.

It's time that young women have a handbook that explains the real goals and agenda of the feminists plus a non-feminist roadmap to a happy life. My co-author, Suzanne Venker, and I have provided this in our new book, *The Flipside of Feminism: What Conservative Women Know and Men Can't Say*, which dives right into the middle of the current buzz about the meaning of feminism, and its harm to women, men, marriage, and society. Suzanne Venker belongs to a younger generation, and our book is designed to give the facts of life to the younger women and men who didn't live though the heyday of radical feminism in the 1970s and 1980s, as I did.

6

The American Food System

How I Fell in Love With a Fish[*]

Dan Barber

Executive chef and co-owner, Blue Hill, 2000– , Blue Hill at Stone Barns, 2004– ; born New York, NY, 1969; B.A. in English, Tufts University, 1992; degree in classic culinary arts, French Culinary Institute (FCI), 1994; chef and restaurant worker in California, France, and New York City, 1994–2000; food writer, with articles appearing in The New York Times *and* Gourmet, *among other publications; appointee, President's Council on Fitness, Sports, and Nutrition; named best chef in New York City (2006) and America (2009) by the James Beard Foundation.*

Editor's introduction: In this TEDTalk, Dan Barber discusses his wish to offer delicious as well as sustainable fish on his menus. This is a difficult task because supplies of wild fish have been depleted and fish farms are polluters, he points out. He describes a fish farm, Veta La Palma, in the southwestern corner of Spain, where the fish are not fed, and where birds, natural predators of fish, are welcome. In contrast to agribusiness, this farm works along with rather than against nature and produces high-quality food in the process.

Dan Barber's speech: So, I've known a lot of fish in my life. I've loved only two. That first one, it was more like a passionate affair. It was a beautiful fish, flavorful, textured, meaty, a best-seller on the menu. What a fish. (Laughter) Even better, it was farm-raised to the supposed highest standards of sustainability. So you could feel good about selling it.

I was in a relationship with this beauty for several months. One day, the head of the company called and asked if I'd speak at an event about the farm's sustainability. "Absolutely," I said. Here was a company trying to solve what's become this unimaginable problem for our chefs. How do we keep fish on our menus?

For the past 50 years, we've been fishing the seas like we clear-cut forests. It's hard to overstate the destruction. 90 percent of large fish, the ones we love, the tunas, the halibuts, the salmons, swordfish, they've collapsed. There's almost nothing left. So, for better or for worse, aquaculture, fish farming, is going to be a part of

* Delivered on February 9, 2010, at Long Beach, California. Reprinted by permission.

our future. A lot of arguments against it. Fish farms pollute, most of them do anyway, and they're inefficient, take tuna. A major drawback. It's got a feed conversion ratio of 15 to one. That means it takes fifteen pounds of wild fish to get you one pound of farm tuna. Not very sustainable. Doesn't taste very good either.

So here, finally, was a company trying to do it right. I wanted to support them. The day before the event I called the head of PR for the company. Let's call him Don.

"Don," I said, "just to get the facts straight, you guys are famous for farming so far out to sea, you don't pollute."

"That's right," he said. "We're so far out, the waste from our fish gets distributed, not concentrated." And then he added, "We're basically a world unto ourselves. That feed conversion ratio? 2.5 to one," he said. "Best in the business."

2.5 to one, great. "2.5 to one what? What are you feeding?"

"Sustainable proteins," he said.

"Great," I said. Got off the phone. And that night, I was lying in bed, and I thought: What the hell is a sustainable protein? (Laughter)

So the next day, just before the event, I called Don. I said, "Don, what are some examples of sustainable proteins?"

He said he didn't know. He would ask around. Well, I got on the phone with a few people in the company. No one could give me a straight answer. Until finally, I got on the phone with the head biologist. Let's call him Don too. (Laughter)

"Don," I said, "what are some examples of sustainable proteins?"

Well, he mentioned some algaes and some fish meals, and then he said chicken pellets. I said, "Chicken pellets?"

He said, "Yeah, feathers, skin, bone meal, scraps, dried and processed into feed."

I said, "What percentage of your feed is chicken?" thinking, you know, two percent.

"Well, it's about 30 percent," he said.

I said, "Don, what's sustainable about feeding chicken to fish?" (Laughter)

There was a long pause on the line, and he said, "There's just too much chicken in the world." (Laughter)

I fell out of love with this fish. (Laughter) No, not because I'm some self-righteous, goody-two shoes foodie. I actually am. (Laughter) No, I actually fell out of love with this fish because, I swear to God, after that conversation, the fish tasted like chicken. (Laughter)

This second fish, it's a different kind of love story. It's the romantic kind, the kind where the more you get to know your fish, you love the fish. I first ate it at a restaurant in southern Spain. A journalist friend had been talking about this fish for a long time. She kind of set us up. (Laughter) It came to the table a bright, almost shimmering, white color. The chef had overcooked it. Like twice over. Amazingly, it was still delicious.

Who can make a fish taste good after it's been overcooked? I can't, but this guy can. Let's call him Miguel. Actually his name is Miguel. (Laughter) And no, he didn't cook the fish, and he's not a chef. At least in the way that you and I understand it. He's a biologist at Veta La Palma. It's a fish farm in the southwestern corner of Spain. It's at the tip of the Guadalquivir river.

Until the 1980s, the farm was in the hands of the Argentinians. They raised beef cattle on what was essentially wetlands. They did it by draining the land. They built this intricate series of canals, and they pushed water off the land and out into the river. Well, they couldn't make it work, not economically. And ecologically, it was a disaster. It killed like 90 percent of the birds, which, for this place, is a lot of birds. And so in 1982, a Spanish company with an environmental conscience purchased the land.

What did they do? They reversed the flow of water. They literally flipped the switch. Instead of pushing water out, they used the channels to pull water back in. They flooded the canals. They created a 27,000 acre fish farm—bass, mullet, shrimp, eel—and in the process, Miguel, and this company, completely reversed the ecological destruction. The farm's incredible. I mean, you've never seen anything like this. You stare out at a horizon that is a million miles away, and all you see are flooded canals and this thick, rich marshland.

I was there not long ago with Miguel. He's an amazing guy, three parts Charles Darwin and one part Crocodile Dundee. (Laughter) Okay? There we are slogging through the wetlands, and I'm panting and sweating, got mud up to my knees, and Miguel's calmly conducting a biology lecture. Here, he's pointing out a rare Black-Shouldered Kite. Now, he's mentioning the mineral needs of phytoplankton. And here, here he sees a grouping pattern that reminds him of the Tanzanian Giraffe.

It turns out, Miguel spent the better part of his career in the Mikumi National Park in Africa. I asked him how he became such an expert on fish.

He said, "Fish? I didn't know anything about fish. I'm an expert in relationships." And then he's off launching into more talk about rare birds and algaes and strange aquatic plants.

And don't get me wrong, that was really fascinating, you know, the biotic community unplugged, kind of thing. It's great, but I was in love. And my head was swooning over that overcooked piece of delicious fish I had the night before. So I interrupted him. I said, "Miguel, what makes your fish taste so good?"

He pointed at the algae.

"I know, dude, the algae, the phytoplankton, the relationships, it's amazing. But what are your fish eating? What's the feed conversion ratio?"

Well, he goes on to tell me it's such a rich system, that the fish are eating what they'd be eating in the wild. The plant biomass, the phytoplankton, the zooplankton, it's what feeds the fish. The system is so healthy, it's totally self-renewing. There is no feed. Ever heard of a farm that doesn't feed its animals?

Later that day, I was driving around this property with Miguel, and I asked him, I said, "For a place that seems so natural," unlike like any farm I'd ever been at, "how do you measure success?"

At that moment, it was as if a film director called for a set change. And we rounded the corner and saw the most amazing sight, thousands and thousands of pink flamingos, a literal pink carpet for as far as you could see.

"That's success," he said. "Look at their bellies, pink. They're feasting." Feasting? I was totally confused.

I said, "Miguel, aren't they feasting on your fish?" (Laughter)

"Yes," he said. (Laughter) "We lose 20 percent of our fish and fish eggs to birds. Well, last year, this property had 600,000 birds on it, more than 250 different species. It's become, today, the largest and one of the most important private bird sanctuaries in all of Europe."

I said, "Miguel, isn't a thriving bird population like the last thing you want on a fish farm?" (Laughter) He shook his head, no.

He said, "We farm extensively, not intensively. This is an ecological network. The flamingos eat the shrimp. The shrimp eat the phytoplankton. So the pinker the belly, the better the system."

Okay, so let's review. A farm that doesn't feed its animals, and a farm that measures its success on the health of its predators. A fish farm, but also a bird sanctuary. Oh, and by the way, those flamingos, they shouldn't even be there in the first place. They brood in a town 150 miles away, where the soil conditions are better for building nests. Every morning, they fly 150 miles into the farm. And every evening, they fly 150 miles back. (Laughter) They do that because they're able to follow the broken white line of highway A92. (Laughter) No kidding.

I was imagining a march of the penguins thing, so I looked at Miguel. I said, "Miguel, do they fly 150 miles to the farm, and then do they fly 150 miles back at night? Do they do that for the children?"

He looked at me like I had just quoted a Whitney Houston song. (Laughter) He said, "No. They do it because the food's better." (Laughter)

I didn't mention the skin of my beloved fish, which was delicious, and I don't like fish skin. I don't like it seared. I don't like it crispy. It's that acrid, tar-like flavor. I almost never cook with it. Yet, when I tasted it at that restaurant in southern Spain, it tasted not at all like fish skin. It tasted sweet and clean like you were taking a bite of the ocean. I mentioned that to Miguel, and he nodded. He said, "The skin acts like a sponge. It's the last defense before anything enters the body. It evolved to soak up impurities." And then he added, "But our water has no impurities."

Okay. A farm that doesn't feed its fish. A farm that measures its success by the success of its predators. And then I realized when he says, a farm that has no impurities, he made a big understatement, because the water that flows through that farm comes in from the Guadalquivir river. It's a river that carries with it all the things that rivers tend to carry these days, chemical contaminants, pesticide runoff. And when it works its way through the system and leaves, the water is cleaner than when it entered. The system is so healthy, it purifies the water. So, not just a farm that doesn't feed its animals, not just a farm that measures its success by the health of its predators, but a farm that's literally a water purification plant, and not just for those fish, but for you and me as well. Because when that water leaves, it dumps out into the Atlantic. A drop in the ocean, I know, but I'll take it, and so should you, because this love story, however romantic, is also instructive. You might say it's a recipe for the future of good food, whether we're talking about bass or beef cattle.

What we need now is a radically new conception of agriculture, one in which the food actually tastes good. (Laughter) (Applause) But for a lot people, that's a bit too radical. We're not realists, us foodies. We're lovers. We love farmers' markets. We love small family farms. We talk about local food. We eat organic. And when you suggest these are the things that will insure the future of good food, someone somewhere stands up and says, "Hey guy, I love pink flamingos, but how are you going to feed the world?" How are you going to feed the world?

Can I be honest? I don't love that question. No, not because we already produce enough calories to more than feed the world. One billion people will go hungry today. One billion—that's more than ever before—because of gross inequalities in distribution, not tonnage. No, I don't love this question because it's determined the logic of our food system for the last 50 years.

Feed grain to herbivores, pesticides to monocultures, chemicals to soil, chicken to fish, and all along agribusiness has simply asked, "If we're feeding more people more cheaply, how terrible could that be?" That's been the motivation, it's been the justification, it's been the business plan of American agriculture. We should call it what it is, a business in liquidation, a business that's quickly eroding ecological capital that makes that very production possible. That's not a business, and it isn't agriculture.

Our bread basket is threatened today, not because of diminishing supply, but because of diminishing resources. Not by the latest combine and tractor invention, but by fertile land; not by pumps, but by fresh water; not by chainsaws, but by forests; and not by fishing boats and nets, but by fish in the sea.

Want to feed the world? Let's start by asking: How are we going to feed ourselves? Or better, How can we create conditions that enable every community to feed itself? (Applause) To do that, don't look at the agribusiness model for the future. It's really old, and it's tired. It's high on capital, chemistry, and machines, and it's never produced anything really good to eat. Instead, let's look to the ecological model. That's the one that relies on two billion years of on-the-job experience.

Look to Miguel—farmers like Miguel. Farms that aren't worlds unto themselves; farms that restore instead of deplete; farms that farm extensively instead of just intensively; farmers that are not just producers, but experts in relationships. Because they're the ones that are experts in flavor too. And if I'm going to be really honest, they're a better chef than I'll ever be. You know, I'm okay with that, because if that's the future of good food, it's going to be delicious.

Thank you. (Applause)

Ending Hunger*

The People and Congress

David Beckmann

President, Bread for the World, 1991– ; born Kearney, NE, Feburary 22, 1948; un-dergraduate degree, Yale University; M.Div., Christ Seminary; M.S., London School of Economics; served in a church-supported development program in rural Bangladesh, 1975–76; senior liaison to nongovernmental organizations (NGOs), World Bank, 1976–91; author of books, including Grace at the Table: Ending Hunger in God's World *(1999);* Exodus from Hunger: We Are Called to Change the Politics of Hunger *(2010).*

Editor's introduction: In this speech, delivered to the National Press Club, the Rev. David Beckmann contrasts the progress out of poverty he has seen across the globe with the situation in the United States, where there has been comparatively little movement. "Even before the recession hit," he points out, "our poverty rate [was] about what it was in 1970." Beckmann calls on the government to do its part, including passing the Child Nutrition Act, which was, as he spoke, moving through Congress. Beckmann argues that a constituency of conscience, moved by God, must be mobilized on behalf of the poor. He offers examples of bipartisan cooperation on assistance for the poor brought about by people of faith.

David Beckmann's speech: Thank you very much. Thank you . . . I am grateful to be here, and I appreciate the interest that all of you have in what we can do to end hunger. I want to start by telling you about a visit that I got to make last year to a really remote part of Mozambique, down on the Pacific coast of Africa. We went up to a little island in Lake Nyasa on a tiny airplane and then we took an old wooden boat over to some lake shore settlements along the lake there in Mozambique. These are really remote places. They were at least 100 miles from the nearest road.

---

* Delivered on September 13, 2010, at Washington, D.C. Reprinted by permission.

Our first stop was a little settlement, not really a town, just a settlement of about 40 mud houses, called Ntembwe. And each house had its own casaba field. The truth is, if your casaba field fails, your family goes hungry. There's very little trade, no electricity, no transportation. As we came to the lake shore, there were about 50 people waiting for us, and they were singing hymns and praise songs. And then we landed and they danced us up to the top of a hill above the lake. And up at the top of a hill is a church that they had made, a mud church. And the woman who had arranged for our visit, then, we had a little preliminary meeting, and she said, "Well, tell these visitors from America how your lives have improved here in Ntembwe." Well, it wasn't obvious to me that their lives had improved very much.

But then somebody said right away, "Well, we're at peace." Because in Mozambique, they have just been through a 16 year civil war. All of these people were repeatedly brutalized, they were repeatedly forced into refugee status in neighboring countries. Now, Mozambique has a good government. Somebody else mentioned their school because ten years ago, they didn't have a school in Ntembwe. Now, almost all the kids, even the AIDS orphans, go to school.

And later, we met three women who had been on death's door because of AIDS. And they are now getting anti retroviral medications funded mainly by the U.S. government. And they're able to take care of their children, they're able to farm, and they're part of the—the church has a group that goes around and does education on HIV and AIDS, and they're part of that group, helping other people deal with HIV and AIDS.

So I was really profoundly encouraged, and I think all of us, in fact, can take real encouragement from what has happened in this really poor place in remote Africa. And the same kind of story can be told in hundreds of thousands of communities around the world. Because the world has made dramatic progress against hunger, poverty and disease over the last 30 years. Across Africa, there are a lot more kids in school. There are 30 million more African kids in school today than were in school ten years ago. The World Bank estimates that in 1980, there were 1.9 billion people in extreme poverty; by the same measure, there are now about 1.4 billion people in extreme poverty, that's still way too many poor people. But I'm struck that hundreds of millions of the world's poorest people have been able to work their way out of poverty.

And since I'm a preacher, I see this as God moving in our own history. This is our loving God answering prayers for hundreds of millions of people. I see this as a great exodus in our own time.

Now, in our own country, as richly blessed as we are, we have not made sustained progress against poverty. But it's clear that if countries as diverse as Bangladesh and Brazil and Great Britain can reduce their poverty rates as they have, the United States can do that if we want to do it. Also, we have in fact been able to reduce poverty in the United States when we tried. The clearest example was from the 1960s and early '70s. It was a period of very low unemployment. President Johnson and then also President Nixon expanded anti-poverty programs, and it worked. We cut our poverty rate in half. But we haven't sustained that level of effort. And so, in fact, even before the recession hit our poverty rate is about what it was in 1970.

Now, the economy has caused a huge setback, with a big increase in the numbers of hungry and poor people certainly in our own country. Because of high unemployment, one in four children in our country now lives in a household that sometimes runs out of food. The government's going to release its new poverty data on Thursday. We know that the data will confirm that there's been a big increase in poverty in our communities. And the setback has been global. Now, more than a billion people, as Alan said, more than a billion people in the world are undernourished. That's more than a billion people who can't afford enough calories to make their bodies function properly.

Now, we have clear opportunities right now to moderate the hunger and poverty that this economic problem has caused. And those same changes would position us for rapid progress against hunger and poverty once the economy starts to recover.

I think God is calling us to change the politics of hunger. Why politics? Because if we're serious about reducing hunger, we need to get our government to do its part. Not that the government can do everything, but we need to get our government to do its part. You may remember that in early August, Congress passed a bill to provide financial aid to the states. I think it was a good bill. It'll keep a lot of teachers from being laid off, and my wife's a teacher. But, at the last minute, really, they decided to finance that bill partly by cutting $12 billion from future funding for the food stamp program. $12 billion is a lot of groceries. In fact, in that one decision, Congress took away from needy people twice as much food as all the food banks and charities in the country will be able to mobilize in a year.

And there wasn't much public fuss. That's why we have to change the politics of hunger. Congress is coming back into session today. And on September 30th, the Child Nutrition Bill expires. So, they have to decide in the next 20 days what they're going to do about the policies of our child nutrition programs. So, are we going to provide more nutritious lunches at school for our children or not? At a time when a quarter of the kids in the country are living in households that run out of food, are we going to strengthen the programs that get food to low income kids or not? That decision is being made right now. The House version of the Child Nutrition Act is much better for hungry kids than the Senate version. But the House leadership hasn't figured out how they want to pay for it. And the Senate is proposing to improve school lunches for kids by making deeper cuts in the food stamp program.

So, I would like people to call your member—call one of your members of Congress and ask them to pass the House version of the Child Nutrition Act. If you haven't got a pen, you might want to get one out because I'm going to give you the phone number in a few minutes.

There are some other issues that are hanging fire for hungry people right now, and they're very feasible things that we could do to help. First, to their great credit, the Obama Administration has launched a world hunger initiative. They are investing in poor farmers all across the world, helping them produce more food, and the initiative has a special focus on child malnutrition. They're using a relatively small amount of U.S. money to leverage investments by other governments around the world, including governments of the countries concerned. Congress is not now on track to provide the money that the President requested for this world hunger initiative.

Second, on this issue I'm less enthusiastic about the Obama Administration. We need to make our foreign aid programs more effective in reducing poverty. And the administration has done some things to make our aid programs better, but they have moved slowly. And it seems that they are seriously considering merging our development programs more fully into programs and efforts that are really focused on our own short-term self interests. That is a bad idea. And again, the way to get to them is to get through Congress.

The biggest poverty issue that's hanging fire right now is tax credits for the working poor. I know a young mother who's working two part-time jobs. She has a three-year-old boy. Last year, she was able to use her tax rebate to enroll in a program to learn how to be a dental hygienist. This is what we want; to reward people who are working but are poor and to help them move forward with their lives and the lives of their kids. But the tax rule that benefited her last year will expire unless Congress acts. So in this big debate about taxes, let's not forget the tax credits for the working poor. So have you got your pencils ready? Also people watching on C-SPAN, I hope. The number of the capitol switchboard, I'm serious, is 202-224-3121. It's easy. You call, you ask for one of your members of Congress. You'll get a staffer and you tell him or her that you want to see passage of the House version of the Child Nutrition Act by the end of September.

And if you want more information on that issue, or these other hunger issues, here's another thing you can mark down. Bread of the World's website is bread.org. You can find out more and you can become more active in changing the politics of hunger by contacting us.

Finally, we've got a big election coming up this year. November 2nd is important to all of us and it's really important to hungry and poor people. And as we decide who to vote for, one consideration should be which of these candidates is going to be good news for hungry and poor people? It's not guesswork, you ask them. "What do you think about the Child Nutrition Bill? What do you think about the World Hunger Initiative? What do you think about foreign assistance reform? What do you think about tax credits for the working poor?"

What we need is a much stronger constituency for hungry and poor people. And I think a lot of that surge in constituency power needs to come from people who are moved by our consciences, or by our God. Now, a lot of—I think virtually all religious people know that if you want to get close to God, you've got to do right by the poor. It's hard to miss that. We don't all do it, but it's hard to miss the message. But a lot of religious people do not get the—they don't get the idea that God is concerned not just about our individual behavior, but also about our laws and about how we behave as a nation. That is all over the place in the Bible. But for example, when Glenn Beck convened people on the mall a couple of weeks ago, when I read through his speech, this is a point that he just didn't make. That part of what we need to do as religious people is justice for poor people.

Some religious people do get this. Bread for the World itself includes about a million people, mostly Christian people who understand that God is calling them to help poor people and do it in big ways, structural ways. I think the best way for me to tell you about Bread for the World is to tell you about my friend, Pat Pelham, in Birmingham, Alabama. Pat was a young mother in the late '90s and in her morning prayers, one morning, she felt that God was calling her to do something for Africa. Well, she had little kids, what was she going to do?

But her minister suggested, well why don't you help get our church involved in Bread for the World? So she did that and she, together with her friend, Elaine van Cleve, they developed a relationship with their member of Congress, Spencer Bachus. He's a conservative Republican, but he did some things with Bread for the World because of them. And then in early 1999, church people all over the world were energized by the idea that we could write down some of the unpayable (sic) debt of the world's poorest countries, the Jubilee Campaign. And at the same time, Spencer Bachus was named chair of the International Committee of the Banking Committee. So, I called Pat. Within two weeks, Pat and Elaine came up to Washington. They go to the Presbyterian church, but they brought letters from Our Lady of Sorrows Catholic Church to Mr. Bachus. And they convinced him that this was something that ought to happen. And Spencer Bachus became the most effective advocate for debt relief in the U.S. Congress. It's not just a one-time visit. They kept up pressure back home; they recruited other churches, they celebrated his leadership.

At the end of the whole process, there was an appropriations bill. President Clinton signed that appropriations bill and at the signing ceremony he said, "Mr. Bachus, you're from the other party, but we wouldn't be here if it weren't for you." And I used my two minutes to talk about Pat Pelham and Elaine van Cleve and Father Martin Muller, and tens of thousands of other people of faith across the country who had dared to push Congress to do something for poor people when it seemed politically impossible.

What's Bread for the World? We're a collective Christian voice for hungry people. We organize in all kinds of Christian churches, and then we have a secular affiliate, the Alliance to End Hunger, which includes Jewish and Muslim groups, and all kinds of secular organizations. We are bipartisan. We are consciously respectful of people who disagree with us. And maybe most importantly, we win. We win big changes for hungry and poor people. So over the last decade, we helped to triple development assistance to poor countries. We more than doubled nutrition assistance to hungry families in our own country. On both those things, we did a lot of work with President Bush.

Of course, Bread for the World is just a small part of the broader constituency for poor people. And I think we need to say that over the last couple of years, Congress has done some good things for poor people. And at each step of the way, people of faith, people of conscience have been part of the process. In my judgment, the big bills that President Bush introduced right at the end of his term, and that President Obama pushed early in the term to deal with the financial crisis, I think those bills saved us from depression. And we were especially supportive of the Obama stimulus package because half of that money went to programs in which low-income people participated.

We and many other groups helped to win support for that bill. I think health insurance, the expansion of health insurance, is going to keep a lot of people from being pushed into poverty. And it's that logic that led Catholic religious women across the country to support the healthcare bill. It was a tough issue for Catholics because they weren't very satisfied with how the abortion issue was treated. But the support of Catholic religious women was crucial to the passage of the healthcare bill. And so when President Obama signed that bill, he gave the first pen to Sister Carol Keenan.

When Congress took up financial reform, another coalition including a lot of faith groups worked to restrict financial institutions that work with low-income people to reduce the exploitation of low-income people by banks and other financial institutions.

On the Child Nutrition Bill, the food banks, lots of faith groups have been working hard for a couple of years. They're campaigning intensely now. The Jewish Council on Public Affairs has hosted child nutrition Seders across the country. The Lutheran church asked its people to write to Congress on empty paper plates about the Child Nutrition Bill.

Let me just tell you one more story. Maine is an important state because the senators and representatives from Maine are relatively moderate people. So they're often swing votes on these issues that are important to poor people. And I want to tell you about three people in Brunswick, Maine; Helen Small, Ted Bradbury, Christine De Troy. Because they could see how important their representation in Washington often was, they have done a lot to strengthen Bread for the World's network of individuals and churches all across Maine. And they have got a lot of people writing to their members of Congress on issues that are important to hungry people.

Just a few weeks ago, Hellenist Church, which is St. Charles Borromeo Catholic Church in Brunswick, Maine, took up an offering. But it wasn't an offering of money, it was an offering of letters to Congress about the Child Nutrition Act. Now, let me be clear. We do not now have enough political oomph to achieve the changes for hungry people that we should achieve. That's why I'm asking you and other people to become more active on these issues. We're going to try to use the World Food Prize, the book that I've got coming out, to stir up a stronger constituency of conscience on issues that are important to hungry and poor people.

For starters, just take one step, like really do call—let us do call our members of Congress about the Child Nutrition Act. Or, pick out a candidate that you think is a good candidate and help that person to get elected on November 2nd. Or, if you're a journalist, write about some of the issues that are important to hungry and poor people. God uses our modest steps to move through history, to move the world. Jesus said, "You don't even need much faith. If you just have faith the grain of a mustard seed, you can move a mountain." That's my experience.

In our own time, God is moving to overcome hunger and poverty, and I think God is calling us to change the politics of hunger. Thank you. (Applause)

Anxiety, Allure, and the Meanings of Industrial Eating*

Aaron Bobrow-Strain

Associate professor, Whitman College, 2010– ; born Chicago, IL, 1969; B.A., Macalester College, 1992; M.A., Stanford University, 1993; Ph.D., University of California at Berkeley, 2003; lecturer, University of California at Berkeley, 2003; assistant professor, Whitman College, 2004–2010; director, Latin American studies, Whitman College, 2007–08; chair, politics department, Whitman College, 2010–11; author, Intimate Enemies: Landowners, Power, and Violence in Chiapas *(2007);* White Bread: A Social History of the Store-Bought Loaf *(forthcoming, 2012).*

Editor's introduction: In this talk, given at a symposium on "Sustenance" at Texas A&M University's Glasscock Humanities Center, Professor Aaron Bobrow-Strain discusses the alternative food movement. To illuminate the vexed modern relationship between Americans and mass-produced food, he outlines a history of the American consumption of bread, especially the shift from the consumption of mostly home-baked bread to factory-produced bread, and the role played by advertising in that shift. At the turn of the century, in a time of great national anxiety, amid waves of immigration and economic downturns, proper diet was seen as essential to national well-being. Bobrow-Strain suggests some commonalities between historical hysteria about unsafe food and our concerns about what we eat today, noting that emotions are much more in play than we might want to admit.

Aaron Bobrow-Strain's speech: So, about 20 years ago, a complete city kid, I accidentally found myself on a banana plantation on the coast of Ecuador, and head over heels in love with the politics of agriculture and food. I've been working on and studying those issues ever since, mostly in Mexico.

At the same time, I was also getting involved in the U.S., with what you might call the "alternative food movement"—working on [and] then becoming part-owner of a human-sustainable cattle ranch in Arizona. I helped start a clandestine raw-milk co-op that's still in operation; and I sold what may have been the first beef in Tucson explicitly marketed as local-grassfed.

---

* Delivered on April 8, 2011, at College Station, Texas. Reprinted by permission.

As I got older, moved away from Arizona, went to grad school, and had kids, I became the stereotypical backyard chicken-raising, cheesemaking, home canning, farmers' market shopping, community-gardening, artisanal bread-baking foodie. (You have those in Texas, right?)

At the same time, I found myself growing more and more skeptical about the intellectual underpinnings of a lot of food activism in the U.S. It seemed that a lot of it was premised on some variant of the idea that, "if you only knew what I know about how evil your industrial processed food is, you would change."

I started to think that this idea that people would change once they heard "the truth" about their food didn't do justice to people's vexed relation with industrial food; a relationship filled not just with ignorance, but also deeply felt emotional attachments, anxieties, and aspirations.

The "if you only knew" approach also seemed to create a whole series [of] divides between those virtuous people who did know what to eat and those dupes who didn't, something that all too often ends up reinforcing larger social divides around class and race.

So my academic work on food history and cultural politics in the U.S. has arisen of this tension I feel between being a participant in the alternative food movement and being a critic: how can we think about industrial food and food activism in a more nuanced and historically rich way?

A few years ago—thanks to my own obsession with bread-making—that tension morphed into a book project on the 100-plus-year history of battles over industrially manufactured white bread.

Today, I want to talk about a small piece of that history. And I want to do that with an eye toward thinking about what it might have to say about our own present-day struggles over food.

Ok. Let's begin that with an easy question.

What to eat? Something you will all ask yourself a few times today—it's a simple question, right (doesn't provoke any guilt, anxiety, confusion, neuroses . . . no despair)? Hard for us. As a result Americans seem to have an insatiable craving for clear-cut guidelines for what to eat. We kinda love food rules.

Obligingly, in 2009, food writer Michael Pollan compiled an enormous list of food rules gleaned from his readers, into a book *Food Rules: An Eater's Manual*, which it has been a *NYT* bestseller ever since.

In an interview, Pollan admitted that he had a favorite food rule.

"Don't eat anything your great-grandmother wouldn't recognize as food."

This has gone absolutely viral. Becoming a mantra repeated by nutritionists, columnists, environmentalists, gourmet magazine writers . . . Oprah, you name it.

Great rule, concise, homey, gets us thinking. It also sneaks in some really essentialist assumptions about food culture.

Two of my favorite foods are spicy Ethiopian doro wat and anything Mexican made with the dark blue corn fungus huitlacochtle (corn smut, in English). Had either of those? Amazing. Yeah . . . but I'm pretty sure my great-grandmothers would have said they were definitely not food. At least not for civilized humans.

Of course, I don't think the rule was meant to be taken literally. Just to get us thinking about the ways our diets have changed over time. Even if we cut the rule some slack, though, I still find interesting the assumption that, in great-grand-mothers' day, the question of "what to eat" was simpler—more clear-cut. That, at the very least, in great-grandmothers' day people could draw on ancestral wisdom to differentiate between "real" home-style food and bad processed food.

A key point in my book is that Americans' relation to food has always been full of conflicts and anxieties—even in this idealized great-grandmothers' day. In fact, great-grandmothers' dilemmas about what to eat were not as different from ours as we might think.

Let's talk about this. I don't know much about most of my great-grandmothers. But I do know about one. I'd like to introduce her to you.

Florence Farrell. Born in Pittsburgh in 1883; second-generation Irish-American. Mother of seven, married to a self-taught draftsman; living on the teetery edge of middle class respectability.

When Great-Grandmother Farrell asked the question what to eat, the question of what bread to eat would have been fundamental. In the late 19th and early 20th centuries, bread provided more calories in the American diet than any other single food, across class lines, and, to a certain extent, even across ethnic lines.

Even factoring in Asians and Latinos who ate less bread, Americans got an average of 30 percent of their calories from bread during the late 19th and early 20th centuries (by comparison: today, in aggregate terms, we don't get anywhere near 30 percent of calories from any food—not even high fructose corn syrup). An Irish family like the Farrells probably consumed even more of their daily calories—maybe 40 percent—in bread form.

My grandmother and her sister told me that during the '10s and '20s, their mother baked at least a dozen loaves every Monday. It was a festive day and neighbors would often stop by for a taste.

Tellingly, no one remembers what kind of bread Florence liked, but we do know two things: her kids and young folks in the extended family constantly nagged for modern store-bought bread; while her husband P. T. railed against factory loaves, calling them "bags of hot air."

So what did they do? . . . .

By the end of the 1920s, the family had completely switched to bread made in factories, and, by all accounts, they loved it. Sadly, none of my oldest relatives can remember exactly why the family switched, so what I'd like to do for the rest of this talk is to put the Farrell's about-face in a larger historical context.

The first thing to note is that the Farrells weren't alone. Their switch was part of a much larger sea change in the way Americans got their bread.

In 1890, 90 percent of bread in America was baked in homes by women; 10 percent was baked in small, neighborhood bakeries.

In 1930, this had completely reversed. Ninety percent of bread was baked outside the home by men. Only 10 percent was baked in homes.

Bakeries were changing too: in the 1890s, the average commercial bakery produced a couple hundred loaves a day. In 1930, the country's bakeries regularly baked 300,000 a day; and one model bakery set up at an industry expo was said to have topped one million loaves in 24 hours. Small, independent neighborhood bakeries were becoming a thing of the past.

By the early 1920s, the baking industry's business model was also firmly in place: a small number of giant bread conglomerates, producing more or else exactly the same standardized loaves, would compete for market share with massive economies of scale, Robber Baron political tactics, and relentless overproduction.

Looking back at this moment, it's easy to see how industrial bakers could muscle small competitors aside, but how did they convince American consumers to give up on home baking so quickly, especially since it was still cheaper to bake at home until the '40s? What was so wondrous about modern bread?

"Convenience" is an obvious answer, and certainly part of the historical explanation. Baking was arm-breaking work with fickle ovens and inconsistent ingredients. As the owner of the country's largest baking conglomerate liked to brag, just one of his company's mixing machines saved 5,000 women from tedium every hour. Or, as a Polish immigrant woman put it more bluntly, "[Bakery bread was a] God-send for] women. It saved their strength and time for work in the mill."

But, if demands on women's time were the sole reason for the switch to industrial bread, families might have simply replaced homemade bread with equal amounts of store-bought, or even consumed less bread. Industrial bakers knew this, and were deeply concerned. With falling meat prices, relatively inexpensive fruit shipping around the country from California and Central America, and novel new processed foods coming on the market every day, bakers were terrified that bread would get crowded off the American table, no matter how convenient it was.

Instead, something remarkable happened during the first three decades of the twentieth century: per capita bread consumption increased. Modern factory bread wasn't just a more convenient version of the ancient staple, it had taken on new meanings and appeal. A reporter covering consumer reactions to the new bread spoke of housewives' "thrill" at seeing the perfect products of modern factories. Awed consumers flocked to see shining new palaces of automatic baking.

And, when industry spokespeople talked about consumers' embrace of industrial bread during the '20s, they compared it to other Jazz Age fads like marathon pole sitting and barnstorming.

Where did that embrace of industrial bread come from?

A simple answer is advertising. And, to be sure, bakers availed themselves [of] every new innovation in modern marketing to sell bread. But all that advertising could not have convinced consumers to make such a fundamental change in their diet unless it somehow touched a deep emotional chord.

It did. For the rest of this talk, I want to think about two intertwined emotions underpinning the triumph of industrial bread: anxiety and attraction. This is not the whole story—that's a book or more—but it's part.

(Start with a little background on the period we're talking about. If you're a historian of the Progressive Era, this will seem a bit breezy, but I just want to provide a tiny bit of context.)

From the 1870s to the 1920s, a singular convergence of forces rocked the US. Unprecedented influxes of southern and eastern European immigrants, explosive urbanization, rapid technological change, and a series of grave economic downturns strained old social institutions. Thrust into an emerging system of global grain trading and financial speculation, rural America reeled. Urban infrastructure collapsed under demographic pressures. And elites and the poor alike searched for some sense of control over a world turned upside down.

Like many groups faced with great upheavals through history, late 19th- and early 20th-century white Americans scapegoated—placing the blame for turmoil on immigrants and others. Nativism and racial eugenics thrived.

And yet, intertwined with and sometimes inseparable from all the exclusion and vitriol, crusades to rein in the effects of turmoil also produced some of the most inclusive social reforms in U.S. history: child labor laws, worker safety protections, and, of course, landmark food safety laws.

Championing these causes was a rising legion of middle-class social reformers and professional experts armed with an unshakable faith in science and progress. Under their influence, training in fields ranging from medicine to teaching was standardized and professionalized, and new disciplines—sanitation, hygienics, home economics, and public health—were created to extend scientific expertise into new realms.

In the eyes of nearly every branch of this new army of professional experts, Mothers stood on front lines of the battle for social improvement. They conducted the care, feeding, and education of the population, and they governed the most intimate spaces of everyday life. If mothers could be rationalized, most of the nation's problems could be cured, from the hearth up.

In an era when the germ theory of disease was just gaining widespread acceptance in popular culture, domestic hygiene and cleanliness, or rather the lack thereof, topped social reformers' lists of impending threats to society. And, so, from kindergarten classrooms to labor rallies to tenement community centers, reformers set out to convince the nation of its moral responsibility to fight contagion.

As numerous social histories have shown, this idea really took hold in American homes. The slightest deviation from perfect cleanliness was a cause for anxiety—any foothold germs gained in the home could be seen as putting the health of the family, neighborhood, even the entire nation at risk.

What interests me, though, is a less well-known part of this history: the fact that the country's diet provoked just as much anxiety as its hygiene.

Incorrect food choices exposed the population to limitless contagion while inefficient and unscientific diets silently drained the nation's stamina. Indeed, for many of the era's socially-conscious citizens, inefficient diet appeared to be the root cause of nearly all of the nation's moral, physical, and social problems.

Racial eugenicists, reaching the apex of their popularity in the US between the teens and thirties, believed that poor diet constituted clear evidence of genetic unfitness, requiring forceful intervention.

Most home economists and health reformers, however, inclined toward the more optimistic euthenics movement. For them, racial fitness didn't begin and end with genes. It could be achieved by changing physical environments and teaching new habits. Social work and education would teach modern eating habits to the poor, while community food projects would eliminate obstacles to accessing a scientific diet.

Home economists and other reformers called this "spreading the gospel of good food," and, in a fashion reminiscent of many community-garden and anti-obesity campaigns today, well-meaning reformers poured into the country's urban tenements and rural hill countries.

These were well-meaning efforts fueled by confident altruism and a sense that, without immediate reforms, more radical upheavals were on the horizon. In fact, food activists today cold learn a lot from them: marching, boycotting, and pressuring both government and the private sector to guarantee safe food, turn-of-the-century food activists achieved sweeping changes in the way the country ate. They also won incredible victories on the policy level—most famously the passage of the Pure Food and Drugs Act, which is still the foundation of federal food safety regulation. And perhaps even more importantly, hundreds of new state and thousands of municipal food safety ordinances [were passed].

Yet, the gospel of good food was also a metric by which seemingly unruly populations could be disciplined and measured for worthiness. Following expert advice became not just a matter of good practice, but a requirement of competent citizenship—a way to show that you weren't a threat to the health and progress of society.

Even when reformers' efforts to spread the gospel of good food to the poor failed—and they failed a lot—these failures only further reinforced social hierarchies. Rather than using these failures as opportunities for self-reflection (hmm, maybe this means that the poor actually need other things, like higher wages, more than they need our dietary advice) they tended to simply confirm reformers' belief that poverty stemmed from the poor's ignorance (what kind of fool would reject good food?).

Indeed, the failure of efforts to spread the gospel of good food to the poor only deepened aspiring middle- and upperclass folks' identification with scientific eating (we're well off and we eat scientifically, they're poor and reject our efforts to teach them how to eat—clearly we owe our status to our good choices and they owe their status to their bad choices).

OK. With all this in mind, the choice of bakery over homemade can be understood as something more than just a question of taste or convenience.

Centuries of European tradition had linked bread choices with social status, but this was different: the movement for hygienic eating added a whole new level of consequence to food choice: individual decisions about bread didn't just mark class differences, they placed eaters' behavior in relation to the larger health of the nation and proclaimed, for all to see, whether one was fit and responsible—or in need of help and intervention.

The problem for Florence Farrell and millions of other consumers was that it was not at all clear what kind of bread was most scientifically correct. This uncertainty was a source of anxiety.

On the surface, the answer to the question of what bread was most hygienic would have been obvious: home baked bread was better. At the turn of the century, bread from the country's mostly small bakeries was one of the few processed foodstuffs widely associated with poverty rather than affluence, and bakeries themselves suffered under a cloud of suspicion.

Poorly capitalized and facing cutthroat competition, the country's small bakeries slashed any cost possible. They [were] always suspected of whitening flour with things like chalk and alum. And they worked immigrant bakers, literally, to death in damp, super-heated, and unventilated basement bake rooms: 14-to-8-hour days during the week, plus 24 hours on Saturdays were typical.

When sanitary reformers began to investigate bakery conditions, they shocked the nation with what they found. Sensational descriptions of pestilent bakeries filled local newspapers, painting pictures of dark, vermin-infested hovels with raw sewage dripping from pipes into dough troughs, bread cooling on dirt floors, horse manure blowing around, and whole families sleeping on rag piles alongside their chickens, next to the oven. In the worst cases, bakers worked ankle-deep in water and sewage when storms backed up city drains.

Fueled by accounts like this, from the 1890s–1920s we can speak of a full-fledged moral panic about contaminated bread.

Scary stuff. But were small bakeries really that bad? Was bread really that dangerous?

Probably not. . . . Reading pages of testimony and the reports of sanitary inspectors one thing comes clear: while many other pieces of the American food supply—like milk and meat—were threatened by germs, bread was actually fairly sanitary. Sensationalist reports of contaminated bread were just that: sensationalist. But they were also revealing of something important about the nature of food safety fears.

An episode from New York City will make this clear:

Two weeks ago, we celebrated the 100th anniversary of the Triangle Shirtwaist Factory Fire that killed 146 garment workers in New York and sparked an outpouring of concern about workplace safety. After the fire, a Factory Investigating Committee was established to hold hearings on conditions in the city's worst industries—and, along with garment factories and a couple other industries, they focused intensively on small bakeries.

Consumer protection advocate Frances Perkins, who would later become FDR's Secretary of Labor, testified that she had personally inspected one hundred New York bakeries and found the working conditions criminal. As witness after witness confirmed, immigrant bakery workers' lives were nasty, brutish, and short.

But the Factory Inspection Committee was not really interested in hearing this—while they were sympathetic to the plight of immigrant garment workers, they had other intentions when it came to the people whose hands produced the city's bread. With a few exceptions, committee members darted around witnesses' appeals for workplace safety regulations in bakeries, restating the bakery problem as a question of how best to control immigrant workers and protect consumers.

As city Health Commissioner Ernst Lederle argued, "cellar bakeries themselves were not the problem," the problem was that "the people were dirty and careless."

I remember a moment reading through the transcripts of the bakery hearings when it hit me: these folks were not talking about bread safety, they were debating the nature of new immigrants. Visions of food purity were impossible to separate from ideologies of racial purity.

This is the grain of salt with which we must take fears of small bakeries—and a clue to why industrial bakeries flourished. Regardless of whether it was "accurate," the moral panic around dirt, germs, and immigrants was a gift for big industrial bakers.

"I want to know where my bread comes from! I don't want bread from some nameless basement bakery," an affluent woman demanded in this national advertising campaign for Holsum Bread. Or, as another ad from Los Angeles put it more bluntly, "Many bakeries in New York, Chicago, and other cities are being condemned by health officers as unclean and unsanitary. How often do you inspect your bakery?"

This type of appeal touched a nerve, and consumers responded: civic organizations, women's groups, and sanitary activists conducted bakery inspections and drew up "white lists" of acceptable establishments. Modern bakeries were declared civic institutions. Meanwhile, consumers flocked to visit the country's modern new sanitary bakeries. Touring industrial bakeries became a pastime. School teachers even took classes to tour bread factories with the explicit goal of teaching their pupils about the importance of hygiene.

For a population of middle- and upperclass consumers anxious about making the right choices about what to eat, industrial bread was a savior. A savior from a dark, sinister world of threats.

But industrial bread wasn't just a safe haven from food anxiety—it was an attractive spectacle in itself.

And this brings us to the second seduction that Florence Farrell and her family would have experienced: the allure of modern bread.

Consider the precise symmetry of the sliced loaf, each of its pieces "the exact counterpart of its fellows." Calibrated within a sixteenth of an inch, the loaf's tranches articulate a perfect accordion, a white fanned deck. Note the plane of the slice. Each face reveals an intricate lacework unmarred by aberrant holes. There are no unneeded flourishes, no swags added by the baker. If we could, for a moment, let go of our present-day affection for the rustic look of artisanal bread, the sight would take our breath away. Industrial bread exudes a modernist aesthetic, and it didn't get that way by accident.

During the 1920s and 1930s, an obsession with machines and progress changed the look of America's material life. Streamlined design channeled a love of industrial efficiency into the nooks and crannies of Victorian frill and Craftsman style. It began with vehicles; smoothing, tapering, and lengthening their lines to help them slip efficiently through air. It was a seductive look, all speed and glamour, and it spread quickly to other kinds of objects. Irons, pencil sharpeners, and kitchen mixers got lean and smooth.

Bakery engineers were swept up in this too, and responded by smoothing out bread's bulges, squaring off pan bread's flared "balloon tops," and lengthening stubby loaves into sleek Zephyr trains.

They weren't particularly happy about this trend. Industry experts believed that fat unsliced loaves increased bread consumption because people cut larger slices for themselves from them. Whereas with sleek, skinny, and pre-sliced loaves, consumers took the same number of slices, but they were smaller. Eventually, though, bakers were forced to accept consumers' desire for modern-looking streamlined loaves. .

This was more than just a visual style. It was a political statement about the future. Tellingly, a food industry expo in Zanesville, Ohio presented examples of streamlined loaves under the banner of "Utopia."

High-tech foods like streamlined sliced bread promised a future of social harmony built on abundance and efficiency, where the very material constraints of biological existence would be overcome by science. Technology would usher in good society by conquering and taming the fickle nature of food provisioning. Taming the nature of bread—conquering scarcity.

In this context, breadmaking was re-imagined as a charismatic techno-science. Like family health care, bread baking was to be a terrain of control and expert measurement rather than art and aesthetics. References to art, craft, and instinct would pretty much disappear from bakery manuals and cookbooks from the 1920s through the late 1960s.

Scientific bakers proudly trumpeted their ability to tame the unruly nature of bread—their ability to fit living dough into factory assembly lines. These achievements were essential to the economics of monopoly capitalist baking, of course, but they were also something else.

Early 20th century industrial bakers' conspicuous embrace of science was a cultural performance; a theater of charisma, authority, and control. The streamlined loaf wasn't just an object of industrial beauty, it was a carefully scripted display of precision and efficiency—designed to educate consumers about the inferiority of mothers' bread.

A *New York Times* story from the late teens was quite revealing: "I am tired of hearing about that wonderful bread that mother used to make," the story complained. "Mother was a rank fraud as a bread maker . . . Don't you remember how often her bread went wrong? . . . Mother sometimes blamed that on the weather, or maybe on fairies . . . but it [wasn't] the weather [or] the fairies. It was because mother didn't know how [to make bread properly]."

According to leading home economists, mother could still—possibly—compete with even the largest bread factories on price, as long as one considered her labor "free." She couldn't hope to compete on quality or consistency, however; not against the massed forces of assembly-line production, temperature-controlled fermentation, chemical dough conditioners, standardized ingredients, and professional ovens.

Nor should she even attempt it. As a Pennsylvania journalist explained, "The modern woman has out-grown the idea that a mother can best serve her children by slaving for them over the hot stove." Indeed, the reporter continued, time and effort squandered on pointless home baking was "responsible for most domestic misery in the country" and possibly dangerous to families' health.

A good housewife wasn't a baker, she was a professional manager making smart choices to maximize her family's health and prospects—leaving baking to the experts who churned out perfect, clean loaves every time. As the Chair of the University of Chicago's Home Economics Department predicted: in the past, women were judged by their ability to make good bread, in the future they would be judged by their skill at buying it.

Ok, so let me pull all this together and try to imagine the pressures and ambitions that might have shaped the Farrell family question of what bread to eat:

1. When the home economist I just quoted above said women would be judged, she really meant it. Food choice had become a high-stakes exercise that shaped how you were positioned in a society geared up to defend against internal and external threats. Were you a responsible citizen or a weak link requiring intervention?

2. In a moment obsessed with both food and racial contagions, anxiety about what to eat expressed itself as a moral panic about immigrant bakers. Big industrial bakers, with their hardball tactics and economic might, destroyed the country's small bakeries, but well-meaning food reformers paved the way for this destruction to be seen as a good—even lifesaving—thing.

3. Finally, we have industrial bread itself as an alluring cultural spectacle of control, efficiency, and abundance that cast homemade baking in a negative light. Regardless of whether people liked the taste of Mother's bread better, industrial loaves offered a seductive vision of a more perfect world; a world of peace, abundance, and ease.

I'll never know why exactly the Farrells switched to factory bread. They probably didn't fully understand why everyone around them was switching. The question of what to eat is subtle and confusing. But these are some of the emotional investments that would have swirled around their decision.

Of course, these dreams and attachments weren't stable or monolithic: by the end of the 1920s, a competing current of new anxiety erupted across the US. In the minds of many consumers and health experts, bread industrialization had gone too far—it was too pure, too modern; and it was making us fat, dumb, and sick. Even criminal. By the '30s the future of industrial bread was in doubt—how it overcame that is another story.

Today, of course, the anxieties and aspirations about industrial bread that I've just described seem a bit tattered. A lot of us probably feel more connection to the '30s-era critiques of industrial bread than to the alluring dream of it. People who care about the relation between food and society today tend to look to small local farms and hand-made foods as the secret to restoring our health and repairing our communities. So it's tempting to just treat the story I've just told as a curious bit of kitsch representing a set of weird consumer dreams that we've left far behind.

I don't think that's quite true. In fact, I hope I've already got you thinking about how the fervent consumer dreams of the past still haunt the present. I want to end just by highlighting three of these hauntings:

1. It seems pretty clear that anxieties about food safety and contagion still get tangled up in fears of food workers—whether you're talking about Mexican meat packers at a Tyson plant over in Sherman, Texas, or Mayan peasants growing winter broccoli in Central America. More broadly, what comes clear in the story of bread is that food reformers need to reflect carefully on the fact that food anxieties are not always really about food.

2. The desire to save the nation by getting the poor to eat right is very much around these days; our moment abounds with well-meaning reformers who could learn something from the ways that spreading the gospel of good food to the masses ended up reinforcing social divides.

3. Finally, the charismatic image of industrial agriculture and food processing has certainly gotten a little tarnished since the '60s, but it is still around and is one of the hardest emotional attachments to shake. Because it holds out the promise of world peace and abundance achieved through science—a dream that's appealing despite its many failures. We see this being voiced these days by agribusiness critics of slow, local food, who argue that things like heirloom farmers-market tomatoes are all fine and good for elites, but combating hunger, poverty, and global insecurity requires scientific control, efficiency, and scale.

So . . . Charged with these deeply sedimented histories and emotions, the question of "what to eat" can't be contained in easy rules, or glossed through the assumption that "if you only knew how evil your processed foods are, you would change."

What remains to be seen is whether the alternative food movement can effectively counter these affective attachments to industrial eating—create new dreams of good food—without simply reinforcing stark social divides.

Innovation in American Agriculture, Sustainable Solutions to Help Feed the World*

Tom Vilsack

U.S. Secretary of Agriculture, 2009– ; born Pittsburgh, PA, December 12, 1950; B.A., Hamilton College, 1972; J.D., Albany Law School, 1975; mayor, Mount Pleasant, Iowa, 1987–1992; Iowa state senator, 1992–98; governor (D) of Iowa, 1998–2007; Democratic presidential candidate, 2006–07; partner, Dorsey & Whitney, 2007–09.

Editor's introduction: In this address before the National Press Club, Secretary Tom Vilsack asserts that both the productivity and the sustainability of global agriculture must be increased to meet the food needs of a growing population worldwide. He posits that these goals can be achieved while responsibly caring for natural resources. Vilsack outlines a number of recent research initiatives to increase productivity and combat agricultural challenges such as fungi, drought, and flooding. He also touches on the role of agricultural producers in providing renewable energy sources.

Tom Vilsack's speech: Today, the United Nations Food and Agriculture Organization says that 925 million people were undernourished last year. This is an improvement from 2009, but still unacceptably high. Our goal as a nation and international community is clear: to bring down this number by increasing the availability and accessibility of nutritious food around the world.

As we look to the future, this challenge grows even more stark. The global population is on the rise and strong economic growth in developing countries is expanding middle classes and increasing demand for agricultural products. We will have to increase food production by 70 percent to feed a larger, richer global population of 9.3 billion by 2050. What's more, agriculture will play a role in meeting the growing demand for energy—which is expected to increase by more than 40 percent by 2035.

The challenge of feeding a growing global population is real and success not guaranteed.

---

* Delivered on June 13, 2011, at Washington, D.C.

For producers this is a time of uncertainty and constraint as they confront the uncertainty of climate change and face the constraint of limited water resources. We know that past approaches to solving global hunger, which focused efforts on providing food aid, are not enough. We need to increase both the sustainability and productivity of global agriculture so that food is available, accessible and usable to people everywhere in the world.

I strongly believe that our nation, our scientists, our policy makers and—most of all—our farmers, ranchers and agricultural producers have proven they are up to the challenge.

American farmers are the most creative and productive in the world. Each acre we farm has become more and more productive, particularly over the course of the last century. America has moved from subsistence farming of the 1920s and '30s—to the world's largest food exporter today.

This evolution was not pre-ordained. America's producers embraced science in their pursuit of greater productivity. Technologies emerged from the imagination, creativity and hard work of our scientists from USDA, Land Grant Universities, and the private sector.

Principle Number One—the solution to global food security lies in innovation, arising from research and development.

Higher productivity need not come at the expense of conserving our natural resources. America's farmers have taken steps to take care of our nation's natural resources. In the last 30 years alone, USDA has worked to help producers reduce soil erosion by more than 40 percent and agriculture has gone from being the leading cause of wetland loss to leading the entire nation in wetland restoration efforts. Our farms help capture carbon emissions, mitigating climate change. Farm lands, pasture, and forests through proper conservation efforts help preserve our water resources and clean the air.

Principle Number Two—the solution to global food security need not be and should not be at the sacrifice of efforts to conserve our natural resources.

Two years ago, world leaders in L'Aquila, Italy, committed to make sustained, increased investments in agriculture development. And the G-20 Agricultural Ministerial which I will attend next week will continue to reinforce and move this agenda forward.

During these two years, the focus and extent of cooperation among world leaders has been remarkable—and it is mirrored here within our own government. Under the leadership of President Obama, the United States Government has pioneered a new coordinated approach to work towards global food security.

Feed the Future, a presidential initiative led by the U.S. Agency for International Development, is smarter and more efficient because it is focused on raising the productivity and incomes of small holder farmers through country-led strategies. It is focused on specific geographic regions and value chains within 20 countries so that we can significantly invest in priority areas where we bring a comparative advantage. It is bringing together the capabilities of multiple parts of the U.S. Government, as well as multilateral partners and private and non-governmental sectors, to build local capacity to sustainably increase global agriculture productivity, improve nutrition, and also foster regional trade.

Through Feed the Future, USDA is closely coordinating its efforts with USAID. In times of reduced financial resources efforts must be focused on core competencies. For USDA in the context of Feed the Future three core areas have been identified: innovation through collaborative research; in country capacity building in areas such as regulations, natural resource management, trade, and extension; and efficient market development through information, analysis and statistics.

Principle Number Three—the strategy to achieve global food security must focus on country identified needs and the core competencies of US departments and agencies of other developing countries, and international organizations.

As we have seen for decades, innovative research is perhaps our best opportunity for game-changing results in global agriculture.

Research in a climate-changing era is working to develop and extend new, improved technologies and methods for agricultural water use efficiency, soil conservation, and the basic productivity of the land on which seeds are sown.

At the same time, innovative genetic research is changing plant breeding by providing us with a better understanding of the genetic basis of high-yielding and stress-resistant crops. To confront heat, pests, soil salinity, toxicity, and new diseases, we are using discoveries about genetic information to better predict and accelerate the results of conventional breeding—selecting untested lines based on genomics rather than just labor-consuming field trials.

In the past few years, USDA research has helped reveal the genetic blueprints of a host of plants and animals, including corn, soybeans, apples, pigs, turkeys, cacao and a grass with great potential as a biofuel crop. In the past weeks alone, we published research with the full genome sequence of two common pathogens that cause wheat diseases which damage crops around the globe. This sort of work allows us to bypass generations of selective breeding and to develop disease-control methods to rapidly bring more abundant, nutritious food to tables around the world.

This new understanding of genetics is having an impact on one of the world's most threatening agricultural challenges—the wheat stem rust known as Ug-99. This devastating fungus is spreading across Africa, Asia and the Middle East with the potential to threaten crops that feed 1 billion people. The United States is playing a key role in the international effort to reduce its damage. We have provided more than 14,000 lines of wheat to be screened for resistance at plots at the Kenya Agricultural Research Institute. And thanks to genetics, we are pre-screening lines of wheat before sending them for field tests, increasing the frequency with which Kenyan researchers are finding rust-resistance in our wheat and moving us closer towards developing new Ug-99 resistant cultivars.

Today we are taking another step to strengthen our capacity to combat Ug-99. USDA and USAID are celebrating the groundbreaking of a new USDA Ug-99 research greenhouse at the University of Minnesota, a significant commitment on the part of the U.S. government under the Feed the Future initiative to provide a more stable grain supply worldwide.

Other USDA genetic science helped lead to a flood-tolerant rice variety that shuts down during flooding conditions, but resumes growth afterwards. Developed in conjunction with the University of California and the International Rice Research Center in the Philippines, new varieties are helping transform the food security in Feed the Future focus countries such as Bangladesh.

At the African Growth and Opportunity Act Forum last week, USAID and USDA were proud to announce that through the Feed the Future initiative, the U.S. Government will support an African-led partnership focused on controlling aflatoxin. Over 4.5 billion people in the developing world consume dangerous levels of aflatoxins, which are toxic and carcinogenic. This project, paid for by a broad array of international and local public and private sector organizations and foundations, including $12 million from the U.S. government, will help develop comprehensive regional strategies to limit the effects of aflatoxins on health and economic growth.

Other USDA-funded projects are looking at heat and drought tolerance in beans, addressing vitamin A and other nutrient deficiencies that cause problems for millions of children with new corn and potato varieties, and improving fruits, vegetables and specialty crops like cacao and table grapes. This sort of advanced development holds incredible potential for improving sustainable production and nutrition and raising farm incomes both here at home and across the globe.

And because of our belief in the value of global innovation and collaboration on agriculture, the genetic information that forms the basis for much of this work is available publically—and every year USDA distributes, at no cost, over 150,000 accessions from our seed banks to researchers at home and around the globe.

This research is not just a domestic effort. Much of the best research is being done in conjunction with international partners and non-profit funding. And as tight budgets threaten funding for this work at home and abroad, it is critical that we not only advocate for continued investment in this sort of innovation, but that we encourage private and non-profit sector funding as well. At the G-20 meeting of Agriculture Ministers, I look forward to engaging with my counterparts on how we continue to sustain support for such critical research and innovation globally.

But research alone will not feed the world. People will. Farmers and ranchers—and the chains of individuals who will help harvest, package, ship, sell and prepare food will.

To meet future challenges, we must help farmers adopt the latest seed technology, improved irrigation systems and land and animal management techniques. We must help them appropriately apply fertilizers, pesticides and herbicides if need be. We must help them regulate the safety of their food systems, and engage in the global trading system so that food supply can reach demand.

Food security efforts must be country-led and country-driven and focused at the local and community level. We want to engage smallholder farmers in villages to learn their ideas about developing the agriculture sector, so that we can help them with technologies, techniques and crops that fit their culture and lifestyle. Our focus must reflect an understanding of the role of women in farming, who account for between 60 and 80 percent of food production in most developing countries.

And while we improve productivity, we must also ensure that food makes it from farms to mouths. We must help communities and nations build safe water systems, [and] strong post-harvest infrastructure like roads and cold storage, ensure safe food supplies, and encourage vibrant local markets with transparent information and improved financial services.

National and regional governments have an enormous role to play in this effort. In the United States, our land-grant universities and extension agents have helped producers practice successful farm management and marketing and even helped them form cooperatives. The USDA Foreign Agricultural Service engages with Ministries of Agriculture in over 150 countries around the world to enable trade, support policies based on strong science and help disseminate sound management practices in less developed countries.

Today, through the Feed the Future initiative, we are focused on building capacity in countries like Bangladesh, Haiti, Ghana, and Tanzania, as well as regions in East Africa and Central America. These initial focus countries and regions were selected because of the strength of their political institutions and vision for confronting hunger. They have all committed to increasing their own investment in agriculture so our investments generate significant leverage.

Ghana, for example, currently loses 30–40 percent of its grain supply after harvest because of inadequate commercial and on-farm commodity storage and handling facilities. To help tackle this challenge, USDA is collaborating with several Land-Grant University specialists to develop and deliver a series of training and capacity building programs to improve storage systems on and off the farm and minimize moisture losses.

USDA's Borlaug and Cochran Fellowship programs expose international counterparts to American agricultural systems and innovation, supporting the critical human capacity that underpins growth. For example, in Kenya, the Cochran Fellowship program has helped the Kenya Plant Health Inspectorate Service adopt a port-of-entry inspection system similar to what we use in the United States. This is providing direct benefits to the Kenyan economy as America is now importing some of their fresh vegetables. And it has the potential to make a big difference in the region, as Kenyans who have been trained through the USDA program are teaching pest risk procedures and assessments to government agricultural officers at other East African nations.

USDA food aid programs are also driving agricultural productivity increases and raising the incomes of farmers. This year alone, they will benefit more than 5.2 million people in the developing world. USDA's Food for Progress Programs in places like Malawi, Guatemala, and Tanzania are building cooperatives, supporting extension, linking producers with buyers, and increasing market information and developing agricultural finance systems.

And our McGovern-Dole Program invests in the future by increasing school attendance, literacy and food availability for children in 30 countries around the world, while also building capacity to design, manage, and fund sustainable national safety net systems—like the SNAP and school lunch programs that are so successful in America—to underpin longer-term economic growth.

And as we work to develop agricultural economies we must remember that sound agricultural policies—here in the United States, in other G-20 countries, and in the developing world—are founded on good information.

That is why another priority for food security, which I look forward to discussing with my counterparts next week, must be increasing transparency in agriculture systems. That means establishing data collection, information, and regulatory systems so that nations can make more informed decisions to establish sound policies, respond to changes in food supplies, and reap the many benefits of agricultural trade.

The United States supports the United Nation's efforts to improve global agricultural statistics to provide accurate and timely market information and forecasts. And we support in-country efforts to improve data collection and analysis in many countries.

The U.S. Government is working to bolster national agricultural data systems and institutions in Feed the Future nations so that countries can carry out their own food security assessment, monitoring and analysis functions. In Nigeria, USDA is helping with a pilot project to improve sampling methods and data collection techniques. And in places like Guatemala, we're supporting market information systems so that farmers can make informed decisions.

As these new capabilities and systems take hold around the world, we believe that not only will there be less waste and fewer hungry people, but the global community will be better able to mitigate and respond to crop failures and famines.

Countries will be able to make more informed agricultural policy choices. As we watch a substantial increase in global commodity prices for the second time in the past few years, it is a good reminder of the importance of embracing transparency and free movement of food supplies. These measures will get food to the people that need it most, and help to smooth price spikes.

The bottom line is that with transparent systems in place, farmers around the world—from those tilling an acre or two in Central America, to a large row-crop operation in the American Midwest—will be able respond to changing markets and grow what is most profitable for their family and most needed by neighbors, countrymen and global compatriots.

The policies adopted by the international community are critical to creating a successful environment to collectively meet the challenge before us. At the G-20 agriculture ministerial next week, we will establish priorities, and agree on ways to increase the effectiveness of international agricultural systems, information, and investments.

It is significant that the G20 leaders have singled out the importance of food security and are grappling together with how to address the problems of high food prices. I know that they are interested in long-term solutions to improve productivity, and I am hopeful that we will have constructive conversations about additional thoughts on how to meet the growing global demand for food.

And so I will head to the G-20 meeting optimistic about what can be accomplished, and committed to the role of American innovation in driving sustainable intensification of agricultural production and improved nutrition around the world.

In the end, progress on these issues is good for America. It means improved economic opportunities as developing nations grow economically and engage in the global trade system. And it means stable nations and fewer threats to our national security.

Working to eliminate food insecurity across the globe—through innovation, hard work and partnerships—will provide incredible economic benefits and natural resource enhancements to developing and developed countries alike. It will increase political stability in conflict- and poverty-stricken regions, and put countries around the world—and our global community—on a path to future prosperity.

But agriculture's role goes beyond feeding and clothing the world. Producers are increasingly being called on to help provide renewable sources of energy.

Here in the United States, we are looking to biofuels, in particular, to help confront the challenges of providing adequate sustainable energy supplies, generating economic growth in rural communities, and mitigating the impacts of climate change.

In some cases, the same goals can be met by biofuels production in the rest of the world. As the FAO Bioenergy and Food Security Project has shown, bioenergy production and use in the developing world isn't automatically good or bad. Instead, when managed carefully, considering not only energy needs, but environmental needs, economic growth and food security, bioenergy can promote food and energy security by driving investment and increasing incomes in rural areas. To help nations—especially developing countries—reach the right balance, the Global Bioenergy Partnership recently announced a set of measurements and tools to promote the production and use of bioenergy as a way of encouraging sustainable development.

This is a clear reminder that we have to move beyond the all-too-common debate pitting food against fuel, and figure out how to meet both challenges—energy security and food security. The truth of the matter is that corn-based ethanol does not deserve the scapegoat reputation that folks often attempt to assign it. During the great run-up in food and commodity prices in 2007 and 2008, American biofuel production played only a minor role—accounting for about 10 percent of the total increase in global prices.

Combating hunger and feeding the world, particularly the children, is one of the great challenges of our day. Giving a child the opportunity for a brighter, more productive future affects not only the individual child, but the community where that child is raised, the country where he or she lives, and the entire world. This is a moral issue, and we are proud to be engaged in work that gives children around the world an opportunity to follow their dreams.

Cumulative Speaker Index: 2010–2011

A cumulative speaker index to the volumes of Representative American Speeches for the years 1937–1938 through 1959–1960 appears in the 1959–1960 volume; for the years 1960–1961 through 1969–1970, see the 1969–1970 volume; for the years 1970–1971 through 1979–1980, see the 1979–1980 volume; for the years 1980–1981 through 1989–1990, see the 1989–1990 volume; for the years 1990–1991 through 1999–2000, see the 1999–2000 volume; for the years 2000–2010, see the 2009–2010 volume.

Index

About the Editor

Currently a member of the editorial staff of *Art in America* magazine, **BRIAN BOUCHER** earned a bachelor's degree in art history at Vassar College and a master's degree from the Williams College Graduate Program in the History of Art. To his knowledge, he has no relation to the famous hockey player of the same name. In addition to numerous reviews and articles in *Art in America* and other art publications, he has also written, for *New York* magazine, the unlikely story of his cross with a wanted man on the run from the law: "My Roommate the Diamond Thief: He Found Me on Craigslist; I Found Him on America's Most Wanted." He lives in New York City.